Kamchatka Fly Fishing
and Visitors Guide

By Rene Limeres

**Kamchatka Fly Fishing
and Visitors Guide**
By Rene Limeres

©2017 By Rene Limeres

All photos by Rene Limeres unless otherwise noted.
Kamchatka Region Maps by Mike Boruta
Illustrations by William Hickman, Dan Mills, Rene Limeres and Galina Volgina
Design/Layout by Robert Jacobson, Alaska Dreams Publishing

1ST Print Edition June 2017
ISBN numbers:
ISBN-13: 978-0-9987394-0-3
ISBN 10: 0-9987394-0-5

**Ultimate Rivers
P.O. Box 15
Healy, Alaska, USA 99743
907-441-2080**
http://www.ultimaterivers.com

E-Book version available.
Please visit http://www.ultimaterivers.com for links.

Table of Contents

ACKNOWLEDGMENTS

Many kind friends, colleagues and fly fishing enthusiasts contributed valuable material and other support for this guidebook, for which the author wishes to express his deep indebtedness. Foremost among them, longtime Russian business associate and dearest friend, Galina Volgina of **The Climb, Ltd**., for her ceaseless efforts to secure the necessary information and other materials to make this guide complete. Without her unfailing support and considerable contributions, this book would never have been written.

I would also like to thank my longtime friend Igor Shatilo for his considerable input on Kamchatka fish species and locations, and great photos garnered from his many years in the field as a scientist and fishing guide. Premier fisheries scientist and friend Victor Bugaev gave generously of his encyclopedic knowledge of Kamchatka fishes, through his numerous donated publications, countless e-mails, discussions and a particularly memorable stay he made possible one July at his research facility on lovely Azerbaje Lake. For this, I am deeply grateful.

I wish also to express my heartfelt thanks to the local talent for their generous donation of fine photographs and other material which greatly enhanced the book: Irina Kruglykova, Alexander Bichenko, Igor Shatilo, Sergei Markov, Eugeny Lukovnikov, **Utgard Ltd**. and many others. Gennady Lazerev contributed valuable information on Kamchatka's trees and forests. And Margarita Kulakova provided very useful fish identification keys for Kamchatka salmon, trout and charr. Arcadie Mamonov of **Fisherman's Orbit Shop** in Petropavlovsk shared his considerable expertise on local conditions around the Petropavlovsk area. Sergei Lutkin kindly offered a stay at his fish camp on the Avacha River. Thanks as well to my American colleagues for the information and photos they shared: Will Blair at **Best of Kamchatka; ** Paul Allred of **Ouzel Expeditions;** Peter Soverel of the **Kamchatka Steelhead Project**; and Ryan Peterson, Mike Mercer (and others) at **The Fly Shop.**

There were many others who provided valuable information and/or support during the long process of creating this book: My Alaska partner, Goo Vogt (who kept me focused through one of the most difficult times in my life); Mark Dudley of **AirRussia.US;** and Martha Madsen of **Explore Kamchatka.** Not to be overlooked, of course, are the many fine Russian guides, cooks and interpreters I worked with on so many great fishing trips across Kamchatka. Without their help, support and camaraderie, I would have never made it to where I am today in my knowledge of the rivers and fishing of the Kamchatka Peninsula: Genye, Velodya and Ludmila at **Vulkan Tours**, and, Sasha, Andre, Sergei (Big and Little), Viktor, Nadya and Alla at **The Climb**. And finally, it would be totally remiss of me not to acknowledge the hundreds of kind, trusting souls who fished with **Ultimate Rivers** over the years, thus allowing me the privilege of exploring this last great frontier of wild trout angling. Thank you so much, everyone, (including those whom I may be overlooking here)!

PREFACE

KAMCHATKA—LAST FRONTIER OF COLD WATER ANGLING

As the last remaining wild stream fishing along our north Pacific coast was exploited during the last part of the twentieth century, it was inevitable that American anglers turn their attention to the largely unknown, vast territory lying west of Alaska in the remote provinces of Russia's Far East. These two regions, after all, share a common history and many similarities in terrain, climate, culture and natural resources. Rumors of great fishing in the rivers across the north Pacific had tantalized the adventure angling fraternity for decades, magnified perhaps by the hopeless inaccessibility created by the Iron Curtain.

The ideological divide that kept the U.S. and Russia at odds with each other for so long finally began to unravel, and lands that had been closed to all visitation were slowly opened to inquiring westerners. Because of its strategic military importance, the Kamchatka Peninsula was one of the last places in Russia to officially welcome foreigners, and it wasn't until the early 1990's that the first groups of American anglers got a chance to wet their lines in the streams of this former forbidden area. What they found exceeded their expectations. Here was a province of rivers— hundreds of clear flowing and utterly pristine drainages— running hither and yon across a rugged land of incomparable wild beauty, filled with smoldering volcanoes, snow-capped peaks, verdant meadows and birch forests. What made this paradise even more desirable was the rather obvious fact that Kamchatka's rivers, like those in Alaska, were blessed with amazingly abundant salmon, trout and charr populations that, due to isolation, had survived, virtually intact, the ravages of civilization. Could this be the next and last great frontier for cold water stream angling?

In the ensuing years, a hardy band of adventurous guides, scientists and sportsmen have set out to find the answer to this question, exploring rivers, setting up camps, doing research and sampling the fishing everywhere they go. The work of these pioneers, if nothing else, has confirmed that the initial euphoric observations on Kamchatka's potential were not only true but perhaps somewhat understated. For not only does the peninsula hold the last great stronghold of unexploited wild stream fishing, it also presents a rather unique opportunity to the enlightened world community: the chance to study, enjoy and preserve entire unaltered ecosystems within the vitally important north Pacific maritime region.

If fly fishing for trout and salmon is your passion, then surely at some point in your career, Kamchatka will call you to its shores to experience the penultimate excitement in your sport. The lover of nature and wilderness, too, will find it hard to resist the siren call of magnificent, undisturbed landscapes, unique geomorphic features, and abundant wild animal life. For the adventurous spirit in us all that yearns for a place—somewhere!—that inspires and challenges and has not yet been tainted by the excesses of our mass culture, Kamchatka is such a place. But it won't be for very long! We hope this guide will prove useful in your exploration and enjoyment of one of the last great places for wild fishing and outdoor adventure.

Rene Limeres
Denali Park, Alaska 2016

INTRODUCTION TO KAMCHATKA

Imagine yourself on a windswept stretch of crumbling tarmac, in Far East Russia, as a giant helicopter fires up its turbines and signals the start of a fishing adventure of a lifetime. The immense rotor springs to life and the sound and excitement soon become almost unbearable as you and your trip mates scramble inside to find a seat amidst a mountain of gear and enough food and vodka for a small army. The powerful machine lifts the impressive load with ease, and you are soon whirling above a landscape unlike any you've ever seen before. Through forested hills of birch and meadows of wildflowers, against a backdrop of smoldering volcanoes and colossal, icy peaks, countless sparkling streams ramble, with no visible signs of man to mar the scene. Where are all the fishermen, you wonder, with all this good looking water and rumors of big trout?

The big chopper flies on through this endless, dreamy landscape, to the headwaters of an impressive looking stream, cascading down a steep, rocky valley. The pilot puts you down on a long sliver of gravel above boulder-strewn rapids, and before the plane is barely emptied, it seems, one of your buddies has rigged up and has a fish on. It's a rainbow trout, by God, a giant one, jumping and careening as only rainbows can do! The fish soon gets away, but no matter. There are plenty more just as big and

9

willing in the miles of stream you will have all to yourselves in the days ahead. For you, lucky soul, are in one of the last earthly paradises for the wild trout angler, a place where fishing fantasies come true, unlike anything you can imagine—Kamchatka!

Steeped in mystery and isolation, the Kamchatka Peninsula has long been an inspiring dream for would-be adventurers. From the days of Vitus Bering, it has been a fabled land of fire, ice, fur, and fish, beyond the farthest reaches of mainland Siberia. It extends over 700 miles from the eastern tip of Asia into the north Pacific, just beyond the sweep of Alaska's Aleutian Islands. Shaped somewhat like a spear point, at its widest, some 300 miles across, it has a landmass with surrounding islands of approximately 182,000 square miles, larger than the state of California, and almost all of it total wilderness.

From its southernmost Pacific shores at latitude 51 degrees north to its northern border with the Asian mainland at 65 degrees, Kamchatka's terrain encompasses everything from rolling temperate forests and lush meadows to alpine, volcano-studded headlands to barren arctic tundra. Surrounded by three ocean bodies— the Okhotsk Sea along its west coast and the Bering Sea and Pacific Ocean along the east—this is a northern maritime province, with long, cold, snowy winters and cool, damp and cloudy summers. Only its innermost region, the "central valley" of the Kamchatka River between the two main mountain ranges, has any measure of continental climate and vegetation.

As one would expect, much of Kamchatka has the same look and feel as parts of neighboring Alaska. The dense forests of birch, alder and willow and thick understory of cow parsnip, fireweed and wild rose brambles could easily be mistaken for somewhere in the southcentral mainland of America's 49th state. Likewise, the barren tundra and sparse trees that predominate in the northern Koryak region seem so much like areas in the western and northern regions of Alaska.

But much of Kamchatka is also different and unique. Forged in the crucible of the Pacific's "Ring of fire", the peninsula has abundant volcanism evident in the dozens of volcanoes scattered up and down its mountainous core—some 29 or so still trailing plumes in the sky—and hundreds of hot springs and other geothermal features, equaled in number and impressiveness only by those of Iceland. Kluchevsky, the dominating, classic cone-shaped volcano of the massive Klyuchi Group at the northern end of the eastern volcanic chain of mountains is well over 15,000 feet in elevation, the largest active volcano in all of Eurasia. And the "Valley of Geysers" in Kronotsky Preserve and nearby Uzon caldera with hundreds of steaming thermal pools and mud cauldrons rivals America's Yellowstone.

Many of these spectacular features can be accessed from the road system or via short helicopter ride from key hubs, and thus are a major attraction to eco-adventurers the world over.

Adding to the abundant topographical beauty are more than 400 glaciers, several colossal mountain ranges, thousands of rivers and lakes, extensive, marshy coastal plains and hundreds of miles of rugged, rocky coastline. With abundant wildlife rivaling and, in some ways, even surpassing that of Alaska, Kamchatka's natural wonders include unique sanctuaries like the phenomenal Kurile Lake/Ozernaya River system, the most abundant sockeye salmon rearing habitat in Asia and one of the world's best places to observe brown bears and eagles.

Populated by approximately 330,000 hardy souls, predominantly transplanted Russians (with native groups making up only 4% of the total) who live mostly in and around the largest city and main hub of Petropavlovsk, Kamchatka is essentially deserted once you leave its sparse road system. The economy, like that of Alaska, is built on resource extraction, with fishing, mining and lumbering the mainstay and a small amount of farming, cattle and reindeer herding and fur trapping. It is only recently that a small tourist industry has taken hold to service the growing needs of a world hungry for exotic and unspoiled vacation destinations.

One of Kamchatka's main attractions of course, and the key focus of this book is the phenomenal fly fishing potential of the hundreds of clear flowing streams along its coast, many of which have never been adequately sampled by modern anglers. The peninsula's location, physiography, and climate have created what are perhaps the finest stream fishing conditions on the planet, with thousands of miles of perfect wade-and-cast, sight fishing for abundant trout, charr, grayling and six species of salmon. (Unlike much of the water in Alaska that is too deep, swift or glacially silted for good fly fishing.) And the richness of the stream biota includes abundant aquatic insect life for some of the best dry fly fishing west of Montana.

But fishing this new Valhalla presents challenges unlike any other destination in the world. Aside from sampling some of the easier accessed streams around Petropavlovsk and other towns, anglers visiting Kamchatka face a daunting lack of infrastructure and services, in addition to the barriers of a foreign language and culture, making it extremely unlikely to have a safe, enjoyable and productive vacation without the help of an experienced local outfitter/guide. Connecting with the right organization to help you experience the best of Kamchatka's fishing is essential; but equally important to your success and appreciation, we feel, is a basic understanding of the region's terrain, climate, resources, history, and culture.

It is to this end that we have compiled all the information presented in this book, to give prospective fly anglers and other tourists a feel for the unique flavor of the Kamchatka Peninsula and all it has to offer, and present useful guidelines on how to best plan and enjoy an adventure in what is surely one of the most appealing and least spoiled destinations on the planet. We have included details on many of the most notable area attractions besides fly fishing, for those interested, as well as information on some of the major activities available for tourists. For folks wanting to learn more about Kamchatka's many attractions and activities, we encourage them to contact some of the agencies and organizations listed.

It is our sincere hope that you can take the time to familiarize yourself with and eventually enjoy many of the unique opportunities that this developing frontier holds for lovers of outdoor adventure, wild nature, and travel to foreign lands. In doing so, you will not only enrich yourself but also the lives of many of the good people of Kamchatka, who, beyond their immediate economic needs, yearn, like you, for interaction with different cultures and the chance to make new friends. By reaching out to other lands, the world becomes a smaller place and the prospect for lasting peace and understanding among nations grows. If this book can help in a small way to further that cause, then we will consider our efforts more than repaid.

ABOUT THIS BOOK

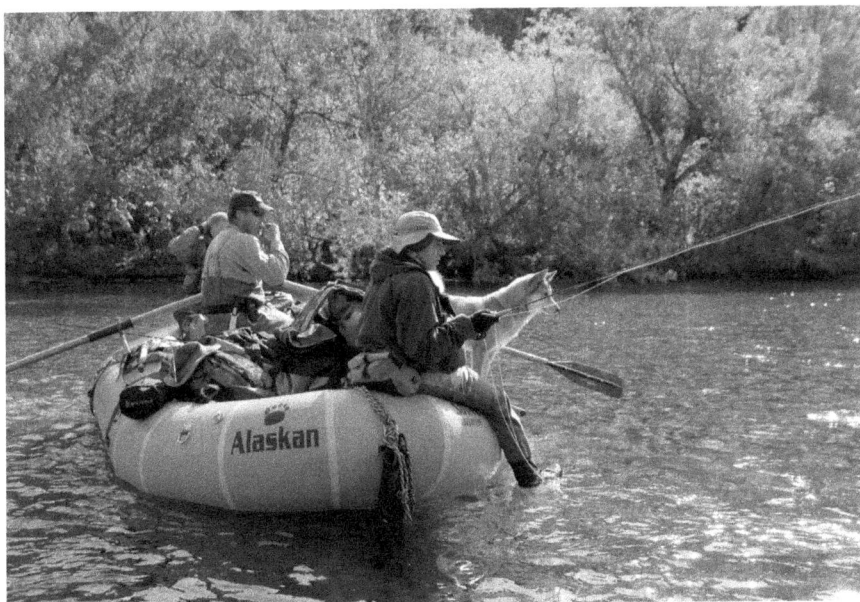

Float fishing the Pymta River in southern Kamchatka

This book represents one of the first attempts to describe and catalog the extraordinary fly fishing opportunities of the Kamchatka Peninsula in the context of its unique setting and the many challenges presented by one of the last remaining angling frontiers of the world. We have compiled what we hope is the most up-to-date and accurate information from numerous sources—our own experiences, those of other guides, sport anglers, local fishermen, pilots and hunters/trappers, articles in scientific journals and conversations with some of Kamchatka's most respected fish biologists. Readers should understand that much of the material in this book represents the current state of knowledge on a vast and still very much unexplored region, with fly fishing potential of countless rivers still uncharted, and many particulars of fish biology still undetermined. Use the information in this guide only as a starting point for your individual exploration, making sure to check with local sources for the most current information on conditions before heading out to fish, especially to remote locations. (Note: It is especially important to contact locals for latest conditions before fishing the more remote waters of central and northern Kamchatka.)

We begin our discussion of Kamchatka's fabulous fly fishing with basic descriptions of the peninsula's most important freshwater game fishes- their ecology, status, habits, best fishing locations & times, most popular fly fishing techniques/patterns, etc. Readers wanting more information on general habits and most popular fly fishing techniques, patterns and gear for most Kamchatka species are encouraged to consult the definitive reference on game fishes of Alaska: *Alaska Fishing: The Ultimate Angler's Guide, Deluxe 3rd Edition,* for many of the general characteristics and angling strategies for the species native to both neighboring provinces are the same.

Overviews of the peninsula's three main regions are provided, with emphasis on the major highlights and areas of interest for fly fishers. Included in these region sections is information on the rivers and streams that have proven most noteworthy so far for fly angling. (As noted, readers should keep in mind that these descriptions are far from conclusive and that many more streams, particularly in the more remote areas, may offer outstanding possibilities for fly fishing.) As much as possible, we give details on available species, conditions, access, suitability for river running, fishing pressure, and other aspects important to anyone contemplating fishing these waters. Also included in this book is a section on basic techniques and gear for Kamchatka fly anglers, and some comprehensive trip planning information and insider's tips for anyone interested in visiting Kamchatka.

We encourage you to contact and support the visitor service organizations we've cited, all of whom have been most sharing of their Kamchatka angling expertise, knowledge of local waters and other aspects of importance to inquiring anglers and other tourists. Your tourist dollars support these companies and other aspects of the local economy as well as the continued development of a new management ethic that recognizes and seeks to preserve a sustainable resource of the highest quality and value— the incomparable fly fishing of one of the last great places for wild cold water stream angling.

Readers Note: If you have information or personal experience pertaining to the fly fishing of the Kamchatka Peninsula (or any other outdoor activity) that adds to or conflicts with anything you have read in this book, we want to hear from you! It is our desire to update and expand the content in this guidebook to keep it as accurate and complete as possible. You can be part of this process and receive acknowledgment and complimentary copies of future editions. Contact the publisher for details.

OVERVIEW OF THE KAMCHATKA PENINSULA

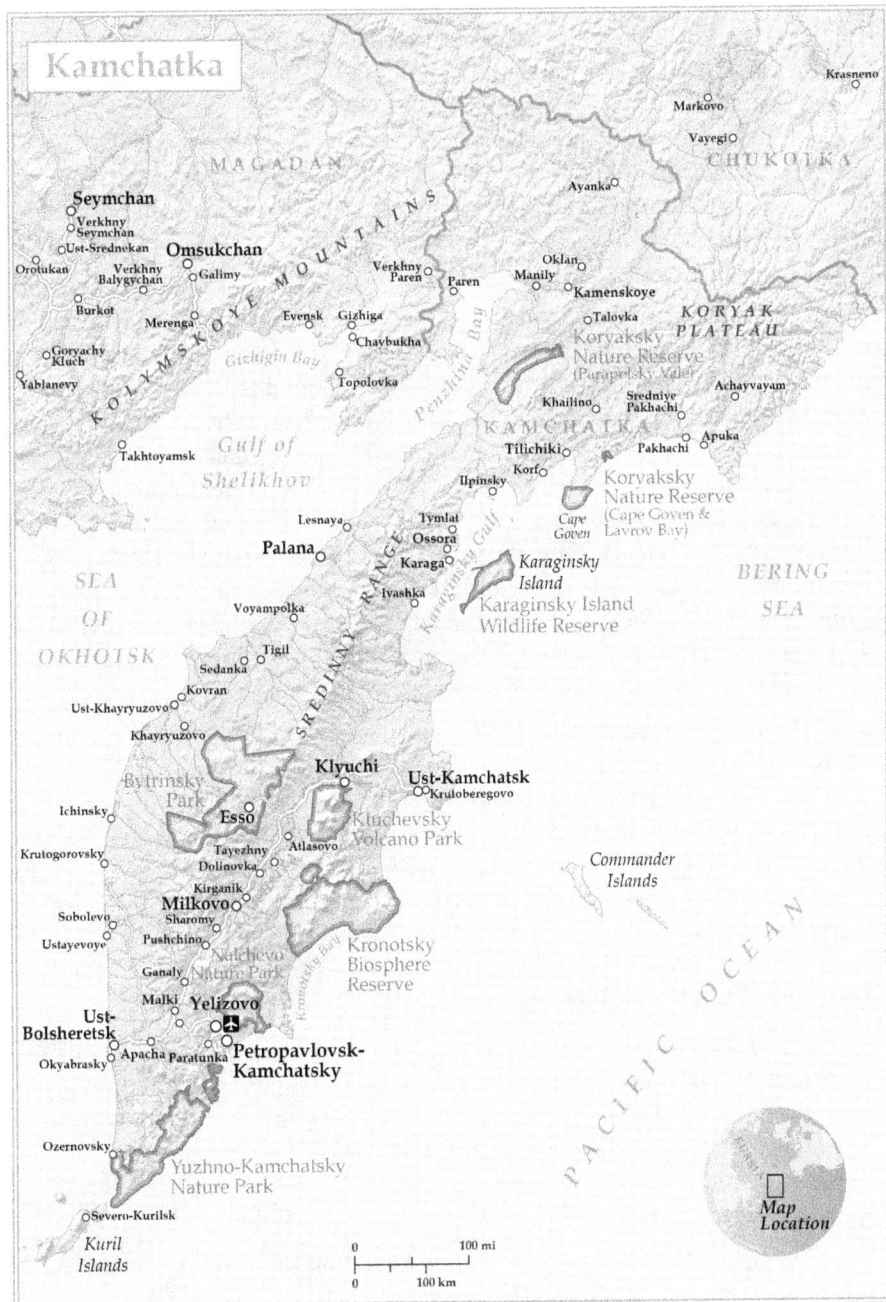

Kamchatka

Krasneno

Markovo

Vayegi

MAGADAN

CHUKOTKA

Ayanka

Seymchan
Verkhny
Seymchan
Ust-Srednekan **Omsukchan**

Orotukan   Verkhny   Galimy   Verkhny   Paren   Manily
Balygychan   Paren   Kamenskoye

Oklan

Burkot   Merenga   Evensk Gizhiga   Talovka   *KORYAK*
Goryachy   Chaybukha   Koryaksky   *PLATEAU*
Kluch   Nature Reserve
Yablanevy   Topolovka   (Parapolsky Vdel)   Achayvayam

Khailino   Sredniye
              Pakhachi

KAMCHATKA

Takhtoyamsk   *Gulf of*   **Tilichiki**   Pakhachi   Apuka
               Shelikhov   Korf
                            Ilpinsky   Koryaksky
                                                     Nature Reserve
                            Lesnaya   Tymlat   *Cape*   (Cape Goven &
                                       Ossora   *Goven*   Lavrov Bay)
               Palana   Karaga

SEA   Ivashka   *Karaginsky*
OF   Voyampolka   *Island*   *BERING*
OKHOTSK   Tigil   Karaginsky Island   *SEA*
               Sedanka   Wildlife Reserve
                    Kovran
Ust-Khayryuzovo
     Khayryuzovo

                                 Klyuchi
                                 OUst-Kamchatsk
Ichinsky   *Bytrinsky*   Kruloberegovo
            Park   **Esso**
Krutogorovsky   Tayezhny   Atlasovo   Kluchevsky
                        Dolinovka   Volcano Park
                        Kirganik
             Sobolevo **Milkovo**   *Commander*
                        Sharomy   *Islands*
Ustayevoye   Pushchino
             Ganaly Nalchevo   Kronotsky
             Malki Nature Park   Biosphere
Ust-   **Yelizovo**   Reserve
Bolsheretsk   O✈
Okyabrasky Apacha Paratunka **Petropavlovsk-**
                              Kamchatsky

Ozernovsky   *PACIFIC OCEAN*

            Yuzhno-Kamchatsky
            Nature Park

     Severo-Kurilsk
Kuril   0   100 mi
Islands
                               0   100 km

Map
Location

Kamchatka's Physiography

Kamchatka's spectacular landscape was sculpted at the dawn of time by titanic forces—the intense pressure and heat created by the collision of continent-sized plates of the earth's crust (the northwest movement of the Pacific plate into the Eurasian continental plate). The resultant uplift and convergence created two rugged ranges of volcanic mountains that comprise the core of the peninsula and one of the most seismically active zones in the world (containing some 129 volcanoes, 29 of them active, along with dozens of geysers, hot springs, fumaroles, mud cauldrons and other features).

The Sredinny, or Central Range, is an ancient chain of mountains that forms the spine of Kamchatka, extending over 600 miles along the center of the peninsula, with elevations from 4800 to5400 feet in the south, decreasing to 1800 to 2400 feet in the north. It contains 120 volcanoes, but only two active, Ichinsky (10,863 feet) and Khangar (6000 feet). The Vostochniy, or eastern range, fronts the Pacific Ocean and Bering Sea, and is younger and more seismically active. Some of the more prominent live volcanoes it encompasses are: Mutnovsky (9969 feet), Gorely (5487 feet), Avachinsky (6951 feet), Zhupanovsky (8874 feet), Karymsky (4608 feet), Kizimen (7455 feet), Kronotsky (10,584 feet), Kluchevsky (15,437 feet), Tolbachik (11,046 feet), and Shiveluch (9849 feet). Kamchatka's glaciers, 414 in all, covering 334 square miles, are found on the highest summits of the Central Range and slopes of the tallest volcanoes.

The eastern headlands of the Vostochniy fall abruptly to a rugged, indented coastline of rocky bays, fjords, and small peninsulas. The western, Sea of Okhotsk side is more a gradual and extensive slope from the crest of the central range, with numerous, long river valleys that dissect the foothills, terraces and low-lying wetlands that comprise the west Kamchatka plain. Between the eastern and central ranges lies the Central Kamchatka plain and long, broad valley of the Kamchatka River.

Land of Rivers and Lakes

One of the most striking features of the landscape is the abundance of fresh water. Kamchatka's rugged topography and ample precipitation give rise to thousands of rivers, streams and creeks, and lakes and ponds almost beyond counting. And because of the lack of industry and sparse population, almost all of these waters are totally pristine. Only a handful of them receive any measure of recreational use, mostly by locals.

The upper courses of Kamchatka's mountain rivers are swift, rocky and single-channeled as they carve steep valleys into bedrock. They slow and widen as they emerge from the surrounding foothills, and become braided as they enter the lowlands along the coast. (The gravel streambeds of the middle and lower sections of these rivers are what provide so much spawning habitat for salmon.) Many of these rivers form extensive lagoons at their terminus with the sea. On the western, Sea of Okhotsk side, the largest of these drainages are the Penzhina (443 miles), Bolshaya (175 miles), Tigil (180 miles), Icha, and Vorovskaya. On the northeast coast, emptying into the Bering Sea are the Ozernaya (124 miles), Ivashka, Karaga, Anapka, Valovayam and Apuka (185 miles) rivers. The biggest Pacific Ocean drainages include the Kamchatka (471 miles), Avacha and Zhupanova (130 miles) rivers.

The physical character of these streams—their size, clarity, swift flows and shallow to moderate depth— plus the fact that many are spring fed, makes them ideal for salmon, trout, and charr, as well as perfect for the fly fisherman. With their classic conditions, these many productive drainages represent what is undoubtedly the greatest reserve of high-quality wild stream fishing left in the world. Nowhere else—not even fabled Alaska— will you find such a concentration of perfect wade and sight fishing water and abundant fish populations. And presently, only a small share of this treasure trove has been exploited by anglers.

The lakes of Kamchatka are many, but surprising few are of the size seen in neighboring Alaska. Many of these small, shallow impoundments have been formed by old craters and calderas (Khangar, Kronotsky, Kurile, etc.), or lava dikes (Palana). But most are glacial in origin or develop in peat bogs. The largest lakes in Kamchatka are Nerpiche (173 square miles) and Kronotosky. The deepest is Kurile Lake at 1004 feet.

Kamchatka's Climate

Due to its location and physiography, Kamchatka has a highly variable climate of predominantly northern to subarctic maritime conditions, with seasonal influxes of continental air masses (due to its proximity to the mainland of Asia). This is especially noticeable in the sheltered central lowlands of the Kamchatka River valley, which see the coldest (to minus 40 F. in winter), hottest (up to two months of 70 degrees F. or more in summer) and driest weather (15 inches average annual precipitation) on the peninsula. Frigid ocean currents and prolonged ice cover (up to eight months on the Sea of Okhotsk) delay real spring in Kamchatka until late May and early June and keep most summers cool, damp and cloudy. This is especially true for northern Kamchatka, which lacks the high mountains to shield from the marine layer, and has from 150-260 cloudy days each year. Generally, the weather is more severe in the west than the east, due to the adjacent, icier Sea of Okhotsk.

Winters in Kamchatka are snowy, long and cold, varying in severity with location, but persisting from late October or early November into April (and sometimes beyond) in much of the peninsula. Temperatures along the eastern coast seldom dip below zero. The largest amount of precipitation, up to 97 inches per year, falls on the eastern and southern mountain slopes of the peninsula; the lowest amount, 12 to 15 inches, on parts of the central valley.

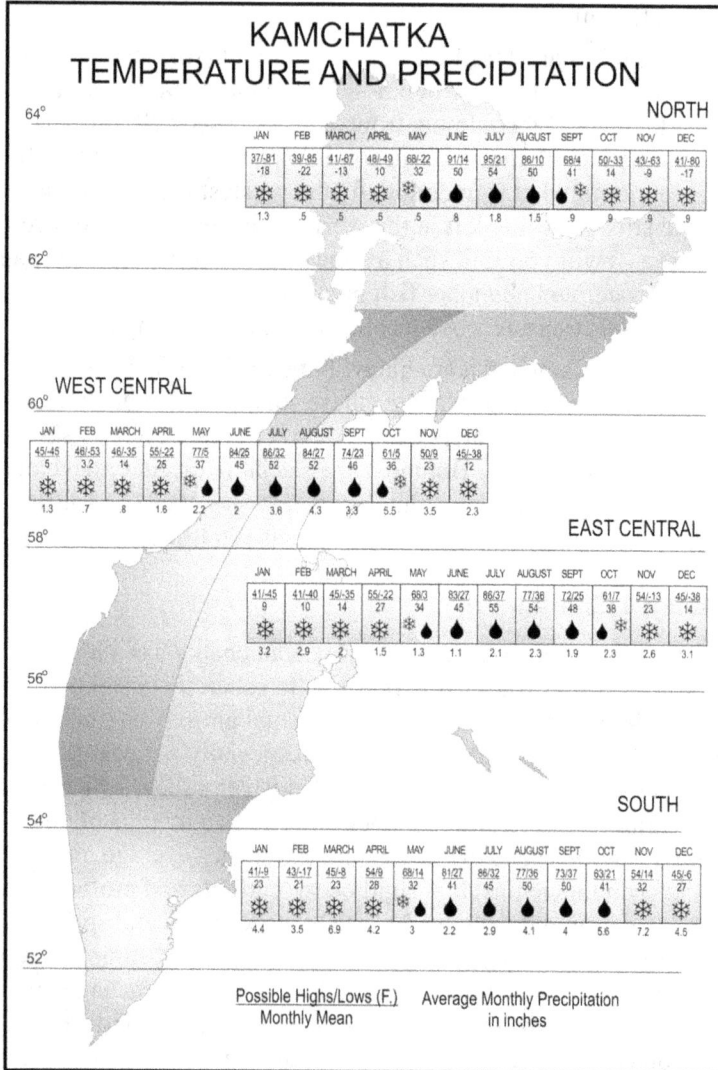

KAMCHATKA TEMPERATURE AND PRECIPITATION

NORTH

	JAN	FEB	MARCH	APRIL	MAY	JUNE	JULY	AUGUST	SEPT	OCT	NOV	DEC
Possible Highs/Lows	37/-81	39/-85	41/-67	48/-49	68/-22	91/14	95/21	88/10	68/4	50/-33	43/-63	41/-80
Monthly Mean	-18	-22	-13	10	32	50	54	50	41	14	-9	-17
Avg. Precipitation	1.3	.5	.5	.5	.5	.8	1.8	1.5	.9	.9	.9	.9

WEST CENTRAL

	JAN	FEB	MARCH	APRIL	MAY	JUNE	JULY	AUGUST	SEPT	OCT	NOV	DEC
Possible Highs/Lows	45/-45	46/-53	46/-35	55/-22	77/5	84/25	86/32	84/27	74/23	61/5	50/9	45/-38
Monthly Mean	5	3.2	14	25	37	45	52	52	46	36	23	12
Avg. Precipitation	1.3	.7	.8	1.6	2.2	2	3.6	4.3	3.3	5.5	3.5	2.3

EAST CENTRAL

	JAN	FEB	MARCH	APRIL	MAY	JUNE	JULY	AUGUST	SEPT	OCT	NOV	DEC
Possible Highs/Lows	41/-45	41/-40	45/-35	55/-22	68/3	83/27	86/37	77/36	72/25	61/7	54/-13	45/-38
Monthly Mean	9	10	14	27	34	45	55	54	48	38	14	14
Avg. Precipitation	3.2	2.9	2	1.5	1.3	1.1	2.1	2.3	1.9	2.3	2.6	3.1

SOUTH

	JAN	FEB	MARCH	APRIL	MAY	JUNE	JULY	AUGUST	SEPT	OCT	NOV	DEC
Possible Highs/Lows	41/-9	43/-17	45/-8	54/9	68/14	81/27	86/32	77/36	73/37	63/21	54/14	45/-6
Monthly Mean	23	21	23	28	41	45	50	50	41	32	32	27
Avg. Precipitation	4.4	3.5	6.9	4.2	3	2.2	2.9	4.1	4	5.6	7.2	4.5

Possible Highs/Lows (F.)
Monthly Mean

Average Monthly Precipitation
in inches

64°
62°
60°
58°
56°
54°
52°

Around Petropavlovsk-Yelizovo and the lowlands of the Avacha River valley, some of the peninsula's nicest weather occurs. Protected from sea winds by the nearby volcanic ranges, this area attracts tourists with a longer summer, with average daily temperature of 60 degrees F. from July into the first part of September. Autumn there is usually sunny and dry, with temperatures, on average, in the 50's F. from the second half of September into October. Average daily temperatures remain above freezing some years until well into November.

Kamchatka's Vegetation

Despite a severe climate, Kamchatka supports a luxuriant growth of vegetation, due to its mineral-rich volcanic soils, long summer days and abundant precipitation. Great areas of land (30% of the peninsula), particularly in the south and central regions, are covered in forest, typically of large, gnarled stone (Erman's) birch, *Betula ermanii*, which is adapted to heavy snow winters, and the much less common, white birch, *Betula platyphylla*. Lush meadows of tall grasses, herbs and wildflowers abound in areas of disturbance, such as from fire or heavy snow accumulation. On mountain slopes and higher elevations, the birch groves give way to near-impenetrable stands of dwarf Siberian pine (elfin cedar), *pinus pumila*, and shrub alder. River lowlands, as in Alaska, are a haven for fast growing, water-loving species like willow (some 33 species in Kamchatka), alder, poplar and the unique and interesting Chosenia (*Chosenia arbutifola*).

The forest in the central valley is mix of birch (both stone and white), aspen and conifers- the Dahurian larch, *Larix dahurica*, and Yeddo spruce, *Picea ajanensis*. A small, relict stand of Sakhalin fir trees, *Abies gracillis*, found near the mouth of the Semiachik River in the Kronotsky Nature Preserve represents the only conifers growing on Kamchatka's east coast.

In the lowlands of western Kamchatka and throughout the northern Koryak region, lie extensive areas of tundra, similar to western and northern Alaska. Dwarf shrubs of birch, alder, pine and willow predominate there, over a carpet of thick mosses and lichens. Sparse stands of trees, mostly birch, occur on better, well-drained sites.

Kamchatka's History

Due to its remoteness, ruggedness and austere climate, the Kamchatka Peninsula was one of the last lands to be explored and settled by the Russians (though various aboriginal peoples such as Koryaks, Evens, Aleuts, Itelmens, Chukchis, etc., lived there for thousands of years). By the middle of the seventeenth century, enterprising Russian Cossacks had spread to the far corners of eastern Siberia and settled in the Anadyr river basin. Rumors of a land of fire, rich in fish and fur, lying to the south were stoked by accounts of some of the most daring early explorers, including Mikhail Stadukhin, one of the first to sail down the coast (Sea of Okhotsk) and describe some of the lands he encountered. Later, bold Cossacks penetrated this territory and explored south to the Kamchatka River, though few written accounts survive of their forays. The first to actually get credit for making the geographical discovery of Kamchatka (based on the first written accounts of exploration) was Vladimir Atlasov, who, in 1697, lead a squadron of Cossacks and natives on an extremely arduous thousand-kilometer trek from Anadyr to the banks of the Kamchatka river, where he erected a wooden cross to mark the acquisition of the peninsula by the Russian Empire. He later built two forts which served as trading posts in the area, and by the early years of the 18th century, hundreds of Russians were living among the native Kamchadals. Kamchatka by this time was considered part of the Yakutsk district of the Siberian province of Russia.

Curiosity about the extent of Asia and its possible connection to the New World prompted Tsar Peter the Great, in the final months of his life (late 1724 to early 1725), to commission an expedition to Kamchatka and beyond to determine if Siberia was joined to the Americas. Thus were begun perhaps the greatest organized adventures of exploration ever betook by man- the two voyages of Vitus J. Bering, a Dane who had served as a captain in the Russian Navy for twenty years and was appointed leader of the expeditions.

Both voyages entailed a grueling traverse of the vast and utterly wild expanses of Siberia, a long ordeal that inflicted severe losses of gear and men. When they reached the Pacific on the first expedition, Bering's crew built ships and set sail to the east, reaching the southern mainland of Kamchatka in the fall of 1727. The following summer, Bering sailed east and north from the mouth of the Kamchatka River in the ship "Saint Gabriel", following the coast of Asia to latitude slightly above 67 degrees north, beyond the strait separating the two continents, which was later named after him. The lateness of the season prevented his further exploration, and he returned to Kamchatka to spend the winter. He set sail again to the northeast next summer, but thick fog and bad weather hampered his efforts to reach the coast of the new lands. From his observations and numerous conversations with natives, however, he concluded that the two continents were separated and returned to St. Petersburg in 1730 to report to his superiors.

Though he had achieved much in the way of exploring and mapping the hitherto unknown coasts of northeast Siberia and Kamchatka, Bering was met with considerable skepticism from his peers for failing to conclusively prove the existence of a northeast passage. Undaunted, he convinced Empress Anna to commission another expedition, far more ambitious and larger than the first.

The horse-drawn caravans of the second expedition left St. Petersburg in 1733. Included were two naval sections, directed to reach the unknown coast of America and find a sea route to Japan, and four detachments whose mission was to explore and map Siberia and Kamchatka. Two German scientists from the newly formed Russian Academy of Science, Gerhard Muller and Johann Gmelin, were in charge of this branch of the expedition, with the young student Stepan Krasheninnikov, their assistant.

When Bering reached the settlement of Okhotsk on the Pacific, he had two ships built, the Saint Peter and Saint Paul, which he, along with his lieutenant Alexei Chrikov, sailed to Avacha Bay on the southeast coast of Kamchatka in 1740, where he had previously sent supplies and men to build a small settlement, which later became the city of Petropavlovsk. In early June of the following year, both ships left to search for America, Bering in command of the "Saint Peter" and Chirikov in the "Saint Paul." The boats became separated in heavy fog soon after leaving Kamchatka and Bering, after a brief attempt to locate the sister ship, resumed course to the north and east, eventually making landfall near Cape St. Elias, Alaska on the 20th of July, 1741. (His landing party included pioneer naturalist George Steller, who gathered the first written observations and specimens of Alaska's natural history.) Chirikov made it farther south and east to the Alexander Archipelago but was unable to go ashore.

The explorers did not linger long in the new lands, heading southwest to skirt the Alaska Peninsula and Aleutians. Unfavorable winds, dwindling freshwater supplies, and scurvy hindered their progress back to Kamchatka, and Bering and his crew became shipwrecked in early November on one of the bleak Commander Islands off the east coast of Kamchatka. (Bering died there in early December). Chirikov made it back to Avacha Bay by October. Bering's marooned crew suffered heavy casualties over the winter, but built a prow from the remains of the Saint Peter the following spring and summer and sailed it back to Petropavlovsk in early fall 1742.

In 1755, Stepan Krasheninnikov published his monumental book, *"Description of the Land of Kamchatka"*, detailing the geography, native culture and natural history of the peninsula, from his four years of exploring Kamchatka. Russian colonization continued, with settlers and exiles swelling the population to several thousand by the early 1800's. In 1854, the French and British, who were battling Russian forces on the Crimean Peninsula, attacked Petropavlovsk. Although far outnumbered, local forces managed to defend the outpost during the siege. After the Anglo-French forces withdrew, Petropavlovsk was abandoned as a strategic liability, and the naval port was moved to Ust-Amur. The sale of Alaska to the United States in 1867 further decreased Petropavlovsk's importance as a hub for traders and explorers on their way to the American territories. In 1860, the Primorsky (Maritime) Region was established, and Kamchatka was placed under its jurisdiction. In 1875, the Kuril Islands were ceded to Japan in return for Russian sovereignty over Sakhalin. The Russian population of Kamchatka stayed around 2,500 until the turn of the century, while the native population increased to 5,000.

Beginning in 1926, Kamchatka was included in Russia's Far Eastern Territory, administered separately and then later as part of the Khabarovsk district. In 1956, it was given separate status in the USSR. Under the new Russian Federation, as of 2007, Kamchatka Krai (which includes the Koryak autonomous region and offshore islands) is part of the Far Eastern federal district. The city of Petropavlovsk is the capital. In 1991, it was opened to foreign visitors.

KAMCHATKA TODAY

Resources & Economy

The Kamchatka Peninsula, like neighboring Alaska, enjoys a rich bounty of natural resources. Abundant mineral wealth includes numerous deposits of precious metals (gold, platinum, and silver), mercury, complex metallic ores (copper/nickel/cobalt) and coal, oil and natural gas. Plentiful construction materials (sand, gravel, clay, pumice, perlite, building stone, etc.) are also widespread but barely utilized. The peninsula's notorious volcanism creates considerable geothermal potential at numerous sites (only a small number currently being exploited for power generation), along with an abundance of thermal and mineral waters of great value to commerce and personal recreation.

The legendary scenic and biological resources of the Kamchatka Peninsula are, of course, its greatest assets. Foremost among them certainly are the prolific fisheries, providing in waters in and around the peninsula a rich harvest of high-value commercial species (salmon, crab, halibut, pollock, etc.,) in addition to some of the world's last remaining opportunities for virgin cold water sport fishing. The unique landscape features and rich and pristine assemblage of wildlife and plants (918 vertebrate animals and 1168 species of plants) are preserved in some 152 designated Protected Areas (nature parks, refuges, reserves, preserves, monuments, etc., comprising 27% of Kamchatka's land area), six of them of UNESCO World Heritage Status.

The 330,000 or so folks who live in Kamchatka earn their living mostly by fishing, canning, sealing, mining, lumbering, shipbuilding, and woodworking. Fishing and related industries dominate the economy and crabs and salmon are the main catch and exported worldwide. Tourism is of growing and significant importance, given the peninsula's world class reputation among Eco-tourists, fly fishermen, and hunters. A limited amount of timber harvesting (in the Central Valley), agriculture (grain, potato and other vegetable growing; dairy farming, cattle and reindeer herding) and harvesting of wild furs rounds out Kamchatka's economy.

Government

In accordance with the principles of self-government laid out in the Russian Constitution of 1993, Kamchatka is now a democratic republic, with government comprised of administrative, legislative and judicial bodies, organized and run much like the U.S. There is a governor, and mayors, district, city and town councils, judges, representatives, ministers, etc., either elected or appointed. The regional government retains a certain autonomy within the Russian Federation, much like an individual state of the U.S. has in the federal government.

People

Kamchatka's population today is comprised mostly of transplanted Russians, with a minority of natives from five major indigenous groups— the Evens, Itelmens, Koryaks, Aleuts, and Chukchis— that have occupied Kamchatka for at least 12,000 years. They are historically nomadic subsistence cultures, utilizing Kamchatka's abundant fish, game and marine mammals and also reindeer herding. They preserve their way of life today in villages and camps around the peninsula, concentrated mostly in the Bystrinsky district and northern Koryak region.

Russian people, in general, are proud, independent and resourceful. A tolerance for the inadequacies of their government and the deplorable conditions they sometimes must endure is a hallmark trait of their character. So too is their hospitableness to foreigners, though they may lack outward warmth to strangers on the streets.

Language

The official language of the Kamchatka region is Russian. Many of its people, however, speak some English and most tourist companies, large hotels, restaurants and government agencies have representatives capable of conversing in English. With the growth of foreign tourism, other languages like German and Japanese are increasingly spoken.

Currency

The official currency of Kamchatka is the Russian rouble, available in coins for small denominations and bank notes for amounts of 10 roubles or more. (Foreign currency can be exchanged for roubles only at the banks.) Almost all businesses in Kamchatka perform cash transactions in roubles only, with credit cards (VISA and MASTERCARD) accepted only by large hotels, restaurants, and some supermarkets in Petropavlovsk-Yelizovo and other large hubs. ATM machines are available in major businesses and banks in the Yelizovo-Petropavlovsk metropolitan area.

Religion

As part of the Russian Federation, Kamchatka has no official religion recognized by the government. The Russian Orthodox Church has a rich history of involvement in the settlement and development of all of Far East Russia and continues its influence today with a majority of believers in Kamchatka. Their distinctive churches can be seen all across the region. There are also 70 other diverse denominations practicing within Kamchatka.

FRESHWATER GAMEFISHES OF KAMCHATKA

RAINBOW TROUT

Oncorhynchus mykiss

Common names: Mikizha (Russia); rainbow, rainbow trout and "bow" (U.S.); noble trout (Kamchatka), semga (steelhead, Russia)

Description: Beautifully colored and spotted native trout of Kamchatka, similar if not identical to same species found in North America. Grows to 32 inches and 12 lbs.; average size 16 to 20 inches, 1 ½ to 3 lbs.

Range/Abundance/Status: Found over most of southern and central Kamchatka. Locally abundant (frequently with charr) and thriving throughout range

Best Waters: Large, productive salmon rivers with variety of habitat

Best Rivers: Zhupanova, Opala, Ozernaya, Pymta, Icha, Tigil, Tikhaya, Kolpokova, Bolshaya & Kamchatka river systems

Best Fly Patterns: Forage, attractor and egg/flesh patterns; nymph and dry flies (including mouse patterns)

Best Times: Available year-round; best in spring and late summer into fall

The most widespread and popular cold water game fish in the world, the rainbow trout was originally described from wild specimens taken from Kamchatka streams as far back as the late 18th century. (The bigger sea-run forms, steelhead, came to be known as the Kamchatka salmon-trout, or "semga" to the Russians, while the river resident forms were called "mikizha" after the local vernacular.). These far-flung populations of robust native rainbows were "rediscovered" by westerners late in the 20th century as Kamchatka opened up its borders to tourists after the demise of the Soviet Union. Visiting anglers' initial encounters with abundant, big wild trout and near-perfect stream conditions launched the beginning of Kamchatka's sport fishing industry. These beautiful fighters remain the biggest draw for visiting fly anglers the world over, who come to experience some of the best wild fishing left for the species.

Description

The Kamchatka rainbow, in its most common form, is usually easily recognizable, different from any salmon, though it sometimes can be mistaken at first glance for a bright, sea-run Dolly Varden charr. River resident rainbows are sleek and streamlined, with topsides of olive green to gray or bluish-gray, blending into sides of silver or silver-gray that become whitish toward the belly. A pink, crimson or lilac stripe or blush along the midline and gill plate, along with prominent round black markings on the body and tail fin are salient identifying characters. Belly fins are generally pinkish to pearly white. Rainbow fry and parr can be hard to distinguish from young coho (silver salmon), which display similar color and markings. (Rainbow fingerlings have smaller eyes proportionately than coho.) The flesh of the rainbow trout varies from white to pink to light orange-red, depending on diet, and is considered choice eating.

Rainbows that spend time in estuaries and out at sea are generally more robust and salmon-like in appearance, with silvery coloration and fewer markings. It should be noted that appearance can vary with time of year, diet, maturity and location. Spawning brings physical changes, similar to but not as dramatic as in salmon, with a darkening of coloration and moderate jaw kypes in the males.

Much has been made of the hefty size of Kamchatka's rainbows. Average length and weight vary considerably from drainage to drainage (because of life history variation- read on for details), and can be anywhere from 16 to 24 inches and 1 & 1/2 to 4 lbs., which clearly puts Kamchatka's trout on a par with Alaska and other trophy locations. (Which is remarkable considering most of Kamchatka's big trout fisheries do not have large headwater lakes, unlike those in Alaska and the Southern Hemisphere.)

Distribution

The rainbow trout is distributed along much of the north Pacific Rim, from Mexico to Kamchatka. In Russia, the "mikizha" is found throughout most of southern and central Kamchatka, from the Ozernaya River in the east, to the Golygina River in the south, to the Palana River in the northwest. It is especially abundant in rivers with abundant spawning and rearing habitat and large runs of salmon. (The rainbow is not found in any numbers on the mainland along the Sea of Okhotsk, and only sporadically on some of the islands south of the Kamchatka Peninsula.) The sea-run form of the rainbow trout, the steelhead or "semga" in Russian, has a similar, but much more sporadic distribution.

Life History

Kamchatka's rainbow trout, for the most part, shares the same life history as the Alaska rainbow, with some interesting differences. It begins its life in much the same manner as salmon, hatching from eggs laid and fertilized in a gravel stream bed (spawning usually occurs in May or early June). Rainbow fry develop quickly, feeding on insect and crustacean life, and later, when larger, on minnows (sticklebacks and juvenile salmon) leeches, freshwater shrimp, the roe and flesh of spawning salmon and even small rodents. Extremely opportunistic, the adult rainbow trout will feed heavily on any available food source, making extensive migrations throughout its range to exploit seasonally available sustenance. It reaches sexual maturity in three to six years, and data collected show it may live to about ten (rarely longer). Unlike salmon, the rainbow trout can spawn multiple times during its lifespan.

Studies done over the last twenty years or so have turned up a remarkable diversity of rainbow life history variations on the rivers of Kamchatka (and shed light on why the average size is so large on many rivers). Apart from the common form that spends its entire life in freshwater or the less common, but well-known steelhead, which spends most of its adult life at sea, there are mikizha that make short feeding forays into estuaries and some even that go out along the coast for up to several months at a time. The trout populations in many of the rivers studied, it turns out, are a mix of these life history types (six possible life history variations have been identified), with some systems producing mostly steelhead, others mostly river resident fish and some rivers a blend of stream-dwelling, estuary feeding and ocean ranging types. Stream morphology, food abundance, genetics, water temperature regimes and other variables have been proposed as possibly influencing variations in life history. Whether this is a phenomenon unique to the rivers of Kamchatka remains to be determined.

Habits

Rainbows, compared to other trout, are notoriously rambunctious, and Kamchatka trout seem even more reckless than their counterparts in Alaska. They will follow a skittered mouse pattern right into shore, hitting it repeatedly and sometimes even hooking themselves at your feet. Or gorge on salmon roe until their bellies almost burst and the eggs spill out of their mouths as they grab your fly in their insatiable greed for more food. Perhaps the most endearing of the rainbow's traits, next to its spectacular fighting ability (few fish will leap as high or as often when hooked), is its easy arousal and vigorous manner in which it attacks prey. Nothing whacks a fly, lure or bait like a hungry rainbow, especially one that lives in the feast or famine waters of Alaska or Kamchatka! If you should fish during the early or late part of the season when food is relatively scarce, there'll be no mistaking the take of a rainbow for any other creature that swims in these waters.

This is not to say that the Kamchatka mikizha is a guaranteed pushover requiring little finesse to entice it to the fly. In situations of great food abundance, such as on summer salmon spawning beds or one of Kamchatka's prolific insect hatches, the rainbow may become surprisingly finicky, to the point even where it may steadfastly refuse any artificial enticement, much to your frustration. More commonly encountered however, will be situations requiring a careful "match the hatch" strategy, along with better line control to detect the subtle takes from fully sated and barely aroused trout. This unpredictability is one of the hallmark characteristics of the species, a trait that combined with its radiant beauty and supreme lust for freedom, make the rainbow the great game fish that it is.

FLY FISHING KAMCHATKA'S RAINBOW TROUT

In Kamchatka, the rainbow trout is frequently taken incidentally by Russians fishing for salmon, using heavy spinning gear and lures. There is also considerable targeted effort for the mikizha by residents who fish them, along with the peninsula's abundant Dolly Varden charr and (where available) grayling, on light spinning gear, primarily for subsistence. (Poachers also take quite a few incidentally in their illegal bulk netting of salmon.) Currently, the only significant fly fishing effort for the species occurs on the most popular rivers visited by foreign anglers (Zhupanova, Opala, Bolshaya, Ozernaya and others). Dozens of great Kamchatka trout rivers receive little or no fly fishing pressure.

Since Russia's rainbows share so many similarities with trout in Alaska, fly anglers interested in pursuing the Kamchatka mikizha will do well utilizing most of the strategies, gear, and flies used in the 49th state, with some exceptions. Rainbows can be fly fished successfully in Kamchatka from the beginning of open water season (April to May in most rivers) to ice-up (late October to November). Generally, forage, nymph and attractor patterns are most productive during early season fishing, while egg/flesh, attractors and dry fly patterns (including mouse imitations) work best during the warmest months of the year. Fall fish will succumb to forage, attractor, egg/flesh and, when the conditions are right, dry fly patterns.

Since the rainbow is extremely opportunistic and far-ranging in its search for food, the accepted strategy is to target areas that may hold seasonally available food sources: lake outlets, stream confluences, river mouths and estuaries (for spring trout feeding on smolt and other forage); salmon spawning and holding areas (for egg and flesh feeding trout during summer and early fall); deep pools, cut banks, tail-outs, drop-offs, boulder-strewn rapids, sloughs, etc. (forage ambush sites used during the entire open water season); and anywhere feeding trout are observed (such as in areas where hatches occur). Local knowledge, maps, an ability to "read" rivers and polarized sunglasses will be extremely useful for locating feeding trout on Kamchatka's clearwater streams.

Early Season Rainbows: Early season in Kamchatka runs from anytime open water is available (usually April or early May in most southern and central streams) to the arrival of the first salmon in early summer (usually early June). This period can present the most challenging trout fishing conditions of the year, with raw weather, possibly turbid and/or swollen streams and feeding fish that may be difficult to locate. (The trout are usually starving, however, and seldom present any challenge in enticement, once you do locate them.) Traditionally, this is the best time of year for forage pattern fishing (including nymphing), especially early on, as the rainbows will be keyed into larval insect and fish life and most prone to properly selected and presented artificials that mimic early season food items (including mouse patterns!) Attractors can also be used to great effect with these early season trout. Traditional wet fly swings and drifts will produce the most response, using floating or short sink tip lines and additional weight, if needed, to get the fly down. Small fish flies (Alevin, Fry, Parr, Smolt, Muddler, etc.) and Leeches are classic patterns for this kind of fishing, as are nymphs like the Hare's Ear, Caddis, and Stonefly. If you do everything right, expect to take quite a few charr along with rainbows, as the two species share waters and compete for many of the available food sources this time of year.

As spring develops, rainbow trout will begin to gather around their traditional spawning sites: small feeder creeks, headwaters, side channels, lake outlets, etc. Hungry, testy and concentrated in great numbers in some areas, they are easy prey for anglers. As Kamchatka has yet to evolve management that protects rainbows at their most vulnerable time in their life cycle (as Alaska has), it is up to the discretion of anglers to leave these fish alone when they actively begin their spawning activities (usually mid-May into early June). After spawning, the trout, spent and famished, will linger briefly in these areas, and then disperse in search of abundant, seasonally available prey such as sea-bound smolt and the first insect hatches of the year. This can be another great time for fishing, to intercept these particularly hungry trout with a good forage pattern or attractor.

By late May or early June, most streams in Kamchatka will be running high and murky from the rapidly melting headwater snowpack, less than ideal conditions, for sure, but still great fishing possible, as the rainbows are in much better shape and the rising water temperatures bring on more feeding activity. There are still shoals of smolts making their panicked way to the sea in the larger, more productive systems and increasingly more emerging insect life for trout to focus on. And, the first groups of salmon begin entering lower rivers, an arrival of such great importance to the trout that they will literally "shadow" groups of their larger cousins as they make their way upriver to their spawning grounds. Depending on location and conditions, you can do fabulously well this time of year fishing forage, dry fly, attractors or even egg patterns. Best spots to locate trout are in river mouths, confluences, shallow to moderately deep pools, riffle sections, drop-offs and around structure like boulders and log jams.

Summer Rainbows: Real summer in most of Kamchatka begins in late June and continues into September. For trout, these warmest weeks of the year mean frenzied feeding on abundant insect hatches and salmon eggs. By the first or second week of July, most of the streams will settle down, presenting great conditions for wade-and-cast, sight fishing. Dry flies and egg patterns will naturally be the best producers this time of year, with attractors and forage flies usually providing consistent, but lesser results.

Locating feeding trout this time of year is usually no trick and consists of searching for hatches and spawning salmon, two activities not in short supply on the fecund rivers of Kamchatka during the height of summer. Most salmon spawning occurs in the middle to lower sections of rivers, where the gravel substrate and current are ideal for the success of the mating act and survival of the eggs. Look for groups of salmon holding in side channels, pool tail-outs, riffle sections, stream margins, sloughs, under cut banks and other prime locations. Good polarized sunglasses are essential for this task. (If, in a likely spot, you sight a group that does not show signs of moving upriver in a reasonable amount of time, you have probably found some spawners.) If you peer long enough into the water, you may sight smaller, lighter colored shapes moving around the periphery of these areas where the bigger fish are holding. These are the opportunistic charr and rainbow trout that are feasting on the stray eggs that drift away from the nests into the current. (Some of the more bold and swift of these egg pirates can be seen darting into the salmon nests to grab eggs.) Depending on the size of the nest area and number of spawning salmon, there can be dozens of these marauders, so keyed into the color and shape of salmon eggs, they make easy prey for anglers drifting a suitable artificial enticement through their field of vision. A single or double egg fly (Glo Bug, Babine Special), bead egg, or appropriate attractor (Polar Shrimp, Skykomish Sunrise) drifted right above bottom (using a floating line, perhaps with split shot placed a short ways above the fly), is deadly in these situations. Strike indicators, if you fish them, can be extremely useful in this kind of fishing, particularly when using bead eggs.

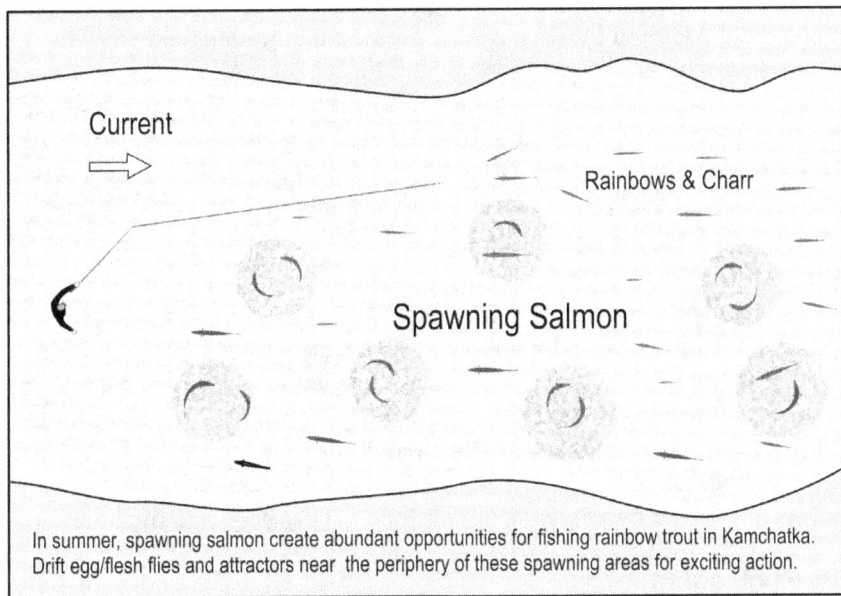

In summer, spawning salmon create abundant opportunities for fishing rainbow trout in Kamchatka. Drift egg/flesh flies and attractors near the periphery of these spawning areas for exciting action.

Note: If you are targeting trout feeding on salmon roe, do not disturb spawning salmon by casting in or drifting through their redds. Instead, cast carefully to the trout holding on the periphery around and downstream of these salmon nests, and if you do accidentally hook one of the big spawners, which happens not infrequently when fishing attractor or egg patterns, break it off immediately.

Locating hatches is not as formulaic, as they can occur just about anywhere and anytime along Kamchatka's rocky streambeds. But in summer, you won't have to work too hard to find some kind of emerging insect activity, especially if you are fishing with a boat. Some of the more common areas to find rising fish are in stream margins, pools, tail-outs, riffle sections and feeder creek confluences. (You may even come upon an area where salmon spawning and hatches are occurring near or even adjacent to each other.) Keep in mind that in Kamchatka, these hatches attract the attention of not just the prized rainbow trout, but also abundant grayling and charr.

Fall Rainbows: Fall in most of Kamchatka's rainbow country comes in mid- to late September, with cooler nights creating a dramatic change in foliage and water temperatures, along with, in addition to waning food sources, a marked shift in the feeding behavior and movements of the peninsula's trout. The last runs of salmon wane, causing rainbows to scour spawning beds for any available eggs and carcasses. (Quite a few rivers in Kamchatka, however, get late runs of sockeye, chum, and silvers, well into September.) Many of these spawning areas, long into fall, can provide great fishing for anglers drifting egg and flesh patterns, tempting trout in the absolute peak of condition, fattened by a summer of gorging, with appetites heightened by the change in season. Egg and flesh flies (Glo Bug, Babine, Flesh Fly, Carcass Fly and others) and egg-like attractors (Polar Shrimp, Battle Creek, Skykomish Sunrise, Kamchatka Special, Cotton Candy, Pink Sparkler and similar patterns) are the ticket to some of the biggest rainbows of the year.

Forage and attractor patterns can also be used on these fat fall trout, with best results fishing areas like pools, confluences, sloughs, under cut banks and around structure (boulders, islands, logjams, etc.), to pick up hungry trout on the prowl as they begin to move from established summer feeding areas to overwintering sites. And don't overlook the Kamchatka fall as a fabulous time for mousing, as the trout become increasingly reckless when their abundant summer food supply begins to dwindle.

Dry Fly Fishing

Even anglers seasoned on the great rivers of the American West, New Zealand or South America will be happy with the dry fly fishing conditions in Kamchatka. Due to the climate and volcanic substrate, the rivers support a surprisingly rich biota of insect life (quite a few species of caddis, stone and dragonflies, some mayflies and numerous midges, black flies, mosquitoes and other insects) and are ideal for fly casting. The timing of these hatches is more spread out than in southern locales, with a peak in intensity during the warmest days of the year (July & August), but sustained throughout the open water season, especially on the more productive rivers. Even on off days of bum weather, if you are fishing with a boat, you can usually locate surface feeding trout within a short distance along the rivers.

As previously noted, rainbows (and charr and grayling) that feed on these abundant hatches can become selective, ignoring other, more nourishing forage available nearby (such as salmon eggs/flesh, rodents, and small fish) and in extreme cases, refusing all but the most carefully matched and presented artificials. Fortunately, these persnickety rainbows are rare, and generally, the mikizha is more than willing to cooperate when presented with a fair imitation of what is on the menu, with no extreme technical prowess or specialized gear required on the part of the angler. (You can leave your fluorocarbon and hero casts back home.) If you do encounter a group of super-snooty rainbows that turn down your best attempts to match the hatch, some of the strategies used in Kamchatka to entice them are to switch to nymphing rigs, dropper fly setups, or even attractors. This sometimes works to jolt them out of their lethargy. Keep in mind, of course, that, similar to Alaska, there are almost always more eager fish available nearby, so don't spend too much time trying to raise overly finicky trout. (See section on techniques and gear for much more information on dry fly fishing in Kamchatka.)

Mouse Fishing

The most exciting and unique "dry fly" fishing in Kamchatka involves skittering rodent imitations across the surface, commonly known as "mousing". This technique employs large, bushy flies constructed of spun deer hair, fur or foam, lifelike creations that mimic any one of several species of Kamchatka's ubiquitous small rodents (voles, mice, lemmings, shrews) that periodically overrun river banks with their numbers and fall prey to marauding trout. The mouse, rat or lemming patterns typically used are best fished on or slightly below the surface, using twitches of the rod to impart lifelike action. Most productive areas are sloughs, pools, rock-filled rapids, under cut banks and around brush piles and logjams. The take of a big trout on these oversized surface patterns is quite dramatic and once experienced, leaves the angler feeling never quite the same about other, more tame surface presentations! The general rule is to let the fish hook itself; otherwise, you may pull the fly from the fish's mouth if you get too trigger happy. A much more intensive fishing technique than drifting or stripping attractors or forage patterns, mousing is usually most productive during the low light of evening and morning and on cloudy days. (See the techniques and gear section for much more information on fishing with the Mouse and other faux rodents.)

An angler twitches a Mouse through some promising water on the Pymta River, southern Kamchatka.

Gearing Up

Most Kamchatka trout anglers bring a 5 or 6-weight, medium-action, standard length (8 to 9 foot) graphite fly rod for headwater and stream fishing, and a 7 or even an 8-weight, medium-action, standard or long (8 ½ to 10 foot) graphite rod for fishing the deeper, swifter water found in the lower sections of Kamchatka's trout rivers, especially the larger ones (Kamchatka, Zhupanova, Bolshaya, Ozernaya and others). Performance-tapered floating and short (5 foot or less) medium-density, sink-tip fly lines work best for almost all the waters you will encounter, along with 9 foot tapered nylon monofilament leaders (Kamchatka's rainbows are not leader shy, so fluorocarbon is not necessary) and 0X–5X (4 to 10 pound test) tippets. Strike indicators and split shot are commonly used. See gear and techniques section for more information on recommended gear for fly fishing Kamchatka's rainbow trout.

Note: Rainbow trout exhaust themselves so thoroughly when fighting that they are easily killed unless handled gently and released quickly into the water. Confer with your guide if you are not entirely familiar with proper "catch and release" techniques, and use micro or barbless hooks to minimize your impact on this world-class resource. (Get more information on minimum impact, catch and release fishing techniques in our section on techniques and gear for fly fishing Kamchatka.)

Recommended Wet Fly Patterns:

Spring: Alevin, Smolt, Fry, Parr and Sculpin (#4–10); Matuka, Woolly Bugger, Leech, Muddler (#4–8); Mickey Finn, Polar Shrimp (#6–8); Hare's Ear Nymph, Bead Head Caddis (#8); Stone Nymph, Mayfly Nymph (#8–14); Bitch Creek #4–8, Bead Head Brassie (#10), Emerger #12

Summer/Fall: Egg Sucking Leech #6–8, Zonker #6–8, Flesh/Carcass Fly #4–6, Black Gnat #4–6, Bunny Bug #4–6, Crystal Bugger #6–8, McCune Sculpin #4–6, Cotton Candy #4–6, Battle Creek #6–8, Kamchatka Special #6–8, Polar Shrimp #6–8, Woolly Bugger #4–8, Glo Bug (Egg) #8–12, Marabou Muddler #4–8, Babine Special #4–8, Skykomish Sunrise #6–8, Bead Egg (5–8 mm with #8–12 egg hook), Crystal Bullet #4–8, Pink Sparkler #6–8

Recommended Dry Fly Patterns:

Wulff #10–14, Stonefly #10, Parachute Adams #14–20, Black Gnat #10–14, Elk Hair Caddis #12–16, Olive Stimulator #12, Mosquito #12–16, Midge #20–22, Cahill #12–18, Yellow Sally #12–16, Red Quill #16–20, Blue Wing Olive #12–18

Mouse (size #4–6): Whitlock's Deerhair Mouse/Rat, Mercer's Lemming, Morrish Mouse, Babine Foamback, Fur Mouse, Wiggle Lemming.

STEELHEAD TROUT

Igor Shatilo

Oncorhynchus mykiss

Common names: Steelhead trout, steelhead, steelie (U.S.); semga (Russia), Kamchatka salmon-trout, noble trout (Kamchatka)

Description: Sea-run, native trout (mikizha) of Kamchatka, salmon-like in size and appearance; 28 to 32 inches and 7 to 12 lbs. average; to 36 inches and 20 lbs.

Range/Abundance/Status: Found west side streams, southern and central Kamchatka. Seasonally rare to common throughout range; Red Book endangered status for Kamchatka populations

Best Waters: Tundra streams along west-central coast

Best Rivers: Utkholok, Kvachina, Sopochnaya, Snotolvayem, Saichik and Voyampolka rivers

Best Fly Patterns: Attractor streamers, forage and egg pattern flies

Best Times: Late September into November

The steelhead trout is the sea-run form of the rainbow trout native to streams along the North Pacific. Called the "salmon-trout" by the first white explorers to reach Kamchatka's shores, this elusive and uncommon fighter, with its hefty size and sea-honed vigor, has become one of the most esteemed coldwater sport fishes in the world, second perhaps only to the regal Atlantic salmon in the fanatical devotion it receives from legions of fly anglers. No other stream fish along the Pacific holds its freedom so dear and fights so valiantly.

Common at certain times of year in only a handful of streams and legally off limits to pursue without special permits (given only to programs associated with scientific research, like The Kamchatka Steelhead Project) the Kamchatka steelhead nonetheless remains a tantalizing possibility for trout anglers. For if by slim chance, you should hook one of these errant, robust sea trout while pursuing late season rainbows, there would be no mistaking it, especially on a light or medium weight rod! Your encounter, no doubt brief but exciting, would give you a taste of what makes these fish the most coveted stream prize in all the North Pacific—legendary power, supreme lust for life and graceful beauty.

Description

Steelhead are generally larger, longer, leaner and more silvery (especially when fresh from the sea) than big resident rainbow trout. Also, their tail fins are generally broader and more fan-shaped, with thicker wrists than those of river rainbows. In the sea or mouths of rivers, steelhead can easily be mistaken for salmon, especially coho or silver, which are of the same size and with similar markings. (Positive identification can be made from a count of the fin rays in the anal fin; the steelhead has eight to twelve rays, most salmon will have 12 to 17). Ocean-fresh steelhead have topsides of shiny gunmetal blue, contrasted with silver-white below the lateral line. A faint blush of pink or rose shading may be present on the gill plates. There are medium-size, black, evenly-spaced, round markings on the back and sides, as well as on both lobes of the tail.

In preparation for spawning, the steelhead's colors become similar to those of resident rainbow trout. The gunmetal blue back changes to olive or gray. A reddish or pink hue intensifies on the gill plates, and the classic crimson stripe begins to show along the lateral line. Males develop, to a lesser degree, some of the physical traits seen in spawning salmon (jaw kypes and ridgebacks). Upon completion of spawning, the steelhead's colors gradually revert to their ocean phase.

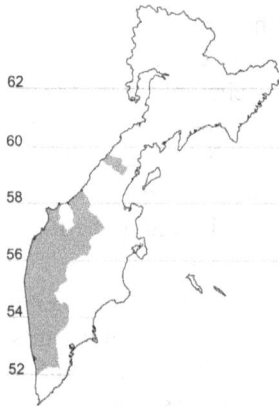

The Kamchatka steelhead, while larger on average than an Alaska sea-run rainbow, generally does not reach the sizes seen in the big river systems of British Columbia and the Pacific Northwest states. Mature specimens average from 26 to 34 inches in length and weigh from seven to 13 pounds, with the largest fish found in the tundra rivers of west-central Kamchatka. Outsize fish in these streams can reach 36 inches in length and 20 pounds.

Distribution

The native range of the steelhead closely follows that of the resident river rainbow along the north Pacific Rim, from southern California to British Columbia and Alaska, and across the Bering Sea to the Kamchatka Peninsula coast. Although migratory rainbow trout variants (fish that make seasonal forays into the salt for short lengths of time) exist in many rivers along both coasts of the Kamchatka Peninsula (and perhaps, to a much lesser extent, in Alaska as well), true steelhead, fish that spend most of their adult lives at sea, are found in sizeable numbers only along the western coast. Small numbers of steelies run in just about every swift, clear flowing mountain stream there, from the Opala River north to the Voyampolka (and perhaps beyond). But the major steelhead runs occur in the slower moving, meandering, tannic-stained tundra streams that flow through the extensive central-western coastal plain. (These streams have more suitable conditions for overwintering survival and successful spring spawning.) These systems, interestingly, lack the headwater lakes that moderate temperatures on the major fall steelhead systems across the Pacific in Alaska (from the Southeast Panhandle to the Aleutians). Never prolific, Kamchatka's small runs of hefty, sea-faring rainbows were listed in the Red Book of endangered flora/fauna of the Russian Federation in the early 1980's, for protection and further study. (Therefore, no Kamchatka steelhead caught by anglers, incidentally or otherwise, may be kept, and must be released unharmed immediately.)

Life History

Comparatively little research has been done on the life history of the Kamchatka steelhead. From what we know, mostly from studies in the eastern Pacific, Kamchatka steelhead rear in freshwater for several years and then migrate to sea, returning several times during their lives to spawn in freshwater. As freshwater juveniles, their feeding habits and behavior are identical to resident rainbows; they subsist on a wide range of available food items—insects, fry, crustaceans, and the roe and flesh of salmon. Roaming the food-rich open sea after leaving freshwater, steelhead feed on diets of various fishes, crustaceans, and squid, and attain large size relative to most resident rainbow trout before returning as mature adults to their natal streams.

Almost all steelhead in Kamchatka, similar to those along Alaska's North Gulf and Alaska Peninsula, are fall run fish, typically entering streams in the fall and overwintering in freshwater before spawning in the spring. These steelhead begin showing up in the mouths of streams sometime in late August (southern streams) or September, peaking in numbers during October, and finishing their immigration in November (or even December in some rivers). Only a very small percentage of Kamchatka's steelhead delay entry into freshwater until spring (much the same as for the more northerly occurring steelhead across the Pacific). Their spawning, as for resident rainbows, occurs in late spring when water temperatures are on the rise, usually late May to early June. Spent adults (called kelts) make their way to sea shortly after spawning, in late spring. Steelhead are capable of spawning multiple times during their lifespan (up to 8 or 9 years).

Habits

Steelhead are notoriously shy, elusive creatures and only moderately social, compared to salmon. They are very sensitive to light and movement when in rivers, particularly in shallow or clear waters, and easily spooked. They are usually more aggressive and prone to enticement when fresh from the sea, and become steadily more aloof in rivers, especially in fall, with dropping water temperatures. They generally do not feed as adults when in rivers but do respond to forage patterns like egg flies and leeches and certain attractors. The take of a steelhead can vary from very hard and aggressive to very subtle and barely perceptible, depending on many factors.

As fighters, steelhead are famously known for their incredible power and jumping ability, outclassing just about every other game fish their size. (Just ask any veteran steelheader for testimonials confirming that fact!) Within the confines of the stream environment, with its numerous hazards, this sterling trait makes them perhaps the most challenging quarry in freshwater fly fishing. Stout gear and stalwart ability with a fly rod are necessary for any measure of success.

FLY FISHING KAMCHATKA'S STEELHEAD TROUT

Because the Kamchatka steelhead is listed in the Red Book of endangered fauna and flora of the Russian Federation, it cannot legitimately be targeted by anglers, except in a limited number of angler-assisted research programs sanctioned by the Russian government. Small numbers of steelhead, nonetheless, are taken incidentally each fall by Russian fishermen targeting salmon and trout on Kamchatka's west side streams, mostly with spinning gear. (Any steelhead taken accidentally must be released without delay or harm.) Almost all fly angling effort for the species is done by foreigners on a few remote rivers targeted by the outfitters running the special steelhead programs.

Fishing fall run steelhead in the North Pacific has never been anything but a most challenging proposition. Unlike fishing for spring steelhead, when conditions are generally more favorable and daily improving, fall steelhead angling occurs during a time of rapidly deteriorating weather (with intense equinoctial storms, especially in Kamchatka), dwindling daylight and fast cooling temperatures. The scenario is often further complicated by late or weak runs of incoming steelhead.

Despite the daunting possibility of high, turbid flows, wicked weather and spotty fishing, more than a few hardy fly anglers have participated in Kamchatka's joint steelhead research programs over the years, and their experiences show that with persistence (and luck) Russian steelies can be taken consistently, using the strategies and gear refined over the years by late season steelheaders in the U.S. Pacific Northwest (including Alaska), who frequently deal with raw weather, challenging stream conditions and fish that are less active and more finicky, once stream waters cool down.

Techniques

As in fall steelheading elsewhere in the North Pacific, Kamchatka's sea-run rainbows are best pursued in lower rivers, where they are bright and often testy, fresh in from the sea. Kamchatka's steelhead waters, similar to those in Alaska, are not large drainages like some of the classic, brawling steelhead rivers of the American Northwest and Canada. The best of them are modest-sized tundra streams that wander out of the foothills of the west-central peninsula on to the dreary coastal flats before emptying into the Sea of Okhotsk. Most of the runs there are comparatively small, in the hundreds or few thousands at most, in the most productive streams in good years.

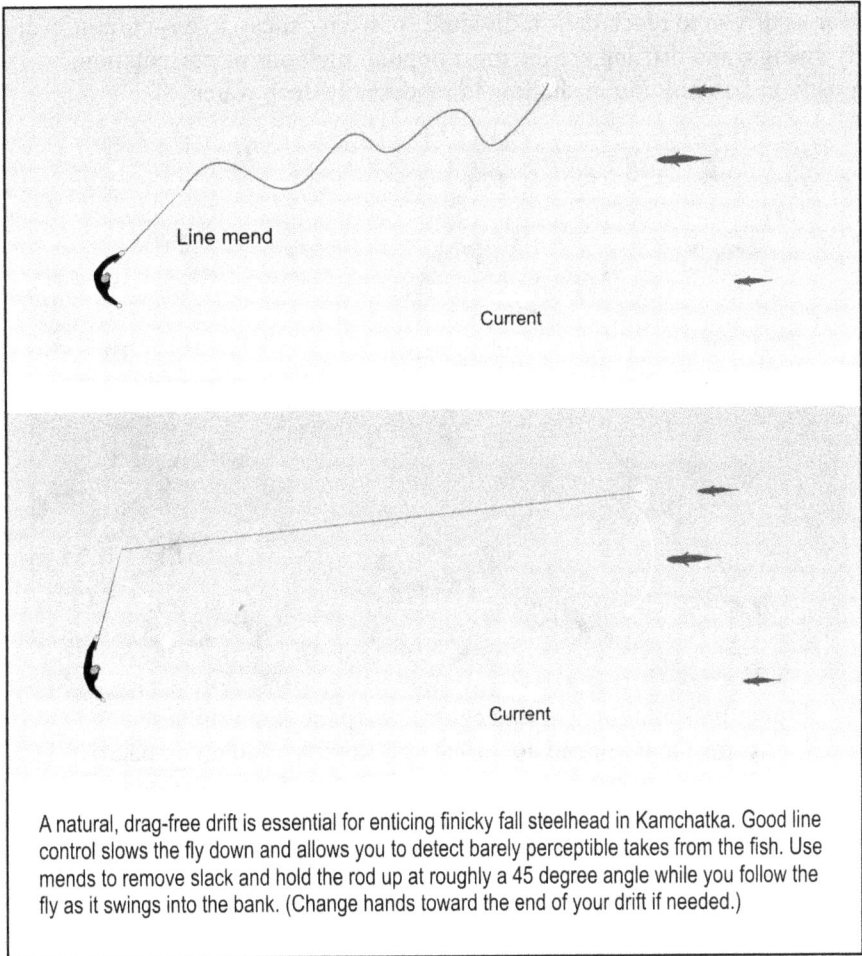

A natural, drag-free drift is essential for enticing finicky fall steelhead in Kamchatka. Good line control slows the fly down and allows you to detect barely perceptible takes from the fish. Use mends to remove slack and hold the rod up at roughly a 45 degree angle while you follow the fly as it swings into the bank. (Change hands toward the end of your drift if needed.)

The main technical challenges for fall steelheaders in this part of the world, like in Alaska, will be locating fish and presenting suitable enticements in a manner that will prompt a take from a creature that can be notoriously aloof this time of year. Most of the Kamchatka steelhead angling effort occurs from early October on, targeting fresh fish that come in on the swell of the fall run. The guides are usually up on the status of the runs and location of fish, and as the steelhead camps are all run with boats, they can take anglers wherever they need to be, which is a tremendous advantage. Steelhead can be found in many of the same river lies that salmon use, as they hold in pools, tail-outs, drop-offs, confluences, side channels, etc. and behind structure like boulders, small islands, etc. (Keep in mind, however, that fall steelhead, unlike salmon or even spring steelhead, are not spawning until the following spring, and therefore not near as driven to reach their individual spawning sites.) Cross-current, wet fly swings, and drifting are the most popular methods of presentation, mostly to fish holding in shallow to moderately deep water.

Ryan Peterson

Proper presentation and line control are paramount in these conditions, for the steelhead are prone to be spooky and uncooperative in these small naked rivers, and the rapidly falling water temperatures aggravate matters, making the fish lethargic and not willing to pursue the fly. Anglers can compensate by modifying their swing technique (see illustration) to work the fly farther downstream and with more natural, drag-free drift, placing it directly in front of their quarry (Mending the line as required to reduce drag and slow the fly). And with the line always under control when fishing this way, the slightest nips from steelhead are felt, increasing hookups. Strike indicators can also greatly increase the angler's advantage in these conditions, allowing greater sensitivity for detecting subtle takes and increasing hookups. Other less common tactics employed for this challenging fishing involve the use of specially rigged leaders, trick drift techniques, long Spey rods and center pinning.

Like late fall steelheading anywhere in the North Pacific, the weather and the quality of the run are major factors that vary widely from year to year. Heavy storms, common in late fall in Kamchatka, can quickly blow out the tundra rivers, making fishing nearly impossible, and as the season progresses, it can easily turn cold and snow. Or you may luck out and enjoy one of Kamchatka's prolonged falls, with Indian summer conditions lingering well into the season, bringing superb conditions for fishing steelhead. But then the trout may not be there in great numbers. In many years, the run comes in "front-loaded," with a strong initial surge that dwindles to a trickle for the rest of the season. Some years it's just the opposite. And then there are years the run never really happens at all. On remote rivers where the only practical access is by expensive helicopter, these ventures are essentially a high stakes crapshoot, where the angler pins his/her hopes on the chance that all the variables will come together to give them a decent shot at some of the last remaining truly wild steelhead in the world. For these few anglers blessed with the means and intense passion, the prize is certainly worth the gamble.

Gearing Up

The standard stick for these Russian fall steelhead adventures, much the same as in Alaska, is a medium-fast action, 8-weight graphite rod, 9 to 10 feet long (or more). Longer rods afford better line control and easier casting, two factors that make them increasingly popular for this kind of fishing. Two-handed Spey rods are especially useful in this regard and are seeing a resurgence in popularity among steelhead anglers.

A high quality, matching reel with good drag and sufficient backing is required. Since you'll probably be casting to fish in water not overly fast or deep, a performance-tapered, floating line mated to a 9-11 foot, tapered sinking leader with 2X to 12 lb. nylon mono tippet (fluorocarbon is unnecessary for these conditions) will be adequate for most situations. For more challenging conditions, a medium-density, short (5 to 7 foot) sink tip line can be used. Interchangeable line tip systems and shooting heads can increase versatility and save time and are commonly used for this kind of fishing.

The successful patterns used on Russian steelhead are mostly attractors, many of them classic Northwest steelhead flies, along with a few standard forage and egg flies. Wise anglers will bring a wide assortment of flies with them (not just the ones listed below) to have just in case the fish do not respond to the standard enticements. (Steelhead have been taken on just about every fly imaginable under the right conditions.) Given how precious the opportunities to hook these elusive fighters may be, it almost goes without saying that you should regularly check all your terminal components— hook, leader, tippet and knots— for any signs of failure, and repair or replace as needed.

Recommended Fly Patterns (sizes #2–8): Polar Shrimp, Woolly Bugger, Practitioner, Leech (all types), Boss, Green Butt Skunk, Zonker, Purple Peril, Freight Train, Egg Sucking Leech, Glo Bug (all colors), Cluster Fly, Mickey Finn, Matuka, Sparkle Shrimp, Rajah, Fall Favorite, Skykomish Sunrise, Popsicle, Silver Hilton

DOLLY VARDEN CHARR

Eugemy Luksamkov

Salvelinus malma

Common names: Goletz, loach (Russia); malma (Kamchatka); Dolly Varden, Dolly (Alaska); charr, bull trout (U.S. Pacific Northwest)

Description: Small to medium-size, stream/lake dwelling (also sea-run) salmonid, common in Kamchatka. Trout-like in form, usually with silver-gray, blue, brown or green topsides and whitish belly, with light pink, red, cream or yellow spots on sides. Average size 12 to 16 inches and 1 to 2 lbs.; to 30 inches and 12 pounds.

Range/Abundance/Status: Found throughout Kamchatka; locally common to very abundant, numbers stable or increasing throughout range.

Best Waters: Larger, more productive salmon streams and lakes

Best Rivers/Lakes: Kamchatka, Opala, Bolshaya, Zhupanova, Pymta, Icha, Tigil and Ozernaya Rivers; Kronotsky and Nachikinsky lakes

Best Fly Patterns: Attractors, nymphs, forage and egg/flesh flies

Best Times: Available year-round, best in spring and late summer-fall

The Dolly Varden is a feisty and prolific game fish of the North Pacific found throughout Kamchatka. It is a species of charr, a group (genus) of salmonid fishes most successful and widespread in far northern waters, occurring across northern Europe, Siberia, Alaska and Canada. Charrs are fishes of incalculable importance culturally and economically, sustaining countless native peoples and providing important sport and commercial fisheries across the North.

In Kamchatka, as in Alaska, the Dolly Varden is ubiquitous, found in nearly every freshwater drainage (the original type specimens for the species came from Kamchatka in the 18th century; *malma* is from the local vernacular), and especially abundant in those with salmon, as they prey heavily on the eggs, flesh and young of their larger cousins. These interesting fish bewilder biologists with complex life histories and uncertain taxonomy. They are very similar in form, life history and habits to the white-spotted East Siberian charr or "kundzha", *Salvelinus leucomenis*, with which they often share waters (see the next chapter for details on these fish in Kamchatka waters).

As a sport fish, the Dolly Varden, when bright and robust, fresh from the sea, is nearly the equal of the esteemed rainbow trout, as it is a swift and hard fighter, yielding its freedom only after a prolonged battle. And with its widespread range, prolific numbers and willingness to take a fly, it provides consistent sport to anglers of all persuasions.

Named after a character from a Dickens novel for its delicate beauty, and incredibly prolific and easily provoked, the Dolly Varden is an inseparable part of the Kamchatka fishing experience.

Description

In form and habit, the Dolly Varden is very much a trout. It has a streamlined, attractively colored body, with slightly forked tail and large mouth for seizing prey. The scales are minute. River or lake resident forms are generally brown, green or gold on the top sides, lightening into a whitish belly, while sea-run fish are more silver grey or bluish. Both forms are daintily spotted, usually in pink, red or yellow, sometimes with blue halos. Light-colored vermiculations on the back are rare. The lower fins are usually yellow, orange or red with white leading edges.

Breeding brings dramatic physical changes. Males develop many of the physical characteristics of spawning salmon, with enlarged kypes and ridgebacks. Coloration darkens on both sexes, accented with brilliant hues of red-orange along lower sides and belly, creating a most striking appearance.

Though generally they average about 1 to 2 pounds in weight and 12 to 18 inches in length, Kamchatka's Dolly Vardens can reach up to 12 pounds and 30 inches or more. Sea-run fish are more robust than resident stream and lake forms, on average. The Dolly Varden has pink to light orange flesh of delicate flavor that makes it highly prized for eating.

Distribution

The Dolly Varden charr ranges throughout the North Pacific, from northern California to Alaska and across the Aleutians to Kamchatka and eastern Chukotka, then south to Japan and Korea. It is astoundingly abundant in certain rivers and at certain times of year, despite decades of overfishing, poaching and even persecution in some waters. In Kamchatka, like Alaska, it is most prolific in the larger, more productive salmon streams or lakes associated with salmon systems.

Life History

The Dolly Varden has many possible life history variations. Research done in Alaska and Kamchatka shows that the majority of mature river fish venture to the sea in the spring each year, returning in late summer to overwinter and possibly spawn. Some fish, however, spend their entire lives in freshwater, either in streams or lakes, and there are even dwarf forms found in headwaters and small spring creeks.

In habits and feeding, the Dolly Varden is very similar to the rainbow trout. It is an opportunistic and voracious predator, feeding on a variety of food items, from small aquatic organisms to insects to salmon fry and eggs and even small rodents. Like the rainbow, it travels considerably within watersheds to exploit seasonally available prey. Sea-run Dolly Varden feed heavily on small fish and crustaceans while out at sea.

The Kamchatka Dolly matures at 2 to 6 years of age, depending on location. Sea-run fish typically spend their first 3 to 5 years in streams before making a saltwater migration. Both resident and anadromous forms spawn in the fall, from late August to the end of November in Kamchatka, though not necessarily every year. Favored spawning sites are main channels, tributary streams, and headwater springs. Spawning and overwintering sea-run Dolly Vardens remain in streams, lakes, and estuaries until late spring. All forms live up to 10 years (rarely more).

Habits

The Dolly Varden charr is a notorious glutton, generally displaying little sophistication in feeding. As such, it can usually, but not always, be tempted with practically any kind of enticement. (Natives have traditionally used berries as bait to catch them and they have been known to hit bare hooks.) They are most easily taken in spring and late summer into fall during times of mass congregation for feeding and spawning. Quite sporting on light to medium-weight gear, the Dolly is a dogged fighter and bores vigorously into the current and spins repeatedly, often hopelessly tangling the leader. (When they amass in great numbers, they can actually be a nuisance when the preferred quarry is the much less common, but more esteemed rainbow trout.)

FLY FISHING KAMCHATKA'S DOLLY VARDEN

Because of widespread availability and fine eating qualities, the Dolly Varden is a very desirable and much sought after gamefish for most Russian fishermen in Kamchatka. Typically it is taken along with rainbow trout and grayling, using light to medium-weight spinning gear and spinners and spoons, on almost all of the more accessible streams and rivers. Only a small percentage of anglers, mostly foreign, pursue the Dolly with fly gear and catch-and- release techniques. Aggressive and usually non-discerning in feeding, the Kamchatka Dolly Varden is pursued with the same gear, techniques and fly patterns used for rainbow trout.

The two most productive times to fish these ubiquitous fighters are spring and late summer into fall. With the melting ice and opening up of rivers in spring, Dollies leave overwintering sites and go on feeding binges, staging in areas with abundant prey (mostly crustaceans, emerging insects and small fish) and cover: river mouths, confluences, lake outlets, estuaries, deep pools, boulder-strewn rapids and other similar areas. Trout anglers this time of year take many Dolly Vardens incidentally while fishing rainbows, as both species seem to compete for the same niche. This is a time for classic nymph and forage patterns fished on a deep drift or wet fly swing through likely areas: Leech, Muddler, Alevin, Fry, Smolt, Hare's Ear, Caddis, Pheasant Tail, Zug Bug, etc. Certain attractor patterns like the Mickey Finn, Supervisor and Polar Shrimp can also be used effectively this time of year. In late spring, many of Kamchatka's Dolly Varden will move en masse to the sea and can be taken in great numbers from holding areas in lower rivers and estuaries, using the same forage and attractor patterns.

Later, the warmest months of the year bring prolific fishing opportunities for Dolly Varden in Kamchatka. Insect hatches peak, and Dolly Varden will target them for selective feeding whenever possible. Also, large numbers of bright, sea-run Dolly Vardens enter rivers with returning salmon this time of year to feed on their abundant roe and flesh and can provide exciting non-stop action in the lower and middle sections of rivers where most salmon congregate (abundant rainbow trout and grayling join in the mix). There is no better time for fly fishing the Dolly and its erstwhile cohorts in Kamchatka!

The Dolly Varden can reach respectable size in Kamchatka, especially in river systems with headwater lakes.

Best fishing strategy this time of year is to locate spawning salmon or surface feeding activity and then fish an appropriate imitation or attractor. When feeding on hatches, the Kamchatka Dolly Varden surprisingly can turn just as finicky as the rainbow trout they share waters with, sometimes refusing even the appeal of a fat egg pattern for a tiny insect. For these special situations, you will need to "match the hatch", sometimes even to the point of tying on a size 18 Midge to get these fish to respond.

For Dolly Vardens keyed into spawning salmon, you can fish the same traditional egg patterns and attractors used for rainbow trout this time of year. Since there is no difference in technique used for these two fighters, you will be casting and hooking up to both Dolly Vardens and rainbows in these concentrated feeding zones, usually in the ratio of three or more to one. (As in Alaska, if you are going to fish rainbow trout in Kamchatka, you will soon learn to love the Dolly Varden.) Also, in many drainages, you may encounter the aggressive "kundzha," or white-spotted charr, mixed in with the Dolly Vardens, so come prepared for a mixed bag of fishing action.

In Kamchatka's clear, shallow waters, polarized glasses are very helpful in locating feeding trout and charr and avoiding spawning salmon. Do not cast directly into the redds (nests); fish instead the periphery of these areas, just downstream or on either side of them to avoid provoking or stressing spawners. And if you should accidentally hook a spawning salmon, break it off immediately! Strike indicators, if you are in the habit of fishing them, can be used to great effect to increase hookups when drifting egg or flesh flies in the vicinity of spawning areas, when conditions are such that you cannot easily sight fish.

As the salmon runs wane and temperatures cool, the Kamchatka Dolly Varden, like the rainbow trout, becomes less selective and more aggressive in its feeding. Insect hatches will occur until late in the season, but with less frequency and duration (calling for many of the same patterns you would use for summer). Look for signs of surface feeding and any late spawning salmon, as many Kamchatka rivers have late runs of sockeye, silver, and chum, and fish those areas intensely, but if you don't locate these hotspots, work the same water you would this time of year for rainbows, in these conditions: under cut banks, on the edge of sloughs, and in deep pools, confluences, stream mouths, boulder-strewn rapids, etc. Charr in fall will begin to make their way to their spawning and overwintering sites, hanging back whenever they can to feed in the most opportune places, but, depending on how late in the season, they may already start to amass in river mouths, tributaries, deep pools, etc., still very excitable and fair game unless they are actively spawning (usually mid to late October). This is a great time for flesh patterns and attractors, drifted or fished with a light strip. Forage patterns will work well also, especially very late in the fall. (The general strategy is to fish slower and deeper as the water gets colder.) The beauty of these fall fish as they develop their striking spawning coloration is hard to describe, and the thrill of bringing one to hand is certainly a significant part of the mystique of late season fishing in these waters.

Gearing Up

Kamchatka's Dolly Varden is best pursued with light to medium-weight gear. Use a 4 to 6-weight, medium-fast action graphite fly rod (7 to 9 foot) with a high-quality matching reel loaded with performance tapered floating line for most situations. (A heavier rod and/or medium-density, short sink tip lines can be used for more extreme conditions.) A 9-foot, tapered leader and 2X to 5X mono nylon tippet (fluorocarbon is not required) are most commonly used. Additional weight in the form of split shot or wrap lead can be added as needed to achieve proper depth on wet fly presentations.

Dolly Vardens, under most conditions, can be taken on just about any fly imaginable. They are especially fond of egg/flesh patterns, bright attractors and classic nymphs and dry flies. Dropper fly setups can be deadly on Kamchatka's Dolly Vardens. Use microbarb or barbless hooks and catch-and-release techniques to minimize stress and physical damage to the fish.

Recommended Fly Patterns

Spring: Leech, Muddler, Woolly Bugger, Alevin, Fry, Smolt, Parr, Mickey Finn, Supervisor and Polar Shrimp, in sizes #6–10; Nymphs-Hare's Ear, Stonefly, Bitch Creek, Brassie, Caddis, Mayfly and Zug Bug, in sizes #6–16

Summer: Irresistible, Elk Hair Caddis, Stimulator, Parachute Adams, Emerger, Hare's Ear, Scud, Cahill, Mosquito, Gnat and Midge, in sizes #10–18; Babine Special, Glo Bug, Bead Egg (8–12mm), Battle Creek, Polar Shrimp, Egg Sucking Leech, Cotton Candy, Kamchatka Special and Krystal Bullet, in sizes #6–12

Fall (sizes # 4–10): Polar Shrimp, Egg Sucking Leech, Zonker, Kamchatka Special, Battle Creek, Skykomish Sunrise, Bunny Flesh Fly, Pink Sparkler, Woolly Bugger, Leech, Muddler, Matuka, Copper and Orange and Fall Favorite in sizes # 6–10; Gnat, Midge, Elk Hair Caddis, Emerger, Adams, in sizes #10–18

EAST SIBERIAN CHARR

Malkov/Shatilo

Salvelinus leucomaenis

Common names: "Kundzha" (Russia); east Siberian charr, Sakhalin charr, white-spotted charr, charr (U.S.)

Description: A large, predatory charr of Kamchatka and northeast Siberia, similar to Dolly Varden. Body streamlined with large head and jaws and prominent teeth. Usually silver-gray, dirty brown or bronze on top and sides, with whitish belly. Has large, irregular silver, cream or yellowish spots on sides; minute scales. Average size 14 to 20 inches and 1 to 2 lbs.; to 36 inches and 20 pounds.

Range/Abundance/Status: Found throughout much of Kamchatka, especially western drainages of the Sea of Okhotsk; locally rare to common, status of populations throughout much of range undetermined.

Best Waters: Slower flowing, productive salmon rivers with extensive estuaries

Best Rivers: Kamchatka, Zhupanova, Pymta, Kol, Kolpokova, Icha, Saichik, Sopochnaya, Bolshaya, Tigil, Penzhina and Ozernaya rivers

Best Fly Patterns: Attractors, egg/flesh flies, and forage patterns

Best Times: Spring and late summer into fall

The East Siberian charr or "kundzha" is a unique species of charr found only in northeast Asia and in many Kamchatka rivers. Very similar to the Dolly Varden, this white-spotted charr is a fine game fish, capable of reaching respectable size and a powerful fighter on light to medium-weight gear. Though nowhere near as common as the ubiquitous Dolly, the Kamchatka kundzha is most frequently encountered during summer and fall by anglers fishing for trout and salmon, and is increasingly viewed as an exotic highlight to the fabulous fishing on Kamchatka's streams and rivers. And aside from a handful of drainages along the southern coast, most of Kamchatka's better kundzha waters get little or no pressure from anglers.

Description

In form and habit, the kundzha very much resembles a Dolly Varden. Coloration varies considerably with location and age. Mature sea-run specimens are usually silver-gray or silver-brown on topsides, blending into silver-white on the belly. The markings, faint on fish just out of the sea, are large, oval, silver or cream colored spots. The scales, like those of other charr, are minute. The back is marbled with beautiful large, silver, cream or yellowish vermiculations. The lower fins are dusky gray, yellow-brown or orange, with white leading edges. Fish that have been in rivers for some time have darker coloration, with markings much more prominent. Breeding brings marked physical changes to the kundzha, similar to those seen in other salmonids. Body coloration darkens considerably, to deep brown or almost black in some specimens, and large jaw kypes and ridgebacks develop. The lower fins lengthen and grow wider.

Kamchatka kundzha on average are slightly larger than the typical Dolly Varden, with sea-run individuals 14 to 20 or more inches and 1 to 2 pounds common, and fish up to 28 inches and 8 lbs. or more possible in many of the larger rivers. (In some very productive systems, like the Zhupanova River on the southeast coast, kundzha can reach sizes of 33 inches and 15 lbs.) Their flesh, like that of the Dolly Varden, is pink or orange and delicately flavored, making them choice eating, whether fried, baked, grilled or smoked.

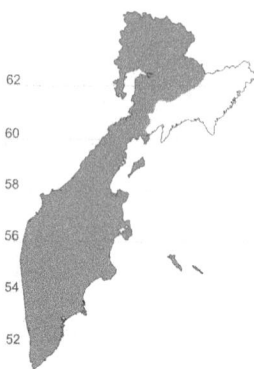

Distribution

The east Siberian charr is found along the coast of northeast Asia only, from the Kamchatka Peninsula (all western, Sea of Okhotsk drainages and eastern drainages to Gulf of Korf) down the mainland along the Sea of Okhotsk to southern Primorye and over to Sakhalin, the Kurils and Hokkaido and the Honshu islands of Japan. Never as prolific as the Dolly Varden, it is most successful in larger, slower moving, productive streams with extensive lagoons. In most of its range, it shares waters and competes with the more prolific Dolly Varden.

Life History

Very little research has been done on the white-spotted charr. We know that, like the Dolly Varden, the kundzha is an opportunistic and voracious feeder that resides in rivers and streams, with a common sea-run (diadromous) life history variation. Much like the rainbow trout and Dolly Varden, it feeds on any available food source, from small insect larva to salmon roe to small fish or even rodents. It also preys heavily on juvenile salmon where present. Sea-run forms subsist primarily on crustaceans and small fish on their forays in near-coastal marine waters.

Most northern populations, like those in Kamchatka, go to sea for part of the year (up to 4 months), beginning as early as their second year of life (but usually at 3 to 4 years). Resident and even dwarf resident forms are found in some rivers and streams of the peninsula, and there may even be some lake-dwelling forms. Most sea-run kundzha stay near the coast, returning to streams in late summer (late July and August) to spawn and overwinter. Favored sites for spawning (from late August through October) are similar to those used by Dolly Vardens and rainbows, and the kundzha, like its cohorts, can spawn multiple times in its life. The maximum lifespan of the kundzha in most Kamchatka rivers studied is about twelve years.

Habits

The kundzha, like the Dolly Varden charr, is an aggressive, reckless feeder and usually easily tempted with all manner of enticements. It is quite frequently found in small groups along with rainbow trout and Dolly Vardens, feeding on seasonally available food sources such as fry, smolt and salmon eggs. On occasion, they can even be tempted to the surface with large floating patterns like the Mouse, Wog, Bomber, etc. (They will seldom feed exclusively on insect hatches like the Kamchatka Dolly Varden charr is known to do, however.) Like Dolly Vardens, Kamchatka kundzha will aggregate in fall in river mouths, pools and confluences in preparation for spawning and are easier to target at this time. They put up a surprisingly good fight when hooked, even more dogged than their cousins, the scrappy Dolly Vardens, and large specimens can be quite a challenge on light to medium-weight gear, especially in larger rivers with swift current.

FLY FISHING KAMCHATKA'S KUNDZHA

Because of their relative scarcity compared to rainbow trout or the prolific Dolly Vardens, the handsome white-spotted charr is considered a very unique and desirable species by most Russian fishermen in Kamchatka, who usually take them incidentally while fishing for salmon, using spinning gear and bright spoons and spinners. They are an incidentally taken but highly esteemed sport species for most foreign fly fisherman as well. As unsophisticated and vigorous feeders, they are usually easy to tempt with the same strategies and traditional attractor, forage and egg/flesh flies that are used to great effect for Dolly Varden and rainbow trout.

The two best times to fish for Kamchatka kundzha are early spring and late summer into fall. After ice-out, kundzha will be found and taken in the same locations as Dolly Vardens and rainbow trout, as they advantageously feed on emerging life such as small fish, crustaceans, insect larvae, etc. Larger sea-run fish will begin to stage for their migration out of freshwater (usually May & June in most Kamchatka rivers). Forage patterns and attractors work best for kundzha this time of year, flies like the Leech, Woolly Bugger, Muddler, Smolt; Hare's Ear, Caddis and Stonefly nymphs, Mickey Finn, Supervisor, Coronation and others, fished with a standard downstream "wet fly swing" or on a drift. Best areas for spring kundzha are river mouths, estuaries, lake outlets, stream confluences, deep pools, drop-offs, etc. Use additional lead or denser lines, if necessary, to get down into the "strike zone."

During the warmest months, kundzha are an available bonus to the exciting mix of fishing available on Kamchatka's rivers. You may take a few incidentally when fishing the hatches this time of year for trout and Dolly Varden, but generally, kundzha are not inclined to surface feeding. (They will hit mouse patterns and other large floating flies sometimes, however.) They will attack egg/flesh flies and egg-like attractors such as the Babine Special, Polar Shrimp, Battle Creek, Bunny Fly, Kamchatka Special and others. Later in the summer and early fall; you will encounter the larger super-predatory sea-run kundzha, often incidentally when fishing big rainbow trout or silver salmon. The larger and more productive rivers that see ample numbers of these big sporting charr returning to spawn and overwinter are prime locations. Look for these outsized, aggressive kundzha in big pools and stream mouths, along the edge of sloughs, below islands and other structure and in deeper main channels, the same holding areas you would target for silver salmon. Use the same flies you would fish for silvers—Egg Sucking Leech, Coho Fly, Zonker, Supervisor, Alaskabou, Flash Fly, etc., in sizes #2–4.

Later in the fall, kundzha, like Dolly Vardens, will start to mass near their spawning areas and can be easily provoked with attractor and forage patterns. You will find them around confluences, in pools, sloughs, river mouths, side channels and slower riffle sections (but don't disturb any kundzha that may have already begun spawning). Some of the more productive late season patterns for kundzha are Egg Sucking Leech, Zonker, Woolly Bugger, Fall Favorite, Smolt, Mouse, Polar Shrimp and Skykomish Sunrise, in sizes #2–6.

Gearing Up

Because of the possibility of hooking Dolly Vardens, rainbows and even salmon when fishing kundzha, Anglers should be prepared with medium-weight fly gear. In smaller streams, a 5 or 6-weight, medium-action graphite fly rod (7 to 9 foot) should be adequate, but in larger rivers with more current and potentially bigger kundzha, a 7 or even an 8-weight rod is recommended. A high quality, matching reel loaded with adequate backing and a performance-taper floating line or a short (3 to 5 foot), medium-density sink tip will be adequate for most presentations. Use a 7 to 9-foot tapered leader and 3X to 0X (6-10 lb.) mono nylon tippet (fluorocarbon is not required for fishing kundzha).

Kundzha, like Dolly Vardens, will take an astonishing variety of fly patterns. They are especially fond of bright attractors, egg/flesh flies, and forage patterns. They will occasionally hit surface presentations and are taken incidentally when mouse fishing for rainbows. Use microbarb or barbless hooks and catch-and-release techniques to minimize stress and harm to the fish.

Recommended Fly Patterns (sizes #2–6): Smolt, Fry, Minnow, Muddler, Leech, Woolly Bugger, Mickey Finn, Supervisor, Coho Fly, Polar Shrimp, Kamchatka Special, Glo Bug, Hare's Ear Nymph, Brown Caddis Nymph, Stonefly Nymph, Bead Egg, Bunny Fly, Battle Creek, Egg Sucking Leech, Skykomish Sunrise, Zonker, Mouse, Bomber, Wog, Fall Favorite, Alaskabou and Deceiver

KAMCHATKA GRAYLING

Igor Shatilo

Thymallus arcticus mertensi

Common names: Harios (Russia); grayling, Kamchatka grayling (U.S.)

Description: Small (12 to 14 inches and less than a pound average), stream-dwelling salmonid, common in much of Kamchatka, similar in form to whitefish, but with huge dorsal fin.

Range/Abundance/Status: Found throughout northern Kamchatka and into the central valley and Bystraya River drainage; locally rare to abundant, populations stable in most drainages

Best Waters: Larger, more productive salmon streams, central to northern Kamchatka

Best Rivers: Kamchatka, Bolshaya, Penzhina, Ozernaya and Naichika river systems

Best Fly Patterns: Forage, attractor and dry fly/nymph patterns

Best Times: Available year-round; best in summer

An abundant and widespread salmonid game fish, the grayling with its giant top fin is an unmistakable denizen of fast flowing, pristine northern waters. A voracious top feeder, it is revered by many an angler for its willingness to take a dry fly. The Kamchatka grayling, first described from wild specimens by French naturalist Achilles Valenciennes in the early 1800's, is considered a subspecies of the much more abundant and widespread Arctic grayling, *Thymallus articus*, found across Alaska, Canada, and northern Siberia.

Like grayling elsewhere, the Kamchatka subspecies provides abundant sport in waters often deficient in surface action. With its exotic appearance and gamey disposition it is a most desirable quarry, and an essential part of the Kamchatka angling experience. For maximum enjoyment of these plucky fighters, fly anglers should pursue them with ultralight gear.

Description

Possessing a streamlined, whitefish-shaped body, with trademark sail-like, oversized dorsal fin, the Kamchatka grayling is hard to misidentify. The body color varies, usually silver-gray, bronze or black on top (including dorsal fin) and upper sides, blending to grayish white (or bronze) on lower sides and belly. Markings are usually absent, but if present, consist of sparse black specks along the sides. The large dorsal fin, like that of the arctic grayling, may be decorated with blue and light orange stripes and spots. Scales are large, as on a whitefish, and the tail is strongly forked and usually bronze or gray in color. Pelvic fins may be marked with rays. The mouth is small with fine teeth. Kamchatka grayling flesh is white and firm and makes excellent eating.

Unlike the peninsula's salmon, trout and charr, Kamchatka grayling exhibit very little changes in physical appearance during breeding season other than a possible darkening of color. They generally do not reach the size of larger specimens of Arctic grayling from the big rivers of Siberia and Alaska. Average size is 12 to 14 inches and much less than a pound, with lengths up to 20 inches and weights to 3 pounds possible on large mainland rivers, but in Kamchatka, 18 inches and 2 pounds is the expected maximum.

Distribution

The Kamchatka grayling is found in most streams of the northern half of the peninsula (and to Anadyr Bay on the Siberian mainland), and in the extensive Kamchatka River basin and Malke Bystraya River in the central-southern region. Isolated populations occur on the mainland along the sea of Okhotsk. It is most abundant in the middle to lower reaches of rivers where gradient eases, and there is slower, deeper water and more varied and abundant food sources. Unlike trout and charr, the grayling of Kamchatka does not leave freshwater seasonally in search of food and usually spends its entire life within a relatively small river area.

Life History

Research on the Kamchatka subspecies shows it to be a late-maturing (5 to 8 years), slow growing grayling, with potential lifespan of 13 years or more. Like other arctic grayling, the Kamchatka grayling is an opportunistic feeder, utilizing a variety of food items depending on age, location and time of year: invertebrate aquatic organisms (leeches, crustaceans, mollusks and insect larvae), flying insects, small fish, salmon roe & carcasses, and even small rodents. It spawns in late spring to early summer, from the end of May to July in most of the peninsula, choosing small tributary streams or mainstem channels for mating. (The grayling does not build a nest or redd like the salmon but instead makes a slight depression in the bottom for its eggs.) After spawning, it moves up or down river to avail itself of the choicest feeding sites during summer. Like the rainbow and charr, the Kamchatka grayling heavily exploits the roe and flesh of salmon in years of heavy runs.

In the fall with cooling temperatures and dwindling food, the Kamchatka grayling, like its counterparts throughout the North, migrates from its summer feeding areas to overwintering sites in deep holes and channels of the lower river mainstem and (if present) tributary lakes. These migrations in mass numbers during fall, much the same as the spring spawning gatherings, are a time of great vulnerability to overfishing and poaching in some locations. During Kamchatka's long winter, they amass in areas of upwellings and deep water and thus can survive, despite the massive ice cover that suffocates most of the rivers.

Habits

Grayling have distinct habits that set them apart from the other resident river species found in Kamchatka. Their most famous trait, other than their penchant for surface feeding, is the vigorous manner in which they seize prey, sometimes leaping completely out of the water to pounce on some hapless bug or other critter. Another grayling trademark is the way they space themselves throughout holding water, each fish guarding roughly the same amount of area, with the larger, more dominant grayling usually at the head (or back) of a pool, in the most choice feeding zones. When hooked, grayling are absolute masters at using the shape of their bodies and oversized dorsal fins to great advantage in the current, cutting tight circles to maximize resistance to the line, so that an angler is often fooled into thinking he has a big fish on.

FLY FISHING KAMCHATKA'S GRAYLING

The grayling's relative abundance in certain waters and eagerness to take a variety of enticements make it a favorite target of anglers. Most Russians pursue the Kamchatka grayling for sport and food, using light spinning rods and small, bright spinners. They are also taken incidentally during outings for larger and more prestigious quarry (salmon, charr, and trout). A growing number of resident anglers are discovering the joy of catch and release fishing for grayling using flies. An assortment of traditional dry flies and nymphs is most commonly used, along with some well-known and productive attractor and forage patterns.

Most anglers locate groups of feeding grayling, which are usually easy to spot along rivers and streams (grayling make a show of taking prey, especially insect hatches), then present suitable imitations from their fly patterns on hand. If you can't locate feeding grayling or insect hatches, which is typically the case when fishing early or late in the season, the standard strategy is to fish forage, nymph, dries and attractor patterns through likely holding areas. Grayling like to position themselves in places where they can hide from the current and ambush prey. Look for them in rocky riffles of shallow to moderate depth, under cut banks, behind large rocks and boulders, along current seams and drop-offs or the edge of deep pools, and in lake outlets and river mouths. Polarized glasses can be of great help locating fish in these situations. Some of the best traditional searching patterns for this kind of fishing are Muddler, Leech, Woolly Bugger, Fry, Minnow, Gnat, Mosquito, Hare's Ear, Black Stone, Bitch Creek, Cahill, Midge and Caddis (larva & dry). Hook size should be #8-16 (remember, grayling have small mouths). Many anglers rig dropper flies with great results when fishing this way. (See the technique section for more details on nymph, forage pattern and dry fly fishing.)

Grayling are known to be quite forgiving when it comes to presenting them with an artificial that may not quite "match the hatch." But at times, frustratingly, then can become quite selective when feeding, or mysteriously go off the feed without warning, which is why you should always have a good assortment of patterns from which you can select a suitable enticement. Extra-long leaders and fluorocarbon are not necessary, however, as the Kamchatka grayling is not the least bit leader shy. The number of grayling you can raise with a "hot" fly in a good stretch of water when the conditions are right can be truly amazing. It is not unheard of to take a dozen or more fish from a single long pool or riffle.

In addition to the peak of insect activity, the height of summer on most of Kamchatka's rivers and streams brings considerable feeding opportunities for grayling and other resident species in and around abundant spawning salmon. It is important not to disturb salmon on their redds, so fish only around the periphery of any spawning activity you see. Egg and flesh patterns like the Glo Bug, Battle Creek, Babine Special, Bead Egg, Flesh Fly, etc., will be most productive drift fished, with egglike attractors like the Polar Shrimp, Skykomish Sunrise, Egg Sucking Leech, Krystal Bullet, Kamchatka Special, etc., almost as effective, fished on a drift or with a light strip. Strike indicators, if you use them, can help increase hookups in this kind of fishing when conditions are more challenging. Quite often this can be the most exciting (and varied) fishing of the year, with a variety of voracious fighters— rainbows, charr, and grayling— vying for your flies in the intensely competitive feeding binges that occur around these spawning salmon.

Later in the fall, grayling leave their summer feeding areas (shallow riffles, pools, headwaters and tributaries) and start heading toward their overwintering sites. Keep an eye out for late spawning salmon (silver, sockeye, and chum salmon usually) and insect hatches for concentrated fishing action, but be prepared to swing flies (attractors and forage patterns) through likely holding areas as a backup strategy for catching late season grayling. Many of the largest grayling are taken in late summer and fall in areas where grayling stage or overwinter: deeper mainstem pools, river mouths, lake outlets, confluences, etc.

Gearing Up

Ideally, for maximum enjoyment, Kamchatka grayling should be fished with ultralight gear. Use a 4-weight or smaller, medium-fast action fly rod (7 to 8 ½ feet) with matching reel and WF floating line, along with a 9-foot tapered leader and 3X to 7X mono nylon (fluorocarbon is not necessary) tippet for most conditions. Additional weight can be added as necessary for depth control on wet fly presentations. A medium-density, short (2 to 5 foot) sink tip line can be used for nymphing grayling in very deep water (large pools, river mouths, and lakes).

Grayling, along with perhaps the Dolly Varden, can be taken on the largest variety of patterns of practically any freshwater sportfish, and Kamchatka's version is no exception. You would be hard-pressed to find a fly they wouldn't hit at some time or another, even oversize patterns (like the Mouse) don't seem to deter them, surprisingly, given the small size of their mouth. To minimize stress and injury to the fish, consider using microbarb or barbless hooks when fishing them.

Recommended Fly Patterns

Dry Fly (size #8–18): Mosquito, Black Gnat, Adams, Emerger, Midge, Stimulator, Elk Hair Caddis, Red Quill, Cahill, Irresistible, Wulff, Humpy, Bomber.

Nymph (size #8–12): Brassie, Hare's Ear, Stonefly, Midge, Caddis, Mayfly, Bitch Creek, Zug Bug.

Forage: (size # 6–12) Leech, Muddler, Fry, Alevin, Smolt, Glo Bug, Bead Egg, Babine Special, Scud.

Attractor (size #8–12): Egg Sucking Leech, Woolly Bugger, Fall Favorite, Polar Shrimp, Mickey Finn, Krystal Bullet, Copper and Orange, Skykomish Sunrise, Zonker, Kamchatka Special.

KING SALMON

Igor Shatilo

Oncorhynchus tshawytscha

Common names: King or king salmon (Alaska), "chavitcha" (Russia), chinook (U.S Pacific Northwest)

Description: A large, robust Pacific salmon found in the rivers of Kamchatka. Sea-bright specimens metallic dark blue, black or greenish back, silver sides and silver-white belly, with irregular, moderate-sized black markings on topsides and both tail lobes; Kamchatka fish average 15 to 20 lbs.; to 50 lbs., or more possible.

Range/Abundance/Status: Locally rare to common along much of Kamchatka's coast; status of certain populations uncertain due to lack of data and possible overfishing (including poaching)

Best Waters: Large, clear-flowing, productive coastal river systems with moderately fast current

Best Rivers: Bolshaya, Kikhchik, Pymta, Kol, Kolpokova, Icha, Tigil, Apuka, Pakacha, Kamchatka, Ozernaya, Avacha, Zhupanova and Opala rivers

Best Fly Patterns: Oversize attractor, egg and forage pattern streamers

Best Times: Early summer (late May to Mid-July)

The grandest and most esteemed of all Pacific salmon, the "chavitcha," king, or chinook is an angler's prize, particularly for fly fishermen, who consider it one of the greatest challenges of their sport in salt or fresh water. A fish of historical importance for native peoples along the entire North Pacific Rim (first noted in 18th-century literature by American and Russian explorers who witnessed the great ceremony attached to the capture of these first salmon of summer), the king salmon has also provided for the development of substantial commercial and sport fishing industries. Never particularly abundant (especially along the Asian coast), the king nonetheless provides a few lucky fly anglers from the world over a chance each summer to match wits and brawn with the undisputed monarch of the salmon family. In Kamchatka, only a handful of rivers receive any targeted effort for the species, leaving dozens of streams untouched and ripe for the probing fly.

Description

King salmon are the largest species of Pacific salmon, reaching weights of 50 pounds or more, and lengths of 45 inches, though their average size in Kamchatka and much elsewhere is less (15 to 20 pounds and around 33 inches for Kamchatka). When fresh from the sea, their appearance can be very similar to other Pacific salmon like silver (coho), pink or chum, especially with smaller immature or precocious adult fish (kings can mature and return to rivers to spawn as early as one year of age). The topsides are usually a metallic purple-blue, black or green, with bright silver flanks and whitish belly. There are moderate-sized, cross-shaped black markings covering the back and both lobes of the tail fin and the gum line is dark. The body is deep, with large head and jaws and powerful tail; the teeth on mature fish well developed.

Spawning king salmon turn dusky red to copper or brown (sometimes with black or purple shading), with males developing hooked jaws, ridged backs and more dramatic markings/coloration. Juvenile king salmon are hard to distinguish from other small salmon, trout or charr, but normally have wider parr marks, tinted edges on the adipose fins, and moderately forked tails. Especially prized for their eating qualities, king salmon are a valuable commercial species and especially sought after by sports and subsistence fishermen. The flesh, rich and flavorful, is usually deep orange-red but can vary to pink or even white in some locations and times of year.

Distribution

King salmon are found along most of the north Pacific, from central California to Kotzebue Sound in western North America and from Hokkaido, Japan to the Anadyr River in Asia. The least abundant of the Pacific salmon, they occur in greatest numbers from British Columbia to the Yukon River, Alaska. Most of the Asian runs occur on the Kamchatka Peninsula (80-90% of total catch), with only small numbers of kings spawning along the mainland coast. Aside from the Kamchatka River and a few other major drainages (Bolshaya, Tigil, Apuka, Pakhacha), Kamchatka's streams support only small numbers of king salmon.

Life History

King salmon share many of the habits and life history traits of the silver salmon or coho. Both are territorial and aggressive, fond of eating fish and spend their first one to two years (or more) of life in freshwater before migrating to sea. (There are precocious male fish, called "jacks," that become sexually mature at age one onward, some even without going to the sea.) Unlike the silver salmon, however, the king's high sea wanderings can be quite extensive and last for up to five years or more (there are some stocks however, that stay in protected inshore waters), so that fish returning to spawn in fresh water can be up to six or seven years of age and hence larger than any other salmon. (Studies done on commercially harvested fish show that the most spawning kings in Kamchatka are 4 and 5-year-olds.)

For the majority of kings that mature out in the open sea, their diets consist almost exclusively of other fish, particularly herring, sand lance, eulachon, pilchards, pollock, smelts, and anchovies, with seasonal binges on squid, crab larvae, euphausids (krill) and amphipods. They are found in a great range of depths, from just below the surface to more than 300 feet, depending on the season. While at sea, these regal salmon suffer the same depredation as other members of the Pacific salmon clan. They get eaten by larger fish, predatory birds, sea otters, sea lions, killer whales and man.

Run timing varies considerably throughout their range, but in far northern waters like those of Kamchatka, mature kings begin entering stream mouths in late spring (late May), with the peak period of return occurring from June to early July. Most spawning takes place from June into August (and into September with late-running populations). Hens lay from several thousand to well over 15,000 eggs in a shallow nest, or redd, which can be quite substantial in size. Because of their size and power, king salmon are able to utilize many areas in the stream bed that have too strong a current or unsuitable substrate for smaller salmon. As in all Pacific salmon, breeding for kings is a terminal act, with rapid physical deterioration and death soon following.

Habits

As consummate fish predators, the king and silver are perhaps the most easily aroused of the Pacific salmon, succumbing to all manner of enticements in fresh and salt waters. Probably because they are the least abundant of the Pacific salmon, kings tend to be not as social as the other species, and so are usually encountered as solitary individuals or in very small groups. Because of their size (and sensitivity to light), they are inclined to feed and move deeper than other salmon when out in the open sea. This habit carries over when they are ascending rivers. They tend to move, hold and spawn more in main channels than other salmon. Also, especially in clearer and/or shallower water, such as found in many rivers of Kamchatka, they prefer to move up river in subdued light. (They will show themselves in streams, however—rolling, breaching and even jumping —but not with the frequency of other salmon.)

As with all salmon, the king's behavior becomes less predictable the more time it is in fresh water. For this reason, the best fly fishing for them will be had in lower rivers and estuaries, ideally within 20 miles of saltwater. Generally not as vigorous on the take as the silver salmon, the king will sometimes need repeated prompting before it responds to a lure or fly. When hooked, unlike the silver, the king salmon rarely jumps, and instead usually uses its tremendous power and size to best advantage in the strong currents of the main channel. In the swift rivers of Kamchatka, this makes the king salmon an especially formidable adversary on a fly rod.

FLY FISHING KAMCHATKA'S KING SALMON

Most sport fishing effort for king salmon in Kamchatka is done by locals on the larger, more accessible rivers that are known for their ample runs of these much sought-after first salmon of summer. Heavy spin or bait casting gear is used almost exclusively, with large spoons, spinners and plugs being the most common enticements. Fly angling for king salmon in Kamchatka is a rare exercise, usually done only by visiting anglers. Many remote, lesser known drainages with fishable runs and good conditions for fly fishing go unutilized.

As noted, the closer to saltwater you can intercept the king, the better. Fishing at or right above tidewater will put you into kings that are at their testy best, yet concentrated in predictable holding areas that can be worked to great effect. The trick for fly-fishing kings in Kamchatka (and Alaska) is to find suitable water for fly-casting—neither too deep, fast, nor too turbid— conditions that can be hard to come by in early summer due to high water released from snowmelt. On the larger, more productive king systems like the Kamchatka, Bolshaya, Tigil and others, the mouths of smaller, clearer flowing tributary streams (like the Elovka on the lower Kamchatka River) or side channels and sloughs may present more fly fishing opportunities this time of year than the lower main channel. So too may many other lesser streams along the coast that receive smaller runs, but have more ideal conditions for fly fishing (Kolpokova, Pymta, Opala, Zhupanova, and others.)

The basic techniques and fly patterns used to take king salmon in fresh water are similar to those used for the smaller silver. Large, flashy or bright-colored attractor pattern streamers (sizes #3/0-2) presented right above bottom using traditional, wet fly swings and short or even lob casts, is the most widespread and successful strategy. Sight fishing in shallow clear waters is preferred, but not always possible (especially in early summer), so anglers should work likely holding water—main channels, pools, tail-outs, river mouths, estuaries, drop-offs, sloughs, larger riffle sections, around islands, etc. (see illustration)— as thoroughly as possible to incite fish that are holding or moving through. If you are fishing within a few miles of tidewater, it would be extremely helpful to time your efforts within a few hours of the high tide. Also, when fishing shallower clear rivers, keep in mind that kings feel less vulnerable moving through these areas during the low light of early morning and evening or during darker,

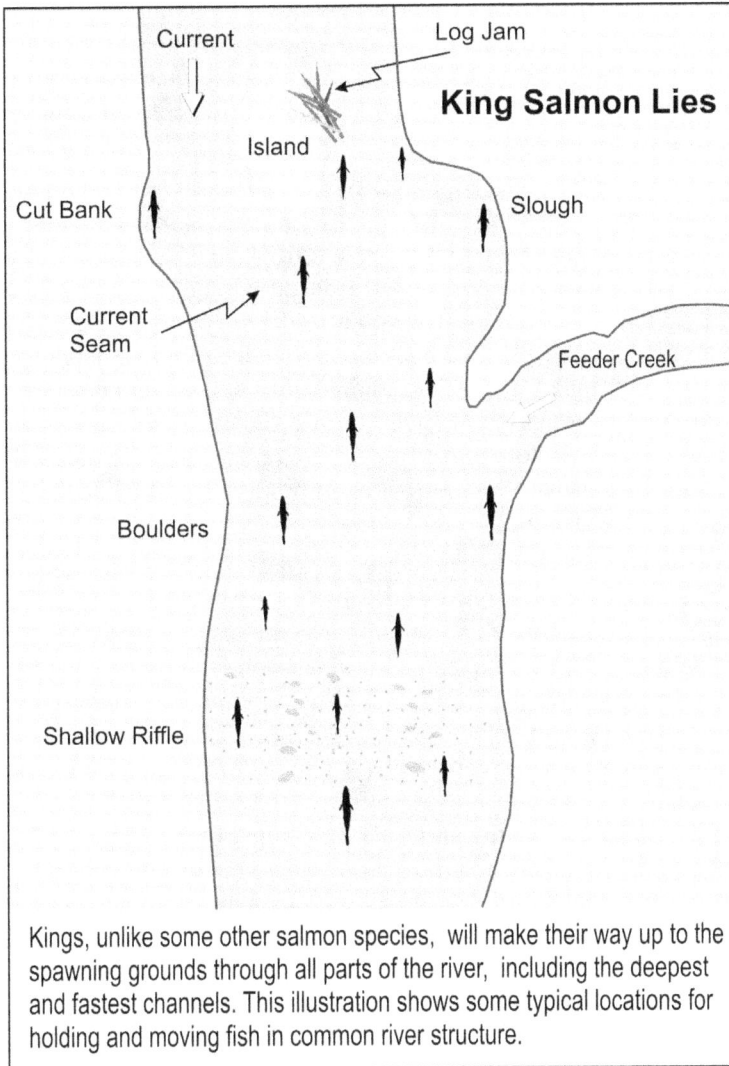

Current

Log Jam

King Salmon Lies

Island

Cut Bank

Slough

Current
Seam

Feeder Creek

Boulders

Shallow Riffle

Kings, unlike some other salmon species, will make their way up to the spawning grounds through all parts of the river, including the deepest and fastest channels. This illustration shows some typical locations for holding and moving fish in common river structure.

overcast days. (High tides on cloudy mornings with a stiff onshore breeze are classic king fishing conditions for lower rivers.)

It cannot be overstated that the single most important thing in fly fishing kings is to present the fly at proper depth, for kings will hug the bottom and rarely respond to an enticement not in the "strike zone" (usually no more than a foot or two to either side and probably even less above/below the fish). Short, slow strips of big, heavy flies on long leaders and, if need be, with additional weight in the form of split shot or two (or some wrap lead) will help keep your fly down. High water levels usually encountered early in the season when the kings are running will be a challenge and may require the use of sinking lines. Generally, a short sink tip (3 to 10 feet) will give you more line control in Kamchatka's swift rivers than a full sink line, but this can be a matter of preference, as some fly anglers do very well managing the longer sink lines in fast current.

The take of a king on a fly in freshwater is usually felt as a bump or more commonly a tightening of the line as the fish clamps down and moves upstream. (The smaller kings, especially "jacks" tend to be more aggressive on the take, much like trout.) Because kings develop very hard mouths once they enter freshwater, you must keep your hooks razor-sharp and use a very hard set when responding to the take of a fish. High-quality line, leaders, and tippets and strong, sharp hooks and sound knots are of special importance when fishing these brutes. Check all your terminal components frequently for signs of stress and replace or fix as needed. (Check your drag also to make sure it is set properly for the line and conditions you are fishing.)

In moderate to swift current, a hooked king of even modest size can quickly get away from you once it gets into the main channel. If you are fishing from a power boat, this is no big problem, as you can chase the runaway salmon with the help of your guide or one of your fishing buddies and regain line and save the fish. But if you don't have any motorized river transport, you'll have no choice but to follow the fish along the bank if it gets deep into your backing. The lower sections of most of the king rivers in Kamchatka, like those in Alaska, present a mix of shoreline structure. Much of it is ideal for wading and walking along, but there may be stretches that are impassable and/or hazardous to the wading angler, especially during the high-water conditions encountered early in summer. Things like log jams, sweepers and downed trees, steep cut banks, heavy brush, etc. It is a good idea to scope out the river bank in the area before you start fishing so you can make a preliminary mental plan of what to do if you hook a nice fish that decides it wants to go back to sea. If there are serious hazards along the bank, you may have to break off any fish that gets too far into your backing, rather than risk injury or drowning.

If you're fishing out of a lodge or with a guide/outfitter, they will undoubtedly have a net at hand to land the fish once it is sufficiently played out. If you don't have a net, you can do just as well by beaching the salmon in some quiet water with a gentle sloping bank. Make sure the fish has spent itself sufficiently before attempting this and that you have a fishing buddy handy to help land the salmon by grabbing the leader and sliding the spent fish up on the bank while you are backing off from the water's edge (You can also grab the salmon by the tail, commonly called "tailing the fish".) Do not pull the fish completely out of the water unless you intend to kill and eat it. Instead, slide the salmon into water deep enough to bathe its gills, but shallow enough that the fish is immobilized by the weight of its body. Because of the hardness of the king salmon's jaw and its teeth, you will need a set of stout fishing pliers to remove the hook (forget the forceps you use for dainty trout). Any fish not kept for eating should be gently released in shallow, calm waters to allow them to recover. (See the techniques section for more information on catch-and-release fishing.)

Line and Leader Setups for Kamchatka King Salmon

9-10 foot specialty tapered sinking leader with 12-15 lb. mono tippet

WF Floating

For less than five feet of water, slow to moderate current. Additional weight (split shot, wrap lead, etc.) may be needed to keep fly on bottom.

7 foot specialty tapered sinking leader with 12-15 lb. mono tippet

Sink Tip

For 4-10 feet of water, moderate-fast currents. Use medium-density, 3-10 foot sink tip line. Extra weight may still be necessary to keep fly in "strike zone".

3-5 foot tapered mono leader with 12-15 lb. tippet

Full Sink

Only necessary for extreme conditions, such as during very high water and/ or when fishing lower sections of Kamchatka's largest king rivers. Use low-medium density lines.

Gearing Up

Hooking and landing the king of salmon on a fly rod is one of freshwater angling's great accomplishments. For a chance of success with Kamchatka's kings, stout, high-quality gear is required. A beefy 9 to 11-weight, medium-fast action, graphite fly rod, 9 to 11 feet long, with a fighting butt section is the recommended stick. It should be matched with a large salmon or tarpon class fly reel capable of holding the line plus a minimum of 150 yards of 30-pound backing. Two-handed Spey rods, 10 to

12-weight, 13 to 15 feet long, can also be used for greater ease of casting and line handling efficiency on some of the larger waters.

A high-performance tapered, full floating line will be adequate for most presentations in waters of shallow depth (five feet or less) and not too swift current, conditions which are commonly encountered on many of Kamchatka's streams. (Use additional weight in the form of split shot or wrap lead to achieve proper depth.) For deeper and/or swifter situations, such as those encountered in the lower sections of Kamchatka's big king rivers, a medium-density, 3 to 10-foot sink-tip is preferred over a full sink line, for better line control. High performance, interchangeable tip systems, and shooting heads can also be used for increased efficiency. Specialty, tapered sinking leaders, 9 to 10 feet long with 12 to 15-pound mono nylon tippets (kings are not leader shy, so fluorocarbon is not required), are recommended for the terminal end of your line system. (If you make your own leaders, use a fairly stiff and hard leader material with minimum stretch for good hooksets and abrasion resistance.)

The king flies used in Pacific Northwest America work very well on Russia's big salmon. Most of these are oversize attractors fashioned of marabou, tinsel, bucktail and chenille, tied on super-sharp, strong hooks, size 2 to 3/0, in colors of cerise, orange, red, pink, yellow, chartreuse, black, green and purple. Giant egg/flesh flies like the King Caviar, King Killer, Bunny Bug and others work well also, exploiting the big fish's natural attraction to roe. And many oversize variations of forage patterns like the Leech and Shrimp tied with hackle, chenille, rabbit fur or synthetics can be used to great effect, as well as traditional saltwater flies like Clouser Minnow, Deceiver, and Coronation.

Recommended Fly Patterns (sizes #3/0–2): Leech (Egg-Sucking, Bunny, Strip, Articulated, etc.), Zonker, Popsicle, Alaskabou, Practitioner, Wombat, Herring Fly, Wiggletail, Outrageous, King Caviar, Polar Shrimp, Candy Cane, Cluster Fly, Deceiver, Bunny Fly, Flash Fly, Everglow, Alaska Candlefish, Seaducer, Clouser Minnow, Shrimp, Coronation

SOCKEYE SALMON

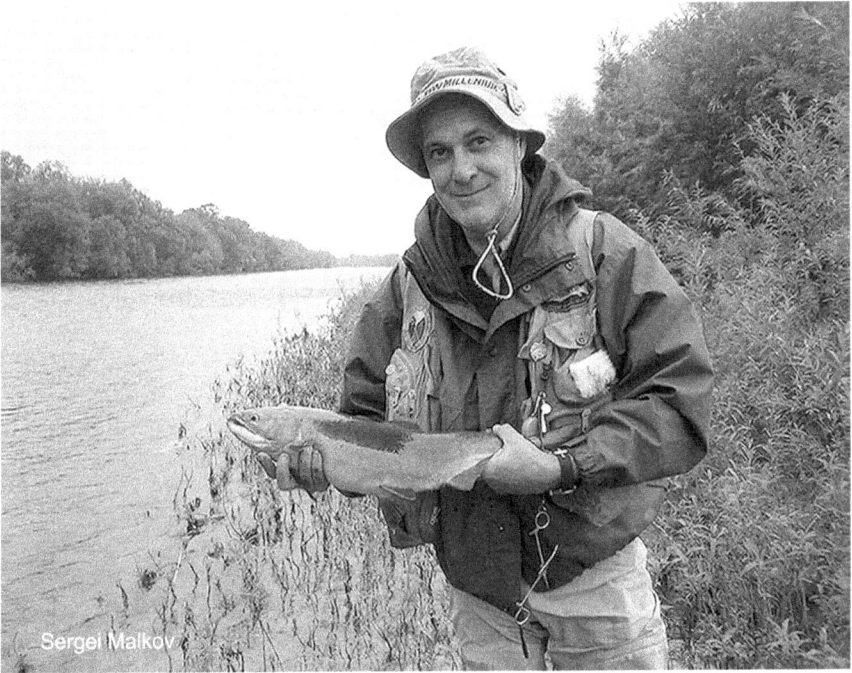

Sergei Malkov

Oncorhynchus nerka

Common names: Sockeye salmon, sockeye (U.S. Northwest); nerka, krasnaya ryba (Russia); red salmon, red (Alaska); kokanee (landlocked form, U.S.)

Description: A medium-sized Pacific salmon, common to many rivers of Kamchatka. Sea-bright specimens have metallic blue, green or gray backs, silver sides and whitish bellies; markings usually absent. Spawning fish strikingly colored, with greenish-black heads and scarlet bodies. Average size for Kamchatka, 22 to 24 inches, and 4 to 7 lbs.

Range/Abundance/Status: Found in varying numbers along much of the coast of Kamchatka, concentrated in a few productive lake and river systems. Status of many Kamchatka runs uncertain due to overfishing (including poaching) and insufficient data.

Best Waters: Large, productive river systems with headwater lakes

Best Rivers/Lakes: Kamchatka, Bolshaya, Palana, Paratunka, Avacha, Kihkchik, Ozernaya, Icha and Tigil rivers; Kronotsky and Tolmachevo lakes

Best Fly Patterns: Sparse bucktail or hackle streamers and yarn flies

Best Times: May to October

The sockeye or red salmon is one of the most prolific and important salmon species in the north Pacific, coveted for its rich flesh, with high food and commercial value. A challenging sport fish—hardwired for grazing plankton, it steadfastly refuses the fly in most situations— this shy salmon possesses legendary fighting qualities when hooked, with amazing strength and jumping capability. Pound for pound, it is perhaps the scrappiest of all the Pacific salmon.

A well-established sport fishery for sockeye salmon exists in the eastern Pacific, in certain areas of British Columbia and Alaska, where sockeyes succumb to special techniques and fly patterns. Kamchatka, home to over 90% of the Asian population of the species, has considerable underutilized potential in many productive, shallow, clear rivers along its coasts. Only a handful of these drainages receive significant pressure, and fewer still see any fly fishing effort.

Description

Sockeye salmon vary little in appearance across their range and so are usually easy to identify. The third largest species of Pacific salmon, they average around 22 inches in length and 4 to 7 pounds in Kamchatka , with streamlined bodies of metallic blue/gray/green on the back, silver sides, and silver-white bellies. Markings on the top sides and tail fins are almost always absent, and this, along with the presence of 30 to 40 fine, closely spaced and serrated rakers on the first gill arch, help positively identify the species. (Sea-bright specimens may closely resemble chum or cherry salmon, but the cherry is generally smaller, more stoutly built and may have fine spots on the topsides and tailfin, while the chum has larger eyes and a gill raker count of only 25.) As the sockeye is predominantly a plankton feeder, teeth on pre-spawning fish are usually less developed than those on other salmon. Juvenile sockeyes have short, dark oval parr marks usually terminating at or shortly below the lateral line. Kokanee, the landlocked form of the sockeye, are very similar in appearance to the anadromous form, but much smaller, reaching about 10 inches average length and rarely exceeding 1 ½ pounds.

Spawning sockeye salmon are among the most striking sights in Nature. The males develop vivid red bodies, greenish-black heads, thick humps and pronounced hooked jaws with prominent teeth. Females are generally more subdued in appearance. Color can vary in intensity and hue in different populations. Red salmon, along with king salmon, are among the most prized fishes for eating, with rich, bright red flesh of unparalleled flavor, whether grilled, fried, baked, smoked, or canned. Their value as a food fish, uniformity in size, and relative abundance has made them a most desirable and economically significant fish for commerce, subsistence and personal use throughout Kamchatka and the rest of the north Pacific.

Distribution

Sockeye salmon were originally found coastally from central California to Point Hope, Alaska (with scattered sightings in the Arctic Ocean) and in Asia from Hokkaido, Japan to the Anadyr River in northeastern Siberia. 90-95% of Asian sockeye salmon stocks are located on the Kamchatka Peninsula, concentrated mostly on the southwest coast (especially the Ozernaya River and Kurilskye Lake) and the Kamchatka River basin in the central valley. Small runs occur on the mainland, along the Bering Sea (north to the Anadyr River) and Sea of Okhotsk.

The third most abundant Pacific salmon, they are found in greatest numbers from the Fraser River in British Columbia to Alaska's Bristol Bay (and in Asia, in the rivers of Kamchatka). The immense and abundant lake-river habitat of the Alaska Peninsula and Bristol Bay hold the world's largest runs of sockeye salmon (that number in the tens of millions). Kamchatka's sockeye salmon runs, while still abundant (commercial harvests in recent years have averaged above 38 million pounds per season), are considered at risk due to overfishing (including poaching) and inadequate management.

Life History

Because of their economic importance, sockeye salmon are among the most studied fish in the world. Their remarkable success as a species stems from an ability to directly exploit the rich blooms of plankton in the North Pacific as a main food source (and utilize the abundant lake and river habitat along adjacent coasts for breeding).

As a general rule, sockeyes are most abundant in rivers with lake headwaters, but they can breed successfully in rivers with springs and small tributary ponds, or rarely, even in estuaries (these fish tend to go to the sea the first summer after hatching). Kamchatka, compared to Alaska, has few large lake and river systems so favorable for mass breeding and rearing. Many of its sockeye populations are thus of the type adapted to breeding in rivers without lakes. Residuals—sea-run fish that for some reason spend their entire lives in freshwater—and true landlocked populations such as the kokanee, exist only in a few places in Kamchatka (Kronotsky Lake).

Mature pre-spawning sockeye salmon begin appearing at the mouths of Kamchatka's rivers in late spring (May to early June), with the peak of the run occurring in early summer (late June and July). Run duration can vary, from early May into late fall (late September into early October) in some systems. Local abundance in the more prolific rivers (Kamchatka and Ozernaya rivers) can be staggering during the height of the runs, choking the waters with millions of salmon. Favored sockeye spawning locations are in stream outlets directly below lakes, in feeder creeks, and along gravelly lakeshores, with peak activity taking place in late summer (late July & August) in most of Kamchatka. In some locations (Kuril Lake), spawning may extend into late fall (October and November) and even early winter (January).

Like the rest of the Pacific salmon, the female sockeye digs the gravel nest, then mates in several bouts of egg-laying that may involve the digging of more than one redd and fertilization by several males. Up to 4,000 or more eggs are deposited and incubate in anywhere from six weeks to five months, depending on water temperature. Breeding is terminal, though fish may linger for weeks after spawning, despite pronounced physical deterioration. Young sockeye fry emerge in early spring (April to May) and usually migrate to the nursery lake by summer. There in the shallows, they feed primarily on insects and crustaceans before moving in schools to deeper waters to consume plankton in the upper water column.

Kamchatka sockeye fry become smolts and migrate downriver to the sea when they are 1 to 3 years of age. Smolt out-migration usually occurs during the darker hours of day in late spring and early summer (May and June).

Once in the ocean, young sockeye grow rapidly on diets of crustaceans, squid, zooplankton, and on rare occasion even small fish such as sand lance, eulachon, herring, and rockfish. In open water, they generally prefer to be near the surface (less than 45 feet deep) a large percentage of the time. Ocean stay of Kamchatka sockeyes varies, but it is usually 2 to 3 years (rarely 4 to 5) and involves lengthy seasonal forays into the western North Pacific and Bering Sea. (A significant number of returning Kamchatka sockeyes are five and even six years of age.) Principal marine predators of sockeye are whales, seals, and man. In rivers and lakes, they are preyed on by charr, trout, coho salmon, sea birds, eagles, bears, and man.

Kokanee: Kokanee, or landlocked sockeye salmon, thrive in large, deep lakes with enough year-round food sources to sustain fish to maturity. These fish are universally small in size, averaging six to 12 inches in length (depending on location), with rare individuals up to 20 inches and four pounds. Unlike landlocked or residual populations of king and silver salmon, kokanee are capable of reproduction and undergo seasonal prenuptial changes much like those of their larger, anadromous cohorts. Breeding occurs in suitable lake bottoms or inlet streams late in the year (October and November). Although most kokanee populations are natural, due to a blockage of outlet streams preventing juvenile fish from migrating to the ocean, there are a few mountain lakes, mostly in southern Kamchatka, that have been stocked with populations of kokanee taken from Kronotsky Lake.

Habits

Sockeyes have some unique and interesting habits that can be exploited by anglers. Along with pinks, they are the most gregarious of salmon, grouping by the thousands for their upstream migrations, where they mill in estuaries, river mouths, lake outlets, sloughs, and pools, to rest from their strenuous journey. Like other pre-spawning salmon, these sexually mature sockeyes frequently breach the surface and jump, in displays that are easily mistaken for aggression, as many an angler has discovered after futile bouts of casting. They tend to hug shorelines as they move up rivers and through lakes, which makes it easier for interception by predators, including man.

The most mysterious and exasperating aspect of sockeye salmon nature has to be their legendary aloofness to enticement by anglers. As plankton consumers, they are not the aggressive, reckless feeders that king and silver salmon are. The standard attractor lures and flies that work so well for other salmon in fresh water, under most conditions are almost always totally ineffective for arousing pre-spawning sockeyes. (Fish that have been in rivers and lakes for a while and are actively spawning are a different story.) Through trial and error, anglers have developed specialized techniques, gear and flies to elicit takes from this shy salmon.

FLY FISHING KAMCHATKA'S RED SALMON

Sockeye salmon are coveted by Russians who take small numbers of them by rod and reel during summer on the major, road accessible rivers like the Paratunka, Bolshaya, Avacha and Kamchatka. Most of these fish are caught incidentally or intentionally, quite often by foul hooking, on spinning gear, using spoons and spinners. Very little fly fishing effort for the species currently takes place, most of it by visiting anglers. Considerable untapped fly fishing opportunity for the species exists on some of the more remote productive streams along Kamchatka's coast.

Despite their passive nature, sockeye salmon, in certain conditions and with the right enticement and technique, can be coaxed to take a fly or lure. Commercial trollers in Northwest U.S. and southern B.C. discovered years ago that certain spoons, hootchies (plastic-skirted jig streamers), streamers, and even bare colored hooks, when trolled slowly and erratically will draw strikes from red salmon, albeit usually not in great numbers. Innovative fly anglers further refined some of the techniques and gear to develop a simple yet effective methodology for taking bright sockeye salmon in rivers. On many rivers, it was found that sparsely tied streamer flies of bucktail, yarn or synthetics, in certain colors (yellow, red, chartreuse, green, orange, pink and white) produced consistent results, although, in a few areas, spoons, spinners, bait and even colored sponge balls seem to work best. Over the years, a new sports fishery developed, mostly in Alaska and Canada, with certain patterns and methods gaining precedence. So far, all indications from fly anglers fishing Kamchatka show that the Russian sockeyes can be taken with the same flies and techniques used in Alaska and elsewhere, though in smaller numbers on most streams, due to the different conditions and lesser runs. As time goes by, no doubt, fly anglers will develop a unique set of strategies and patterns more suited to taking these reticent fish in Kamchatka's waters.

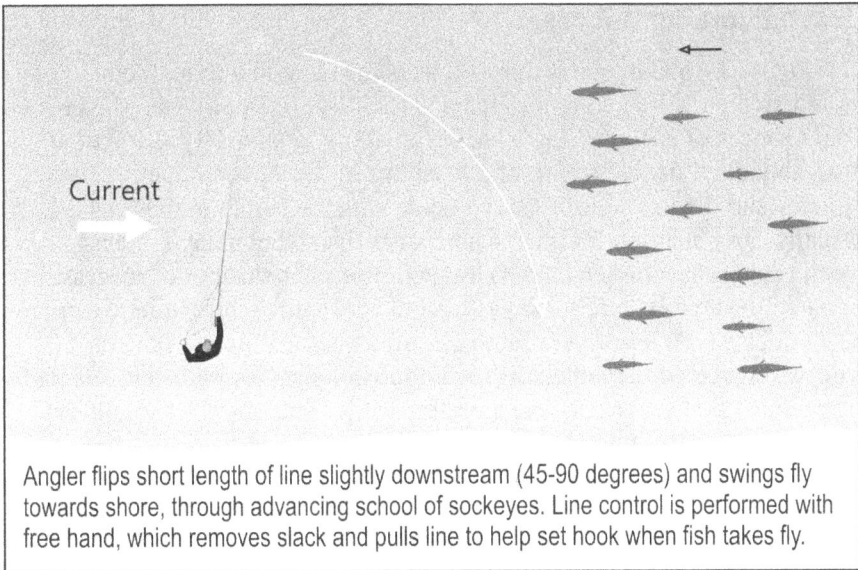

Angler flips short length of line slightly downstream (45-90 degrees) and swings fly towards shore, through advancing school of sockeyes. Line control is performed with free hand, which removes slack and pulls line to help set hook when fish takes fly.

Techniques

The basic technique most used to coerce strikes from sockeye salmon in fresh water is a slightly modified, tight wet fly swing. Anglers use short casts (20 feet or less) to work only water that lies adjacent or slightly downstream of their position. A swing or flip technique is used to lob out the line in one quick motion, thus eliminating back casts and slack. Using the free hand to control the line, the angler pivots to follow the fly as it completes its short arc into shore, paying close attention to the drift. Additional weight, usually in the form of a lead dropper, wrap lead or split shot, is used to keep the fly right above bottom. When the fly swings to shore, the angler flips the line back up to begin the drift again and repeat the whole process. (The entire cast and drift take but seconds; after a short while, the movements become fluid and automatic.)

Sight fishing conditions are obviously ideal for this technique, so fishing shallow clear waters (and having a good set of polarized sunglasses) is very advantageous, but not absolutely necessary. Fishing blind in turbid waters can be done successfully, with careful attention to the drift and quick reflexes to set the hook at the slightest indication of a take. (Some fish will be foul hooked when fishing this way.) It is important to remember that this technique, especially when performed in turbid waters that limit visibility, works best in fast, shallow rivers with great concentrations of sockeyes (see below).

Best Factors for Success

Dense Fish Concentrations Perhaps the most important factor. The more fish there are moving through a particular stretch of water, the greater your chances of encountering a sockeye willing to take a fly. Target the most abundant, fish-concentrating locations in the most productive river systems and time your efforts to coincide with the height of the runs (usually early summer for most Kamchatka rivers, but many systems receive late runs into September) to maximize your chances of success. Some of the areas where sockeyes tend to concentrate in running water are lake outlets and inlets, river mouths, confluences, big pools, sloughs, narrows and below structures like waterfalls, rapids, logjams, and islands. (Remember that sockeyes have a preference for hugging the shoreline as they move upriver, but are easily spooked.)

Shallow, Clear, Fast Waters The most productive locations for hooking sockeye salmon will have water that is shallow (less than four feet deep), clear and with moderately fast current. Lakes, bays, estuaries and other still waters, even if they have great numbers of fish, seldom offer any chances for success. (Rarely will the odd sockeye hit a lure or fly on the edge of a slough or in a lake outlet or river mouth.) The theory is that when jammed tight, the salmon are stressed and more prone to hit flies out of irritation. And when they are concentrated in shallow clear waters, it certainly makes accurate presentation of the fly easier (see below). You can fish sockeyes successfully in waters that are not that shallow, clear or fast, but it is much more difficult.

Reasonably Bright Fish The closer to salt you intercept sockeye salmon, the better. Once in the river for a while, their appearance, behavior, gameness and eating qualities change, mostly not for the better. Sockeyes that have begun their spawning are definitely more aggressive, and will actually chase your fly. But it is not sporting and probably not legal either in most waters, to harass them at this point in their life cycle. If you do accidentally hook a sockeye in bright spawning colors, it's important to free your line as soon as possible. To do this, reel in all slack, point your rod directly at the fish, grab your spool firmly so it can't turn, then yank sharply while moving away from the fish. (Turn your face away while you do this, and always wear eye protection, as the stretched line and fly can tear free and whip back with destructive force, especially when there is lead attached.)

Proper Presentation A fly presented at fish eye level has the most chance of a take, but only for the brief moment, it passes in front of the moving fish's mouth. Sockeyes that have been in fresh water only a short time will rarely if ever, pursue a fly, and only barely nip at it. For this reason, you must use the proper line and, if necessary, additional weight to keep the fly drifting right above bottom. Split shot, wrap lead, and dropper rigs are traditional ways to get your fly down deep, in addition to using very short sink tip lines (long sink sections tend to interfere with the drift).

Tight Lines & Sharp Hooks The take of a sockeye is usually very subtle, almost like a winter steelhead's. A tight line and super sharp hook are essential. In waters where you cannot sight fish, any variation in the drift may signal a connection with a sockeye, so you should be ready for an instant hook-set the moment you feel a bump or change in the tension or direction of the line. Since red salmon have such a powerful instinct for upstream movement, they generally hook themselves once they feel the slightest resistance from the line, so a quick, upward snap of the rod combined with a downward pull on the line with the free hand will usually set the hook. (And hang on! Make sure you have the drag set tight before you hook up, as the first thing that fish will do is panic and rip out line, making for a guaranteed knuckle buster if your drag is improperly set!)

Gearing Up

For sockeye salmon angling in Kamchatka, a stout 7 or even 8-weight, medium-action, graphite fly rod (8 ½ to 10 feet) is recommended. Matching reels should be high-quality, single or compound action, with excellent drag systems. Lines used are generally performance-tapered floating, or medium-density, very short (2 to 5 foot) sink tips, with 7 to 11 foot tapered sinking leaders (fluorocarbon not necessary) and tough mono nylon tippets of 2X to 12-pound strength. Additional weight in the form of split shot, wrap lead, rubber core sinker, or pencil-lead dropper with an 18-inch leader may be used to get the fly down to the proper depth.

Recommended Fly Patterns (size #4–8): Russian River, Comet, Brassie, Sockeye Orange, Sportsman's Special, Yarn Fly, Sockeye Willie, Green Boss, Flash Fly, Supervisor, Krazy Charrlie, Shad Fly, Mickey Finn, Coho Fly, Fall Favorite

PINK SALMON

Oncorhnychus gorbusha

Common names: Pink salmon, pink, humpback or humpy (U.S. Northwest and Alaska), gorbuscha (Russia)

Description: A very abundant, small Pacific salmon, common to the rivers of Kamchatka. Metallic blue or green back, silver sides and whitish belly, with sparse oval black markings when fresh from sea; spawning fish develop grotesque humpbacks and jaws, with brown or mauve topsides and cream-white belly. Kamchatka fish average 2 ½ to 3 ½ pounds and 17 to 22 inches.

Range/Abundance/Status: Found in great numbers along most of Kamchatka's coast; status of most populations secure.

Best Waters: Productive streams and river systems with extensive intertidal habitat

Best Rivers: Bolshaya, Avacha, Paratunka, Zhupanova, Opala, Utka, Khikchik, Pymta, Kolpokova, Ozernaya and Icha rivers.

Best Fly Patterns: Attractor and forage pattern streamers

Best Times: Late June to mid-August

Smallest and least savory of the Pacific salmon, the pink or humpy makes up for a lack of glamor with sheer abundance and willingness to take a fly under most conditions. Noted for accelerated physical changes (and often grotesque appearance) as it nears home waters, this highly social salmon spawns in practically every suitable clear-flowing drainage of the North Pacific, filling bays and river mouths during the height of its spawning run. For fly anglers lucky enough to be in Kamchatka during this time, the feisty pink can provide exciting sport on light gear when encountered close to its prime in intertidal areas or lower rivers, and should not be overlooked

Description

In ocean dress, the pink is a small, sleek salmon with a dark metallic blue or green back, silvery sides, and a white belly. Sparse, medium-size oval spots occur across the back and both lobes of the tail fin. Due to their similar appearance, sea-bright pinks can be misidentified as small (jack) king or silver salmon.

Spawning fish undergo dramatic changes in appearance, often before ascending rivers. Males develop a grotesquely humped back (hence their popular name) and an elongated, hooked snout with enlarged teeth. Females generally show much less changes. Coloration on both sexes darkens to a greenish-gray, brown or mauve on the topsides, with yellowish-white belly and more prominent oval markings.

Pink salmon in Kamchatka average from slightly more than two pounds to almost four pounds in weight and 17 to 22 inches in length. Outsize specimens can grow to seven pounds and 28 inches or more. Size varies with sex (males usually being larger than females), location (fish from northern rivers are usually smaller) and brood year (odd-year pinks tend to be slightly heavier than even-year fish).

The flesh of sea-bright pink salmon has an orange or pink hue and moderately soft texture and is excellent table fare. Pink salmon comprise the bulk of the North Pacific's commercial salmon catch (and over 70% of the salmon harvest in the Far East in recent years) and are a significant subsistence and sport species in many areas. In Kamchatka, with their abundance and availability, they are a coveted catch among urban anglers.

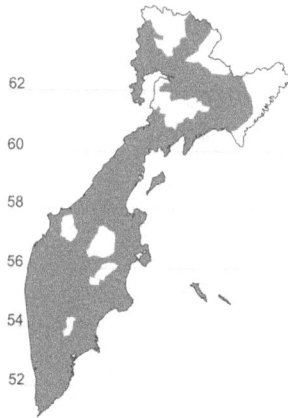

Distribution

The most abundant salmon, the pink ranges along the coast of west North America from Sacramento, California to the Mackenzie River delta in the Northwest Territories, and along the eastern rim of Asia from North Korea to the Lena River in Siberia. Transplant efforts have spread the species to locations as far away as the Scandinavian Peninsula, parts of South America, and the eastern United States and Canada. Major pink salmon populations in Asia are found along the mainland from northern Primorye (Amur River) to the Anadyr River, and on Sakhalin Island, the Kurils and the Kamchatka Peninsula. In Kamchatka, they are most abundant along the southwest (from Cape Yuzhny south) and northeast (from the Ozernay Peninsula to Cape Oliutorsky) coasts.

Life History

Pinks differ from other Pacific salmon in several ways. For one, they have a shorter lifespan, with almost all fish returning to freshwater to spawn after only one winter at sea. (Fish that have spent more than one winter at sea are extremely rare.) In Kamchatka and elsewhere, dominant runs occur during even or odd years on many river systems. These even-year and odd-year fish do not mix and are considered two distinct genetic stocks.

Pinks also show the least affinity for stream life, moving quickly from the river gravels where they are hatched to lagoons and estuaries and thence to the open sea. (In Kamchatka, this occurs from May to July.) The fastest growing salmon, pinks feed on a variety of small organisms when young—larvae, plankton, crustaceans and occasionally insects—eventually switching to a diet of small fishes, squid, and amphipods as size increases.

They spend most of their first summer feeding in near shore waters, then move out into the high seas, where they may mingle with fish from western Alaska. Mature adults begin returning from their offshore feeding grounds to coastal areas in late spring or early summer of the following year (June and July for much of Kamchatka). They typically peak in numbers by midsummer in inshore waters and continue to arrive until early fall, concentrating in huge schools near major spawning streams.

Bright fish may be present in freshwater anytime between June and October, but mostly (in Kamchatka) during July and August. As with other salmon species, the timing of individual runs is greatly influenced by the different water temperature regimes. Actual spawning for most of Kamchatka's pink salmon occurs from mid-July to late August and early September.

Not powerful swimmers, pink salmon tend to spawn in the lower reaches of rivers and creeks, including intertidal areas (pink eggs can withstand a high degree of salinity). During abnormally strong runs with high spawner density, pinks tend to migrate farther upstream than in normal years. "Straying" into non-natal streams for spawning occurs with a much higher frequency than in other salmon.

They can spawn in almost any conditions, from mere trickles of water to major rivers. However, their general preference is for shallow (five inches to three feet deep), moderate-flowing, clear-water streams with clean gravel substrate. A female pink may deposit anywhere from 1,100 to 2,300 eggs in several nests, guarding the area from 10 days up to three weeks. As in other Pacific salmon, breeding for pinks is terminal, and they undergo rapid deterioration and death following spawning.

Habits

The pink is perhaps the most social of the Pacific salmon species (even more so than the sockeye), gathering and moving in great schools, especially prior to spawning. They show themselves frequently— porpoising, jumping and finning near the surface— when amassed during migrations and thus are usually easy to spot and target in bays, lagoons, river mouths, pools, etc. Aggressive when bright from the sea, they are notoriously easy to tempt with all manner of enticements, particularly bright attractor pattern streamers fished with a lively strip. Hard biters, they practically hook themselves and are known for their game fight on light to medium-weight gear, thus endearing them to anglers of all persuasions and skill levels, who can expect to do quite well during the height of the run when fish are concentrated in great numbers.

FLY FISHING KAMCHATKA'S PINK SALMON

In Alaska and most elsewhere in the eastern North Pacific, pink salmon are not as prized as other salmon species by sport anglers. In Kamchatka, however, they are generally given much more regard by local fishermen and frequently taken in lower rivers in late summer, along with other more desirable species like silver salmon. They are a favorite of the young, inexperienced and more elderly anglers, because of their great numbers and ease of capture. Almost all effort for pink salmon in Kamchatka and the rest of Far East Russia is done with spinning gear; few are the fly anglers who purposely go after these small salmon when larger, more exciting quarry is available.

The poor reputation of these salmon is certainly not due to a lack in numbers or reluctance to respond to enticement. They can be so plentiful in certain years during the height of the runs and so aggressive as to become a nuisance to anyone pursuing the more glamorous species available in late summer. Because of the accelerated physical changes they undergo during their spawning phase, pinks should be sought only in near-shore marine waters, intertidal areas and extreme lower reaches of coastal rivers and streams during the early stages of the run (usually the first two weeks or so for the freshest fish in greatest numbers). Some coastal creeks and rivers never see anything other than fish in full nuptial maturity, as the pinks will mill around the stream mouth until ripe and ready. Encounters with fish far advanced into their spawning phase should be avoided.

Ideal fishing locations are the heads of bays, lagoons, river mouths and other intertidal areas, and small, shallow pools and riffles, sloughs and stream confluences in lower rivers with clear or semi-clear water and moderate current flow. Pinks seem to be "on the bite" more often in rivers and creeks with a good flow and at least two to three feet of water. In very slow and still waters, they can be more difficult to catch, especially under bright, clear conditions.

A wide range of fly patterns is used for enticing these diminutive salmon. Dead drift and wet fly swing presentations right above bottom produce the most responses, as pinks are fairly aggressive takers in and out of salt water. (When you encounter schools of these scrappy fighters, you can expect all the action you can handle!) Typically you will hook quite a few fish that are fairly advanced in their spawning phase and therefore undesirable, so it is important to carry an ample supply of flies and leaders to allow for "break-offs." Groups of pinks that appear well into spawning should, of course, be avoided.

Gearing Up

For greatest enjoyment and efficiency when fishing pink salmon, fly anglers should gear down to a 4 to 6-weight, fast-action graphite rod, 8 to 9 feet long, with matching, high-quality reel and performance-tapered floating or medium-density short sink-tip line (2 to 5 feet). A 9-foot, tapered sinking leader and 5X to 2X (4 to 8 pound) mono nylon (fluorocarbon is not necessary) tippet are most commonly used.

Bright and flashy attractor pattern streamers, smaller versions of those used for silver and king salmon, are especially productive with pink salmon, in colors of silver, gold, pink, red, orange, yellow, white, chartreuse, purple, and black. Leech, smolt and egg patterns can also used to great effect, as many anglers take pinks when targeting trout and charr with these flies in lower rivers during mid to late summer.

Recommended Fly Patterns (size #4–8): Comet, Boss, Polar Shrimp, Flash Fly, Alaskabou, Everglow, Coho Fly, Egg Sucking Leech, Crazy Charlie, Krystal Bullet, Wiggletail, Blue Smolt, Coronation, Woolly Bugger, Shrimp, Zonker, Fall Favorite, Supervisor, Glo Bug, Flash Fly

SILVER SALMON

Eugeny Lukovnikov

Oncorhnychus kisutch

Common names: Silver salmon, silver (Alaska); "kizutch" (Russia), coho (U.S. Pacific Northwest)

Description: A medium-sized, Pacific salmon found in most rivers of Kamchatka. Metallic-blue, black, gray or greenish back, silver sides and whitish belly, with small, irregular dark markings on topsides when fresh from sea. Kamchatka fish average 6 to 8 lbs.; rarely to 12 to 15 lbs.

Range/Abundance/Status: Common to abundant along Kamchatka's coast; status of certain populations uncertain due to lack of data and possible overfishing (including poaching)

Best Waters: Larger, productive streams and river systems

Best Rivers: Bolshaya, Kamchatka, Zhupanova, Opala, Pymta, Kolpokova, Icha, Tigil, Ozernaya and Apuka rivers

Best Fly Patterns: Attractor, egg and forage pattern streamers

Best Times: Late summer and fall (August into October)

The silver salmon is one of the most important sport fishes in the North Pacific and comprises a significant part of the commercial and subsistence fisheries as well. Widespread and locally abundant, it's eagerness to take a lure or fly and resolute gameness once hooked (not to mention its fine eating qualities) make it extremely popular with anglers of all persuasions. No other salmon responds to enticement as predictably or as aggressively, and few fish can fight with the same vigor and finesse, especially on medium-weight gear.

First described by Steller and Krasheninnikov during their 18th century Kamchatka explorations, the silver, or "kizutch" as it is called by Russians, makes its eagerly anticipated appearance all along the coast in late summer, continuing to show up well into the fall in many locations. As the last Pacific salmon to make its way up rivers, it adds a final—and often spectacular—highlight to the fishing season, and an important opportunity for locals to finish stocking their larders for the looming winter. Presently, there are literally dozens of rivers along both coasts of Kamchatka with great runs of these last salmon of summer that go begging for any fly angling effort.

Description

A powerfully built, medium-sized salmon, the silver, when fresh from the sea, is very similar in appearance to a small king salmon, with steel-blue, black, gray or greenish back, chrome sides and whitish belly. Faint irregular black markings are sprinkled along the topsides, including the upper tail fin. The scales are medium-sized, like those of other salmon; the gum line is not dark like that of a king. Silver salmon flesh is orange-red, firm and more mildly flavored than that of king or sockeye salmon and thus highly prized.

Like other Pacific salmon, silvers undergo dramatic changes in appearance prior to spawning, particularly males. The body deepens, topsides darken to greenish- or reddish-black, flanks become imbued with dark red or greenish-bronze, and the belly darkens to gray or black. The head and jaws on males become enlarged (kyping) with protruding teeth.

Silvers are the third largest of the Pacific salmon, attaining weights in Kamchatka to 15 pounds or more, but averaging 6 to 8 pounds and 22 to 28 inches in length. (Males tend to be larger than females.)

Distribution

Silver salmon range throughout most of the North Pacific basin, from Hokkaido, Japan (and scattered points south along the mainland to North Korea) north to the Anadyr River, across the Bering Sea and south along the west coast of North America to Monterey Bay, California. Comprising only a small portion of the total Pacific salmon population (less than 10 percent) they are much less abundant along the Asian coast than in the Americas, occurring in greatest numbers on the Kamchatka Peninsula, eastern Sakhalin Island and along the northern mainland, from the Sea of Okhotsk to the northern Bering Sea (Anadyr River.)

Life History

The life history and habits of the silver are similar to other Pacific salmon, but with some interesting differences. They begin their lives in the gravels of stream beds, like other salmon, but spend at least one, and sometimes two or even three years in freshwater before heading to sea. When small, they very much resemble, in appearance and behavior, juvenile rainbow trout. Territorial and voracious, silver salmon parr can commonly be observed (and even taken on small flies) in large schools along stream margins and in side channels and small tributary creeks. In late spring and early summer of their second or third year of life, young silver salmon become smolts and head out to sea. (Naturally occurring populations of small, landlocked silver salmon exist in a few lakes in Kamchatka and elsewhere throughout the North Pacific.) After several months near shore, most of the silvers from Kamchatka migrate east into the North Pacific, mingling with fish from Alaska. They roam this vast sea pasture north and south with the seasons until they mature after one or two years and head back to freshwaters to spawn.

Like the king salmon, the silver is a big fish eater, and once large enough, switches to an almost exclusive diet of finny creatures. In rivers, young coho can inflict serious damage on other important species like sockeye salmon and rainbow and cutthroat trout. Out in the sea, they grow rapidly on steady diets of herring, sand lance, smelt, capelins and other small salmon, with supplemental binges on invertebrates (crab larvae, squid, and shrimp).

The silver salmon shows great diversity in the timing and duration of its spawning runs, to best exploit optimum stream flow and water temperatures. In Kamchatka, the first silver salmon of the season begin appearing in near shore areas and stream mouths in late July, with the largest surge into rivers occurring from August into September. Late running fish trickle in into October on many rivers.

Actual spawning usually takes place late in the fall (from mid-September into October) but can occur as early as August or as late as January or February (or later even) in some areas. Silvers utilize entire river drainages for spawning, from lower reaches right above tidewater to the smallest feeder creeks. After mating and depositing fertilized eggs in a manner similar to other salmon species, silvers die soon after, leaving some 1,400 to 5,700 fertilized eggs per breeding hen, buried in several gravel redds (nests).

Habits

Along with king salmon, silvers are the most aggressive and territorial Pacific salmon. Usually easy to provoke in freshwater with all manner of enticement (males are especially testy), they can be unpredictable when in rivers for some time. Not as gregarious as sockeye or pink salmon, they will congregate in predictable locations prior to spawning, where they show themselves frequently. Look for them milling, breaching and jumping in bays, lagoons, river mouths, lake outlets, pools, sloughs, etc. The take of a silver salmon is usually unmistakably abrupt, felt as a bump or a grab, but as they, like other salmon, develop hard mouths once in freshwater, a strong hookset and razor sharp hooks are essential to keeping them on your line.

One of the traits that endear silver salmon to fly anglers, other than their willingness to take a wide range of feathered enticement, is the spectacular fight they put up when hooked. As previously mentioned, they are not subtle takers and quite frequently will hook themselves, even after repeated nips on the fly. Although most of the silvers you will encounter in Kamchatka are not brutes, weighing but 6 to 8 pounds, they are amazingly strong, boring into the swift currents, jumping repeatedly, and violently side shaking that quite often results in their winning their freedom.

FLY FISHING KAMCHATKA'S SILVER SALMON

The bulk of the sport fishing effort for silver salmon in Kamchatka is done by locals along the major road accessible fisheries—the Paratunka, Avacha, Bolshaya, Bystraya and Kamchatka rivers. Most of these salmon are taken on spinning gear and bright spoons and spinners. Much of the peninsula's best silver fishing, on the more remote rivers and streams, goes underutilized, with only a very small percentage of Kamchatka's silver salmon taken on flies.

As with other salmon, the closer to saltwater you can intercept the silver, the better. Bays and estuaries, river mouths, and lower stream sections, from right above tidewater to about 20 miles from the sea are ideal. Further up into freshwater, the silver's behavior, appearance, and gameness begin to change, mostly not for the better. Fish actively spawning on redds should be left alone and any silvers accidentally hooked in this condition should be broken off immediately.

The basic technique for taking silvers in freshwater is similar to that used for king salmon: deep drift presentations and short streamer swings through holding water—channels, sloughs, pools, river mouths, confluences, eddies, riffle sections, current seams, anywhere these aggressive fish might be resting in or moving through. (Remember that silvers, unlike kings, prefer to avoid moving and holding in deep, swift main channel sections.) Sight fishing salmon in clear water, for more precise casting, is ideal and certainly possible in the clear and shallow waters of many Kamchatka rivers. (Be sure to bring polarized sunglasses.) But if sight presentation is not possible, look for signs of showing fish, as pre-spawning silvers commonly engage in porpoising and jumping. If you take sufficient time to adequately observe the waters and still don't see any signs of salmon, you may have to fish "blind", working all potential holding areas thoroughly (a good rule of thumb is to make three drifts through a lie, then, unless you have some indication there might be a salmon there, move on to new water.) One thing that should be obvious about fishing salmon in rivers is that no matter how dead a stretch of water may seem, it can change dramatically in matter of hours with fresh fish moving up continuously from the sea.

Silver salmon fishing is attractor pattern fishing, as no other salmon responds as readily and energetically to bright streamers as this husky brawler. And a wide assortment of patterns is used to entice them, many of them traditional Northwest steelhead/salmon patterns or gaudy flies developed especially for coho or their bigger, more glamorous cousin, the king salmon. (Since silvers have a very hard mouth, strong, sharp hooks of the highest quality should be used, in size #1/0 to 4.) Big egg and select forage pattern flies like the Wiggletail, Leech, and Shrimp will also work well on freshwater silver salmon.

As with fishing kings, the most important thing to remember about presentation for silver salmon is to get your fly down to where the fish are, which is usually, but not always, a foot or less above bottom. (Silvers will frequently pursue lures and flies through the water column, but to have the best chance at hooking up, you should present the fly right in front of them.) This may entail adding some split shot or switching to a denser line.

Not too long ago, it was discovered that silvers, under certain conditions, could be lured to the surface to take large dry flies. Shallow, clear waters close to the sea seem to be the best areas for instigating this kind of exciting action, with the most productive flies being bulky traditional floaters like the Irresistible, Bomber, Wulff, Elk Hair Caddis or Deer hair Mouse, (size #2-4) or some of the less conventional topwater patterns like Poppers or 'Wogs. Unlike fishing for trout with these big floaters (remember that the silver, like all other Pacific salmon species, does not feed once it leaves the sea), the strategy for silvers is to make short fast strips across current, creating as much commotion and noise as possible. (You may need to make repeated casts to prompt a strike.)

Silvers that have been in fresh water for a time can become finicky, sometimes needing extra provoking to entice a take. For this reason, you should work every likely stretch of water thoroughly (especially if you know there are salmon there) and have an adequate assortment of patterns so you can experiment with different flies if you don't have any success with your tried-and-trues. Silvers will go off the bite entirely for no apparent reason when in freshwater, but sometimes a different retrieve or a strange fly will do the trick. Be especially mindful of your silhouette and the noise you make when stalking these salmon in Kamchatka's clear waters, as they tend to get spooky when they have been in rivers awhile. As noted previously, do not be tempted to cast to fish that are actively engaged in spawning, aggressive thought they may be, as this is not very sporting and may even be illegal.

Because of the hard mouths silver salmon develop in fresh water, a very positive hook set is required when a fish takes the fly. (Make sure your drag is set properly before you hook up, or your knuckles may suffer!) Silvers are incredibly energetic fighters and quite frequently will shake the hook or part your leader with their aerial gyrations, so it is very important to check your terminal components regularly to make sure your hook is still "sticky sharp," your knots snug and your leader not frayed.

For practical reasons (and to prevent potential stress and harm to the fish), unless you are working big water from a boat, there is no need to use a net to land silver salmon. Instead, lead the played out fish into calm, shallow water (by grabbing the leader) and slide it on its side into the shallows. (Leave it in enough water to cover most of its gills.) After you free the hook if you intend to release the salmon, grab it by the tail and gently pull it into deeper water and let it go.

Gearing Up

For Kamchatka's silver salmon, a 7 or 8-weight, medium-action, graphite fly rod, 8 ½ to 10 feet long, with stout butt section, will be adequate for all but the largest rivers (like the Kamchatka). A matching, high-quality reel with a strong drag system and sufficient backing is critical. For most of the situations you will encounter, you will do fine fishing a performance-tapered floating line or, for more challenging conditions, a medium-density, short (5 to 7 foot) sink tip line. A 9-foot, tapered sinking leader with 1X to 3X (8 to 12-pound) mono nylon tippet is recommended (fluorocarbon is unnecessary). Don't forget a sturdy pair of high-quality fish pliers to remove the fly from the silver's hard jaws.

Recommended Fly Patterns (size #4–1/0): Flash Fly, Coho Fly, Polar Shrimp, Leech, Egg-Sucking Leech, Zonker, Woolly Bugger, Maraflash Fly, Krystal Bullet, Alaskabou, Popsicle, Comet, Shrimp, Supervisor, Wiggletail, Everglow, Polywog, Deceiver, Pratitioner, Wombat

CHUM SALMON

S. Malkov

Oncorhnychus keta

Common names: Chum salmon, chum, calico salmon (U.S. Pacific Northwest); keta (Russia); dog salmon (Alaska)

Description: A medium to large Pacific salmon, common in the rivers of Kamchatka. Sea-bright specimens have metallic blue-black or green backs, silver sides, and whitish bellies; markings usually absent. Spawning fish develop calico coloration—greenish-yellow bodies with jagged, vertical black and rouge streaks. Kamchatka fish average 6 to 8 pounds, 22 to 28 inches.

Range/Abundance/Status: Found throughout Kamchatka, most abundant along southwest coast. Status in Kamchatka uncertain; many populations threatened by overfishing and poaching.

Best Waters: Productive rivers with extensive estuaries or bays

Best Rivers: Bolshaya, Zhupanova, Avacha, Kamchatka, Ozernaya, Icha, Tigil, Kolpokova, Pymta, Kol and Kikchik rivers

Best Fly Patterns: Bright attractor pattern streamers

Best Times: June through September

The chum salmon was first described by naturalist Johann Julius Walbaum in the late 18th century, from specimens taken from the Kamchatka River. As a sport fish, it is frequently overlooked by anglers in pursuit of more glamorous quarry, despite the fact that it is an exceedingly game species, especially when bright from the sea. When caught at its peak, pound for pound it is every bit the match of the regal king or sporty silver salmon, and its rich orange flesh makes a feast just as satisfying.

Supporting extensive commercial, subsistence, and personal use fisheries throughout the North Pacific, the chum salmon has always been a vitally important species, particularly for natives. Found in nearly every coastal drainage of Kamchatka, it is more prized by Russians for its roe or caviar than for its flesh or sporting qualities. Nonetheless, anglers should not overlook this humble species for the exciting challenge it can provide on a fly rod when fishing Kamchatka's rivers in summer and fall.

Description

The chum is the second largest Pacific salmon species. Ocean-bright fish may be difficult to distinguish from fresh red salmon since both species have similar form and coloration: streamlined bodies with dark greenish-blue metallic backs, silvery sides, and silver-white bellies (markings are usually absent from both species). Some of the chum's distinguishing characteristics are the ventral fins, which have whitish tips, and the eyes, which are generally larger than on sockeyes.

Spawning chum salmon develop striking calico coloration. The sides darken to a yellowish-brown or green with jagged, vertical streaks of rouge, yellow, and black. The head turns greenish-brown with a touch of golden yellow on the cheeks, and on males, a severe hooked jaw develops, with protruding teeth, which partially accounts for their nickname, "dog salmon" in Alaska. Females develop a dark horizontal band along the lateral line and are generally not as colorful. The pectoral, anal, and pelvic fins all feature whitish tips.

Second in size only to the king salmon, chums have been known to reach weights of 30 to 40 pounds and lengths to three feet along the coast of North America. But in the western Pacific, they run smaller, with the average size for Kamchatka, (the more northerly fish are not as big) being about 6 to 8 pounds and 22 to 26 inches. When fresh from the sea, chum salmon have a flesh color of light orange-red, and are excellent eating, whether grilled, fried, smoked or canned.

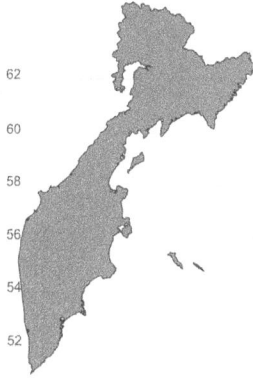

Distribution

The chum salmon has the broadest distribution of any salmon in the world. It is found in Asia from South Korea and the island of Kyushu in the Sea of Japan to the Arctic Ocean as far west as the Lena River in Siberia, and eastward into all coastal drainages of Alaska (including those along the North Slope, to the Mackenzie River of Canada), and down along the Pacific coast to Monterey, California. The second most abundant Pacific salmon (after the pink), the chum in the Far East is most numerous on the mainland—in the Amur River of Primorye to the Anadyr and other rivers along the northern sea of Okhotsk— and on the Kamchatka Peninsula and Sakhalin Island. Along with the pink salmon, the chum is the most extensively propagated fish in the North Pacific, with hatcheries in the U.S, Russia and Japan releasing billions of chum smolts into the ocean every year.

Because of the importance of chum salmon for commercial, subsistence and personal use and subsequent heavy fishing pressure, the long-term status of many of Kamchatka's chum populations is uncertain. Poaching of fish for their roe is a serious problem in most rural areas, as is overfishing in many districts. Stepped-up enforcement efforts and stricter management of recent years hopefully will stem the tide of this depredation.

Life History

Chum salmon have interesting life history adaptations to best utilize a variety of river habitats. Like all Pacific salmon, they begin life in the well-aerated, clear, cold running water of stream gravels. Shortly after emergence in early spring, unlike most of the young of chinook, coho, or red salmon, chum fry migrate directly downriver into estuaries, bays and near shore marine environments. Spending their first summer in these transitional habitats, they grow quickly on diets of small aquatic organisms until they are large enough to survive in the open sea, where they spend the next few years making extensive seasonal forays into the western North Pacific and Bering Sea, living on diets of crustaceans, mollusks, fish, and squid.

Age of returning fish varies between two and five years (most are three or four), with small numbers as old as six or even seven years in the more northerly populations (Kamchatka). Nearing inshore waters, mature chums begin to congregate in schools or runs, according to which river they are bound for. In the Far East, as elsewhere in their range, these mass returns of fish are segregated into early and late runs, so that in Kamchatka, for example, chums can be found in rivers from early summer into the fall (June through September or later), with older fish appearing earlier than younger fish. Actual spawning in Kamchatka occurs mostly later in summer (July and August) but can be delayed into late fall and early winter in some late-running populations. Chums can make full use of all suitable areas along the river for spawning, from right above tidewater to the smallest headwaters. Early spawning fish tend to nest in main channel areas, while late spawners select areas with more consistent water flow (upwellings and springs) for winter survival. Chum salmon eggs are the largest of the salmon, and an average female can carry between 2,000 and 4,000. As in other Pacific salmon, breeding is terminal for chums.

Habits

Chum salmon are generally not as aggressive by nature as king or silver salmon. Found in far greater numbers, they are quite social and more inclined to show themselves during their pre-spawning movements by jumping, breaching and milling, particularly in lower rivers. (They have a propensity, like sockeyes, to hang out in sloughs, pools and side channels.) Sea-bright individuals are the most testy and can usually be prompted to take attractor-pattern streamers and other bold enticements. Chums that have been in freshwater for any time, like all salmon, change dramatically in appearance, gameness, and behavior (most chums will get more aggressive as they near their spawning grounds). The take of a chum is usually more vigorous than that of a king salmon, but not as hard as a silver. They are powerful, dogged fighters, usually boring into the main channel when hooked, where they use their strength and size to great advantage in the river current. For this reason, it is important to have stout gear when fishing them.

FLY FISHING KAMCHATKA'S CHUM SALMON

Because of their large roe and relative abundance, chum salmon are a much coveted and targeted species among Russians, particularly poachers, who illegally take large numbers of fish for caviar all across Kamchatka. Local sport anglers pursue them whenever available, usually with heavy spinning or casting gear. Only a small number of chums are taken by fly anglers in Kamchatka, mostly by tourists. In the eastern North Pacific (Alaska, Canada, and Pacific Northwest states), the situation is much different, with tighter management, more advanced angler ethics and considerable targeted fly fishing effort for chum salmon in fresh water.

Like the other salmon, chums are best taken within close proximity (20 miles or less) of salt water, while still bright and at their peak. The intertidal zone and lower sections of rivers are ideal places to intercept them at their fighting best. (Chums, like sockeye salmon, are usually easy to spot in freshwater with their highly visible displays of pre-spawning behavior. Be sure to have a good pair of polarized sunglasses with you when you fish chums, to make it easier to spot fish.) It is unsporting and may even be illegal on some rivers to target fish that are actively spawning on their gravel redds. Chums that are well advanced into their spawning phase should be broken off immediately if accidentally hooked. To do this, firmly grab the spool of your fly reel with one hand, the rod above the reel with the other, then lower your rod until it is pointing directly at the fish and back off sharply until your tippet snaps. (Turn you head away from the water while you do this, in case the hook tears free from the fish and comes flying back at you.)

Bright attractor-pattern streamers have traditionally been the most productive enticements for chum salmon, in colors of lime green, chartreuse, yellow, red-orange, silver, and purple, along with certain forage and egg patterns. (Hooks should be stout and very sharp, to penetrate the chum's extremely hard jaws and withstand its brute strength.) Flies should be fished near or along the bottom, drifted with the "wet-fly swing" or fished with short, fast strips, through pools, runs, sloughs, confluences or under cut banks, anywhere the gregarious salmon might be holding. Use sinking line (short sink tips preferred) or additional weight in the form of split shot or wrap lead, if needed, to get down into the "strike zone." There is usually no mistaking the take of a chum salmon; because of their hard jaws, a powerful hook set is required to keep them on your line, and your drag must be tightened beforehand to avoid busted knuckles and lost fish.

During the height of the runs in the more productive rivers, it is not uncommon to encounter large shoals of bright fish in the lower sections of rivers, with the potential for providing abundant, non-stop action for fly anglers.

If you've never fished chums, they will surprise you with their dogged strength. A good-sized fish, once it breaks into heavy water, can take you deep into your backing, so it's important to have good gear—a stout rod and a reel with a strong drag—and to know how to use it to keep the fish from getting away from you. (An occasional pursuit along the river bank is not unheard of when fishing these fighters!) Most fly anglers will beach or tail chums they've played to exhaustion, with nets commonly used by the Russians. Your native hosts will likely want to keep some of your catch for eating, and if you've never had fresh, sea-bright chum salmon, let the Russians prepare one for lunch or dinner. (Ask them for barbecue or "shashlik," so you can try chunks of the mild flavored, orange flesh done over a fire.)

Gearing Up

Because of their size and strength and the river currents they are taken in, Kamchatka chum salmon require stout gear. An 8-weight, medium-action, 9 to 10-foot graphite rod and matching, high-quality reel with good drag is recommended. Performance-tapered floating or medium-density, short (5 to 7 foot) sink tip lines will work best for most of the situations encountered in Kamchatka's lower rivers, along with a 9-foot, tapered sinking leader ending in a 0 to 2X mono nylon tippet. (Pre-spawning chums develop very sharp teeth so you might want to bump up to a 12 or 15-pound tippet. Also, in many river systems, you'll encounter mixed groups of salmon during the early part of the season, which might include some king salmon so it may be wise to fish heavier.) Don't forget heavy duty pliers to remove your hook from the chum's toothy jaws.

Chum are notorious suckers for flashy attractors (including some saltwater patterns), particularly hair wing streamers. They will also hit many of the gaudy flies used for their larger cousin, the king salmon. It goes without saying, almost, that, given the chum's sharp teeth and the way it fights when hooked, you should routinely check your terminal components for any signs of stress, especially after playing a fish.

Recommended Fly Patterns (size #1/0–4): Alaskabou, Popsicle, Outrageous, Egg-Sucking Leech, Alaska Mary Ann, Woolly Bugger, Teeny Nymph, Herring Fly, Clouser Minnow, Deceiver, Candlefish, Sandlance, Comet, Polar Shrimp, Flash Fly, Mickey Finn, Wiggletail, Coho Fly, Supervisor, Everglow

CHERRY SALMON

Ryan Peterson photo

Oncorhynchus masu

Common names: Cherry salmon, cherry (U.S.); sima (Russia), masu (Japan)

Description: A small salmon found only in the Far East. Similar in appearance to a small, red (sockeye) salmon when fresh from the sea, with steel-blue, black or gray back, chrome sides and whitish belly. Markings, if present, consist of sparse, small black spots on topsides. Spawning fish unmistakable, with reddish-orange, flame-like vertical bars on sides. Average size in Kamchatka, 16 to 20 inches, 2 to 4 pounds.

Range/Abundance/Status: In Kamchatka, found in rivers of west coast, from Bolshaya to Icha most abundant. (Small numbers may exist along southeast coast and in Kamchatka River basin). Kamchatka status uncertain due to lack of data.

Best Waters: Productive SW Kamchatka river systems

Best Rivers: Bolshaya, Pymta, Kol, Kolpokova, Kihchik and Icha rivers

Best Fly Patterns: Attractor and baitfish patterns; bulky dry flies

Best Times: Late May to mid-July

The cherry salmon (or sima or masu) is a small salmon found only along the coast of Far East Asia. One of the first salmon to make its appearance in freshwater in late spring and early summer, the cherry, unlike the very similar sockeye or red salmon , is not aloof to the fly and can provide exciting early summer sport for anglers fishing southwest streams of the Kamchatka Peninsula. More commonly pursued in the coastal waters of Primorye and Sakhalin and Hokkaido islands farther south, and not particularly abundant in Kamchatka, the cherry nonetheless can provide satisfying diversion for Russians and visiting fly anglers on early season forays in the southern peninsula and should not be overlooked. (Other than the regal Atlantic salmon, the cherry is also the only salmon with a known affinity for the dry fly, making it even more desirable quarry.)

Description

In appearance, sea-bright, mature specimens of the cherry salmon can easily be mistaken for small red salmon or possibly even chums. The back is steel-blue, black, gray or olive, the sides silver, and belly whitish. Markings are not always present and usually consist of sparse, small black specks along the topsides and on the tail fin. The smallest of the Pacific salmon, adult masu returning to Kamchatka's rivers are, on average, from two to four pounds in weight and 16 to 22 inches in length. Fish from rivers farther south (Primorye and Sakhalin) run larger, to 28 inches and 8 pounds.

Like other Pacific salmon, the adult cherry undergoes dramatic changes in appearance once it enters freshwater to breed, particularly males. There is a deepening of the body, and the sides darken to a deep olive-black and become imbued with pink, red or orange, flame-like vertical bars, creating a striking visage. Males develop enlarged jaws (kyping) and teeth. The anal fins of both sexes become broadly edged in white. The flesh of the cherry is bright orange-red and considered a delicacy in much of the Far East, often served as sushi or fried, grilled or smoked.

Distribution

Cherry salmon are found only in the more temperate waters of the northwest Pacific basin, from Korean drainages in the Sea of Japan to the rivers of southwestern Kamchatka. They are particularly abundant in Hokkaido, the Sakhalin Islands and the Primorye region of the Russian Far East mainland (north as far as the Amur River). No measurable numbers occur along the Bering Sea.

The least abundant of the Pacific salmon, masu have been fished commercially for decades by the Japanese and Russians, with limited success at augmentation by hatcheries. Due to declining numbers in recent years, the fishery has been drastically curtailed in many parts of their range. Kamchatka's populations of the cherry salmon, while relatively small, seem stable, though a lack of reliable data hampers any definitive measure of their status.

Life History

The cherry salmon displays the greatest variation in life history of all Pacific salmon. Like the other five species, masu begin their existence in the gravels of cold, clear flowing streams connected to the sea. Feeding on small aquatic organisms and fallen insects and inhabiting sheltered areas off mainstream channels, young cherry salmon grow quickly, and by early summer of their second year of life, most Kamchatka fish are ready for their seaward journey. But depending on stream location, food abundance and other factors, some fish, mostly males, can spend three years or more and, in some rare instances, their entire lives, in freshwater. Cherry salmon that live entirely in freshwater are called Yamame or cherry trout and are greatly prized in parts of the Far East.

In the ocean, anadromous populations of masu (predominantly female) feed mostly on small fish, crustaceans and plankton, and range from the sea of Okhotsk in the warm months, to the north Pacific and Sea of Japan during winter. They migrate back to the rivers of their birth after one or two years at sea, usually entering estuaries and lower stream mouths in Kamchatka sometime in late May to early June, with a peak in early July. Most spawning occurs in late summer (August in Kamchatka) in many of the same sites in the lower river that silver (coho) salmon prefer. (Cherry salmon usually do not spawn in the upper sections.) Unlike other Pacific salmon, the mature masu may occasionally feed in fresh water. Breeding is a terminal act for anadromous cherry salmon.

Habits

The masu is a shy, sometimes moderately aggressive, very social salmon. It amasses in big schools in salt and fresh waters, and feeds on a wide range of food sources, even taking prey as an adult in freshwater. (It is perhaps the only Pacific salmon that can consistently be lured to the surface with dry flies.) Like most other salmon, the cherry will show itself frequently once it enters rivers, so its presence is usually not difficult to determine. It is easily spooked, however, particularly in shallow clear waters, so care must be taken by anglers when pursuing it in Kamchatka's rivers. Though generally not as fast on the take as a testy silver, chum or king salmon, when hooked, the sima fights hard for its size, especially on lighter gear.

FLY FISHING KAMCHATKA'S CHERRY SALMON

Because of its limited range, relatively small numbers in Kamchatka and run timing that coincides with other more desirable species (king, chum and red salmon), the sima or masu does not receive significant attention from sport anglers, unlike elsewhere in the Far East (Korea and Japan), where they are pursued with an almost religious devotion. Russian fishermen usually make incidental catches of them while fishing for king salmon, trout and charr in early summer on some of the more popular road-accessible streams along the southwest coast (Bolshaya, Bystraya and Plotnikova rivers). Almost all these fish are taken on spinning or casting gear, though more and more anglers, including Russians, are discovering how much fun they are when pursued with a fly.

Due to its unique life history and predisposition to feed in freshwater, the cherry salmon makes delightful sport in streams and rivers. In Kamchatka and other locations in the Far East, this small salmon, when bright and fresh from the sea, will hit a variety of attractor patterns and smolt and baitfish imitation streamer flies fished with a traditional "wet-fly swing" through holding water. (See gear and technique section for details on this basic but important presentation method.) As with other salmon, the closer to saltwater you can intercept the cherry, the better. (Anglers should fish them within 20 miles of the sea.) Bays and estuaries, river mouths, sloughs, pools and any other holding areas in lower stream sections are ideal (Look for signs of showing fish; be sure to bring Polarized sunglasses.) Also, since cherry salmon tend to run upriver in schools, you can usually have quite a bit of action from a good stretch of water once you connect with one. (Keep in mind that these salmon will spook easily when in tight schools, however.) Fish in full nuptial colors that are actively engaged in spawning should be avoided, and any salmon in this condition accidentally hooked should be released immediately by "breaking them off," rather than tiring them to exhaustion by playing them.

The cherry is also one of the few Pacific salmon that can, under certain conditions, be coaxed to the surface with a dry fly. Anglers targeting bright salmon right above tidewater have had success using summer steelhead and Atlantic salmon flies, small specialty top water patterns and even some of the more traditional dry flies used for trout. (Some anglers have best results skating the larger patterns; others stick to the drift, especially with the more traditional flies.) Target shallower areas (less than three feet deep) in lower rivers for best chances at enticing these diminutive fighters to the surface.

Gearing Up

For the best sport and efficiency, anglers wishing to pursue cherry salmon in Kamchatka should equip with a 4 to 5-weight, medium-action graphite fly rod (8–9 feet) and matching, high quality, single action reel. A performance-tapered floating line will work for most of the situations encountered, mated to a 7 to 9 foot tapered sinking leader ending in a 2X to 5X mono nylon tippet. (Fluorocarbon is not necessary, as these salmon are not leader shy.) Use split shot, if necessary, to get your subsurface presentations down into the "strike zone." For more extreme conditions, a medium-density, short (5 feet or less) sink tip line should be adequate.

Cherry salmon will take a wide range of attractor pattern streamers and undoubtedly will hit just about any properly presented salmon/steelhead fly under the right conditions. Have a wide assortment on hand for experimentation, especially dry flies. The following patterns are some of the most popular currently used in Kamchatka for the small but willing cherry.

Recommended Fly Patterns

Wet Fly (size #4–6): Coho Fly, Coronation, Deceiver, Clouser, Alaskabou, Crazy Charlie, Smolt, Matuka, Mickey Finn, Purple Peril, Egg Sucking Leech, Candlefish, Supervisor and Crystal Shrimp

Dry Fly (size #6–8): Bomber, Waller Waker, Elk Hair Caddis, Wulff, Humpy, and Irresistible; #2 Poly Wog.

NORTHERN PIKE

Igor Shatilo photo

Esox lucius

Common names: Shuka (Russia), northern pike (U.S.), pike, snake, water wolf (Canada & Alaska)

Description: Large-headed, duck-billed, barracuda-like predator, with yellow eyes and dark green to greenish-gray or brown top and sides marked with longitudinal rows of large oval yellow spots; belly and lower jaws creamy white. Average weight in Kamchatka less than 10 lbs., but can grow to 30 lbs. or more.

Range/Abundance/Status: Found in northern Koryak lowlands; populations locally abundant and stable

Best Waters: Sluggish, productive lowland rivers and associated lakes in northern Kamchatka

Best Rivers: Talovka and Penzhina river systems

Best Fly Patterns: Large attractor and forage imitation streamers (including saltwater patterns); also specialty top water patterns

Best Times: Available year-round; best in late spring through late summer and early fall

The legendary ambush predator of northern backwaters, the pike is an important subsistence and sport species throughout the circumpolar world, including Siberia and northern Kamchatka, where it occurs in the extensive lowlands associated with the largest, most productive rivers. Famous for its utter wantonness in feeding and the depredation it exacts on a variety of hapless prey— from small fishes to rodents to young waterfowl—the northern pike is a challenging quarry on the fly, with great potential size and strength and fearsome teeth. In Kamchatka, it escapes almost completely from any real fishing pressure, except from the few locals based in the small villages scattered across the northern Koryak region. Abundant virgin fishing and potential trophy specimens await the adventurous fly angler willing to take the journey to these far flung waters to match wits with these peerless predators.

Description

The northern pike is easily recognized, as it has quite different shape and markings than the trout, salmon, charr, grayling and whitefish it shares waters with in the Far North. It has an elongated body, with a dorsal fin riding far back towards the tail and a very large head with flattened snout and some 700 dagger-like teeth lining its jaws. The eyes are yellow and the back and sides are dark green, grayish green or brown, with numerous, oval yellowish spots arranged in irregular longitudinal rows. The pike's scales are moderately small and may have a touch of gold to the edges. The belly and lower jaw are creamy white. Dorsal, anal and caudal fins are typically greenish-yellow, in some populations even appearing almost orange or red with dark blotches. The meat is white and flaky and considered quite flavorful, but is also very bony. It is usually eaten fried, baked or boiled.

Northern pike of 65 pounds or more have been recorded in years past from the most productive waters of central and northern Europe. It is not currently known how big northern pike can grow in Kamchatka, but specimens of 30 pounds or more are not uncommonly taken by locals fishing some of the larger, more sparsely fished waters in the lowlands of the northern Koryak region. Average size seems to be less than 10 pounds, similar to Alaska.

62

60

58

56

54

52

Distribution

Pike are found in lakes, ponds, and slower moving streams, all across the northern part of the globe, from the British Isles to the Pacific coast of Siberia and from Alaska to the Atlantic coast of Canada. They are particularly abundant in Alaska, northern Canada, Siberia, and the Scandinavian Peninsula. In Kamchatka, they are found only in the Koryak Region, from the vast Parapolsky lowlands to the upper Penzhina River.

Life History

Northern pike are spring spawners, leaving the cold depths of overwintering areas to seek out warmer, shallow areas right after ice break-up, usually sometime in May or June, depending on location. Lake populations commonly utilize shoreline areas, channels, and sloughs with suitable bottom structure for spawning, but may at times leave the lake environment to nest in slow-moving feeder streams. River populations undergo similar migrations, preferring sloughs and lower reaches of tributary rivers and creeks for reproduction. However, spawning migrations are seldom extensive and generally no more than a few miles. The preferred spawning habitat is shallow, quiet water with emergent vegetation and mud bottom. Spawning occurs during the day in areas no deeper than one or two feet and ceases at night or during periods of heavy cloud cover, rain, and cold air temperatures. Like many other species, pike may return to spawn in the same location every year.

Northern pike in mating are neither very territorial nor monogamous and frequently spawn with several members of the opposite sex. The spawning act is repeated often (every few minutes for up to several hours), as only relatively few eggs are released at a time. Depending on the size and age of the mature female, between 2,000 and 600,000 eggs are released. A ready-to-spawn female contains both large, ripe eggs as well as immature eggs that will ripen the following year.

After spawning, the eggs settle along the bottom, where they remain until they hatch, a period that may range from four or five days to a month, depending on water temperature. After hatching, the young feed off their yolk sacks until they are old enough to consume zooplankton, later switching to a diet consisting of insect larvae and nymphs. Mortality from egg to fry is very high (99.9%), primarily caused by predation from other fish species and birds, competition for food and even cannibalism by larger pike. Before long, juvenile pike begin to forage on small fishes, at which time growth increases dramatically. Rate of growth is fast the first few years and then slows. Also, the growth rate appears to be more rapid in the southern range, progressively slower to the north and largely tied in with water temperature. However, pike in more northern latitudes live to a greater age. Maturity is attained as early as age two, but for the most part not until age three or four.

After spawning, spent adult pikes stay on or near the spawning beds, feeding heavily. At this time, they are particularly vulnerable to anglers. Fishes make up the greater part of the diet of big northern pike and in some areas may be their exclusive food. They are not picky at all about what kinds of fish are consumed, either, devouring whatever is available. Grayling, whitefish and even smaller pike are among the favored species, but juvenile and adult trout and salmon are preyed upon as well. Pike consume mice, shrews, lemmings and large insects without hesitation, and are also serious predators of young waterfowl in some areas.

Habits

The northern pike's voracious, reckless feeding behavior is perhaps its most salient trait and a big part of the mystique that undoubtedly makes it so sought-after as a gamefish. Pike have been known to drive shoals of small baitfish into shallows and up on beaches, decimate entire populations of nesting ducks, and even attack and attempt to swallow fish and other prey much larger than themselves (choking themselves in the process). This savagery is, of course, their undoing in encounters with anglers, who are usually able to easily tempt them with all manner of enticement.

All this is not to say that the northern pike is a total pushover for fishermen, however. There are situations, such as in clear shallow waters, where they exhibit considerable wariness, particularly during bright sunny days, and you may find them hard to locate, and even more difficult to tempt with the standard fare in these conditions. In these situations, pike will avoid wide open waters, and as the day progresses will move into deeper or shaded locations or areas containing weeds or structure. Adjust your fishing strategies accordingly for best results (try fishing during early morning or late evening hours or on overcast or windy days).

FLY FISHING KAMCHATKA'S NORTHERN PIKE

Due to the remoteness of the waters, currently, few pike are taken by fly anglers in Kamchatka. Most Russians fish them with spinning/casting gear or hand lines, using large spoons, spinners, jigs or bait. As in Canada and Alaska, however, northerns can be easily enticed with large attractor and forage patterned streamers (including many large offshore saltwater baitfish patterns), along with a wide assortment of specialty top water and diving flies like the 'Wog, Mouse, Frog, Water Dog, Diver, etc., and even large poppers.

Though they can be taken year-round, northern pike are fished most successfully from spring to fall. Starting after ice-out, spawners position themselves in shallows around weed beds in lakes, ponds, sloughs and streams and are easily targeted by anglers. In many areas, especially on warm days, it is possible to sight-fish, spotting pike suspended right beneath the surface, still and motionless, like driftwood. Short, fast strips— enough to leave a good wake on surface presentations and arouse the attention of nearby pike—are generally most productive. (Anglers should use discretion when fishing this time of year and release all fish taken since the majority of large pike are females and crucial to the well-being of local stocks.)

Sometime after spawning, pike disperse into deeper waters and become more difficult to find. Look for them on the edge of drop-offs, in tributary stream confluences, along weedy or rocky lakeshores, around brush piles in sloughs, and anywhere there is structure of some kind to provide the ambush conditions they favor for feeding. (Keep in mind that the big, older fish are very territorial and will occupy the choicest sites along rivers and lakeshores.) Using watercraft to access better sites on larger rivers and lakes is a definite advantage. Regardless of how you access, avoid totally open water and concentrate your fishing efforts near structure, using fast strips and twitches of your rod tip to impart erratic action to your presentations.

As water temperatures drop in late summer and early fall, baitfish migrations to spawning or winter holdover sites will prompt northerns to leave their summer feeding grounds for more productive locations. They are in prime shape this time of the year and easily provoked with all manner of enticements, as winter looms and stokes a savage hunger and wantonness. Attractor and baitfish pattern streamers are most productive, drifted or stripped through sloughs, stream mouths, lake outlets/inlets, the edges of deep pools and other bait staging areas. This is the best time of year to catch trophy specimens, as fish are in top condition after a summer of abundant food.

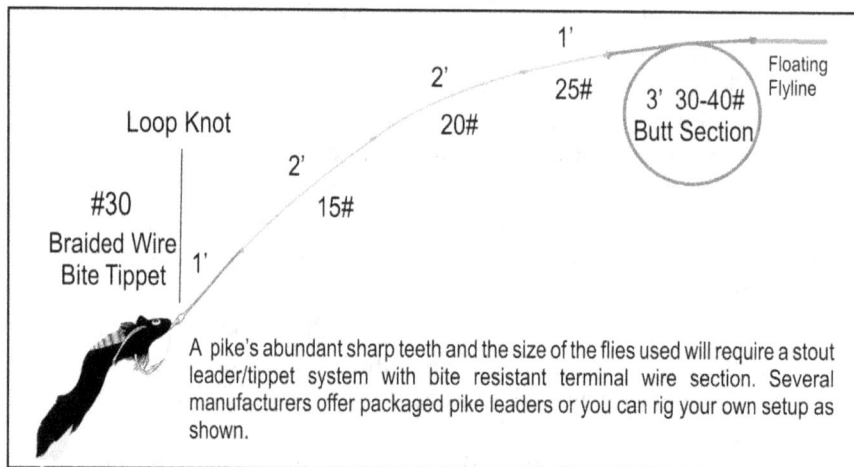

A pike's abundant sharp teeth and the size of the flies used will require a stout leader/tippet system with bite resistant terminal wire section. Several manufacturers offer packaged pike leaders or you can rig your own setup as shown.

Gearing Up

Recommended gear for fly fishers wanting to take on Kamchatka's giant northern pike is at least an 8-weight rod (9 to 10 feet) with good backbone and a matching high-quality reel with a strong drag and sufficient backing (100 yards of 30 lb.). 8 to 9-weight Spey rods (10 to13 feet long) can also be used for more efficient casting and line control. Fly lines for most of the conditions encountered on Kamchatka's pike waters are generally performance-taper floating or, rarely, medium-density sink tip, mated to a stout, specialty tapered nine-foot leader terminating in a 12- to 20-pound tippet with the last 12 inches being strong braided wire (see illustration above). And don't forget to bring along a sturdy pair of large fishermens pliers to safely free the hook from the pike's fearsome jaws.

Fly anglers can expect good results tempting Kamchatka's big, wild northerns with large, bushy surface or diving patterns and oversize attractor and forage imitation streamers. Tube flies and saltwater patterns can be fished with great effect as well. (Flies with a certain amount of bulk are especially useful since they help grip the pike's teeth.) Because of the pike's hard, bony jaws, super sharp and strong, size #3/0 to #4 hooks are recommended. (Check terminal components of your rigging frequently for wear when fishing these brutes.)

Recommended Fly Patterns:

Forage/Attractor (size #3/0–4): Flash Fly, Alaska Mary Ann, Outrageous, Alaskabou, Gray Ghost, Sculpin, Bunny Bug, Clouser Minnow, Pike Fly, Deceiver, Articulated Leech, Herring Fly, Seaducer, D's Minnow, Blanton's Whistler, Baitfish and Tarpon Fly.

Topwater/Diving: Dahlberg Diver, 'Wog, Pike Popper, Mouse, Articulated Lemming, Water Dog, Frog

KAMCHATKA'S MAIN REGIONS

SOUTHERN KAMCHATKA

Southern
Kamchatka

Dolinovka

Mount
Yalutat
2726

Mount
Bragia
6632

Mount
Sokharnaia
1291

Mount
Swad'ch
5056

Klungur
Volcano
6453

Mount
Kudryash
583e

Kirganik

Mount
Shoronskaia
5449

Milkovo

Mount
Ushati
710

Mount
Pamskaia
3324

Mount
Kensoi
4727

Sharomy

Mount
Shergovsky
3362

Mount
Moksni
4835

Mount
Tauishis
7549

Sobolevo

Mount
Voroshkaia
4604

Pushchino

Mount
Kerilkovskaia
5354

Mount
Stol
4042

Ustayevoye

Mount
Kasulga
4793

Mount
Kurgonnaya
4291

Karpinskiy
Volcano
4963

Maly
Semiachik
Volcano
5000

Mount
Kagoniai
6327

SREDINNY

Mount
Prorani Rel
3272

Mount
Khribtakian
6131

Bakening
Volcano
7478

Mount
Timonovskaia
3564

Ganaly

Nalychevo
Nature
Park

Dzenzur
Volcano
7496

Zhupanovskie Mt
Volcano
4511

Mount
Achtia
4639

SEA
OF
OKHOTSK

Malki

Mount
Ostraia
4925

Severnyye
Koryaki

Koryaksky
Volcano
11253

Avachinsky
Volcano
8914

Dalniy

Koryaki

Razdolny

Karymay

Sokoch

Yelizovo

Vulkanny

Kavalerskoye

Nachiki

Sosnovka
Nikolievka

Ust-Bolsheretsk

Apacha

Paratunka

Petropavlovsk-
Kamchatsky

Cape
Shipunsky

Mount
Khrebtovaia
3904

Vilyuchinsk

Vilyuchinsky
Volcano
7129

Avacha
Bay

Oktyabrasky

Mount
Varshina
Moskovstva
3740

Opala
Volcano
8001

Gorely
Volcano
5902

Asachei
Volcano
8264

Mutnovski
Volcano
7867

Mount
Savin
2949

Mount
Skolistwo
3195

Khodatka
Volcano
6689

Mulikova
Bay

Vetchin
Bay

Mount
Kizanel
5169

Kenelich
Volcano
3540

Yuzhno-
Kamchatsky
Nature Park

Zaporozhye

Zhelrovsky
Volcano
8118

Ozernovsky

Pauzhetka

Ilinsky
Volcano
5101

Cape
Senyavina

Vestnik
Bay

Cape
Siluchy

Kambalny
Volcano
6492

Cape
Senyavina

Kambalny
Bay

Mount
Moshkov-ev
1650

PACIFIC

Alaid
Volcano
7674

Cape
Lopatka

OCEAN

Ebeko
Volcano
3793

Severo-Kurilsk

Fussa
Volcano
5813

Chikurachki
Volcano
5958

Kuril
Islands

0   50 mi

0   50 km

117

The southern tip of the Kamchatka Peninsula (from Cape Lopatka north to roughly 54 degrees latitude), is the area most familiar to locals and foreigners. It has most of the peninsula's population and infrastructure, concentrated around beautiful Avacha Bay and the city of Petropavlovsk and nearby Elizovo, along with some of Kamchatka's greatest attractions—wildlife, volcanoes, hot springs and fabulous rivers for fly fishing. This region also has Kamchatka's mildest weather and two spectacular nature parks (both of them UNESCO World Heritage Sites): **Yuzhno-Kamchatsky**, which contains Kurile Lake, largest producer of sockeye salmon in Asia, and **Nalychevo**, with unique and extensive hot spring and mineral water sites and some of the peninsula's most active and accessible live volcanoes. With a range of visitor services unmatched anywhere else on the peninsula, southern Kamchatka can provide an astounding variety of world class outdoor adventures, including some of the best fly fishing for trout and salmon.

The Country of Southern Kamchatka

Kamchatka's twin coasts and dual mountain chains (the ancient Sredinny Range and newer, more volcanic Eastern Range) converge at the southern terminus of the peninsula in a wedge-shaped region of extensive relief and volcanism (5 active volcanoes and numerous geothermal sites, including over 90 hot springs), drained by numerous swift rivers and defined by a rugged eastern coastline of small fjords and bays that is important habitat for many of Kamchatka's sea mammals and birds. The concentration of features and lush landscape give southern Kamchatka a look and feel all its own. Like Alaska's Kenai Peninsula, this area is a showcase for the scenic beauty, productive rivers, abundant wildlife and awesome landforms that characterize the entire province.

Climate, Vegetation and Conditions

The climate here, like most of Kamchatka, has a definite maritime influence, but is milder due to its more southern location, and more varied, with the cloudiest and foggiest weather along the southeast coast (up to 160 days a year) and clearer, more continental conditions in the interior valleys sheltered from sea breezes. In the lowlands of the Avacha valley, around Petropavlovsk and Yelizova, at the foot of the Avacha- Koryak range of volcanoes, some of the nicest weather in Kamchatka occurs, with a longer summer and dry, prolonged fall (daily temperatures into the sixties and seventies from July into the first part of September, with fall foliage usually not evident until the third week in September in most years).

In the verdant countryside of southern Kamchatka, you'll find immense, pure stands of gnarled stone birch (*Betula ermanii*) covering valleys and hillsides (there is no permafrost), abundant meadows of tall grasses, herbs and wildflowers (to ten feet in height) and many species of fast-growing willow, including thick stands of the unique and stately Chosenia, along with abundant poplar and alder along the rivers and streams. Hillsides, ridges and sub-alpine areas are dominated by dense, green swards of Siberian dwarf pine (*Pinus pumilla*), commonly called elfin cedar, to eight feet or more in height. The alpine zones, similar to Alaska, are covered with dwarf shrubs (like arctic willow and dwarf birch), and a profusion of colorful wildflowers, spread over a carpet of mosses and lichens.

Excepting alpine areas and the lowlands along the west coast, a camping and fishing trip in southern Kamchatka means you'll most likely be in the shelter of the forest, with plenty of wood for fires and excellent sites for getting out of the weather. You may have to hack out a spot in the thick, tall brush for your campsite and the insects may be a problem during very warm days in summer and early fall, but generally, this region is comparatively benign for outdoor pursuits during tourist season. (And its winters, while snowy, are usually never too cold to hamper winter sports activities.)

Major Attractions

Southern Kamchatka has so much to offer in the way of outdoor adventure, you can easily spend several summers exploring the main highlights. There are quite a few major active volcanoes and hot springs that can be accessed by road within short drive from the main hubs of Petropavlovsk and Yelizovo. And exciting whitewater rafting on the region's swift and rocky rivers, world class wildlife viewing (for brown bears & eagles fishing for salmon), and even sailing and diving in Avacha Bay and surrounding waters. Not least among the area's attractions, of course, is the fabulous fly fishing, as the southern peninsula contains some of Kamchatka's most important sport fishing rivers, particularly for rainbow trout and salmon. Many of these streams can be reached from the road system (with additional access via 4-wheel drive, hiking or horse trails) or via short helicopter flight from Yelizovo. A wide variety of fly fishing options is available for tourists. Everything from day trips (base out of a hotel or B & B in Petropavlovsk, Yelizovo, Paratunka or Malke) fishing nearby streams with local guides, to short (2-3 day) fishing/camping forays along the road system to multi-day, fly-out fish and float expeditions or lodge stays with some of Kamchatka's premier outfitters.

Access, Infrastructure and Services

The airport at Yelizovo, 12 miles from Petropavlovsk, is the gateway for international and domestic travel to and from the Kamchatka Peninsula. (Not far away, a helicopter base provides almost all of the region's remote access for fly fishing and other activities.) From there, a system of roads, both paved and gravel, links much of this region. Main highways lead from Petropavlovsk-Yelizova to the Central Valley, the Sea of Okhotsk and south along the Paratunka valley to famous area volcanoes and hot springs. (A newly created all-season gravel road built to service a natural gas line leads from Ust-Bolsheretsk up the west coast, providing access to the lower end of many rivers.) From this road system, countless rough 4WD roads and hiking and horse trails lead into the back country, providing still more access to rivers, lakes, hot springs and other attractions.

Major Hubs

Petropavlovsk-Kamchatsky: The city of Petropavlovsk is the administrative, economic, cultural and population center of Kamchatka. It sprawls along the northeast side of scenic Avacha bay, with three immense volcanoes framing the skyline—Avachinsky, Koryaksky and Kozelsky. Situated along one of the world's best ice-free harbors, Petropavlovsk is an important sea port for shipping, fishing and cruise ship tourism. The population of the city is around 200,000 people; its area is almost 15 square miles.

The city's name comes from the two packet-boats "Saint Peter" and "Saint Paul", which sailed to Kamchatka during the Second Kamchatka Expedition, headed by famous Danish explorer Vitus Bering. The vessels entered Avacha Bay in 1740, the official year of the city's birth. There are many memorials throughout the city dedicated to the discovery, exploration and protection of Russia's Pacific territories.

The climate in Petropavlovsk and vicinity is maritime, with wet, cool and foggy summer weather quite common. The fall (from mid- September to mid-October) is usually very pleasant, with many clear, warm, "Indian summer" days and few prolonged periods of inclement weather. Winters are mild compared to Alaska, but usually very snowy, with the city blanketed from November into April.

Petropavlovsk has a full range of visitor amenities, everything from luxury hotels to homestays, fancy restaurants to fast food joints, and luxury spas to beauty parlors. Many prominent sport fishing and ecotour companies are headquartered there. There are groceries, supermarkets, gas stations, banks, theaters, museums and hardware, clothing and sporting goods stores, even a tackle shop (Fisherman's Orbit) with an impressive fly fishing inventory. Presently, however, Petropavlovsk has few businesses that offer rentals on outdoor gear or vehicles of any kind. The city does have great public buses and taxis, with daily service to surrounding communities and points beyond.

Yelizovo: Yelizovo, population 36,000, is the administrative center of the Yelizovsky district, the largest in Kamchatka (16,000 square miles, almost half of it in protected nature territories). Situated in the beautiful birch forests of the Avacha River valley, 20 miles northwest of Petropavlovsk, Yelizovo was founded more than 150 years ago and is now considered Kamchatka's gateway city, because of the international airport located there. (It also has a large heliport that services almost all remote recreational activities in southern Kamchatka.) It is connected by paved road to Petropavlovsk and other hubs to the west and north and serviced by regular public buses and private taxis. A full range of accommodations, groceries & supplies, gas stations, and numerous tourist services are available there, along with notable cultural and historical attractions. (There is also a visitor center located in the bus station downtown.)

Paratunka: The resort community of Paratunka lies some 30 miles west by road from Petropavlovsk-Kamchatsky. Paratunka is famous for its abundant thermal water springs on which numerous recreational and therapeutic facilities have been built. (The mineral water of the Paratunka hot springs is very effective in treatment of various disorders.) It is also located along one of Kamchatka's most popular sport fishing rivers. Visitor amenities in Paratunka are plentiful and varied; there are resorts, sanitariums, hotels, B & B's, outdoor pools, steam baths, restaurants, cafes, etc., along with small grocery stores for supplies. It is a popular destination year-round for folks from Petropavlovsk, Yelizovo, and surrounding communities, as well as tourists, who come to soak and relax in the hot springs or fish the Paratunka River. There is regular daily bus service linking Paratunka to surrounding communities.

Ust-Bolsheretsk: Ust-Bolsheretsk, population 2211, is the administrative center of the Ust-Bolsheretsky district, located along the western coast, near the mouth of the Bolshaya River, 131 miles west of Petropavlovsk. Founded in 1703, Bolsheretsk is mainly a fishing village, utilizing the nearby resources of some of Kamchatka's most productive salmon rivers. Newly developed energy deposits to the north have brought additional economic activity in recent years, but other than a few sport fish camps that operate out of there, tourist services/supplies are minimal. The climate in Ust-Bolsheretsk is definitely maritime, with long winters and short, cool, foggy summers. Ust-Bolsheretsk is connected with Petropavlovsk by a road with regular public bus service.

Fly fishing the Bystraya River in late September during gorgeous Indian summer conditions

Fly Fishing Southern Kamchatka

Southern Kamchatka has some of the peninsula's best fly fishing, along rivers that have become famous for their abundant fisheries, superb conditions and relative ease of access. While it is true that some of these streams get far more pressure than rivers up north, there are still untold miles of water in southern Kamchatka where you can fish without seeing anyone and enjoy a quality of fly angling not equaled anywhere else in the world. Indeed, many fly anglers from the world over return every summer to the same locations in southern Kamchatka, content that there is little to be gained in exploring for better water elsewhere.

The region's milder climate is a big plus. It allows for a richer food base and longer growing season, so the trout reach big sizes sooner (some of the largest rainbows in Kamchatka come from these southern rivers). It also means that insect hatches are abundant throughout the open water season for consistent and outstanding dry fly fishing. Not to mention, of course, is the beneficial effect of nicer weather on camping, hiking and other outdoor activities, especially late in the season

Southern Kamchatka rivers can be fly fished year-round wherever open water can be found, but the season typically runs from April into October. Spring conditions persist until late May or early June when the last of the ice goes out of the rivers and the runoff swells. By late June or early July, the rivers are usually settled with superb fly fishing conditions continuing into October in most years. (West coast rivers are generally slightly behind due to the proximity of the cold Sea of Okhotsk.) Because of the thick vegetation and dense soils, most southern Kamchatka rivers can take quite a drenching before they get blown out in summer or fall. In most years, by mid-October, a creeping snow line and heavy frosts conspire to end all fly fishing in the region.

ALONG THE ROAD SYSTEM

Avacha River

One of Kamchatka's most popular fishing drainages flows through the major hubs of Yelizovo and Petropavlovsk. The 75 mile long, clear **Avacha River** is a lovely, fair-size stream that winds through thick forests of birch, willow, and poplar in an extensive valley lying north of Avacha Bay. It has three swift, rocky forks and numerous access points from the road system. Fishing varies from fair to good, depending on timing and location, for salmon (king, chum, pink and silver) and charr. Rainbows are rare but have been reported from several of its smaller tributaries. The

Avacha makes for a perfect short trip of ½ to 3 days duration, as it can be fished from shore, from a boat or rafted. Many local tourist companies offer varied guided fly fishing services there.

The most popular access points for the Avacha are along the roads on the edge of town (Petropavlovsk), the bridge crossings near Yelizovo and from the rough road leading north of the village of Koryaki. Another, rougher road (and trail) heads north through the forest to the left fork of the Avacha from the village of Razdolny. A float down from one of the access points along the Avacha's upper course, with a takeout at one of the bridges down below, is a popular way of making a multi day outing on the Avacha. (Swift water, abundant sweepers, and submerged logs demand utmost caution and rafting skill, however.) There is also the option of staying at tent camp operations along the lower river that use power boats to access the best water. Best fly fishing conditions on the Avacha are from late June into September.

Paratunka River

The clear **Paratunka River** flows north about 50 miles through an isolated coastal valley known for its abundant hot springs. It empties into Avacha Bay just west of the city of Petropavlovsk and has always been extremely popular with locals who fish it seasonally for salmon (mostly pink, chum and silver) and charr. The village of the same name was built around famous hot springs along the lower river and today contains resorts, sanitariums, dachas (vacation homes), hotels, recreation centers, swimming pools, etc., comprising one of Kamchatka's major recreational areas.

Most popular way to fish the Paratunka is from shore or powerboat, accessing it from the road system (the bridge crossings along the highway from Petropavlovsk to Paratunka and multiple points from the towns of Paratunka and Nikolievka). The lower river, like the Avacha, receives a tremendous amount of pressure. Available guide services include day trips for fly fishing and semi-permanent tent camps. A day outing combining fly fishing and a visit to one of the local hot springs is highly recommended. There are three major thermal sites along the Paratunka: Nizhne-Paratunsky springs by the village Paratunka and Sredne-Paratunsky and Verhne-Paratunsky springs located upriver. Best time to fish the Paratunka is late summer through fall.

Bolshaya River

The **Bolshaya River** system drains the southwest fringe of Kamchatka's mountainous spine and spills into the sea of Okhotsk, about 138 miles west of the city of Petropavlovsk. With character and productivity similar to some of the great rivers of southwest Alaska, the short, broad Bolshaya ("big" river in Russian) and its swift tributaries comprise one of the largest systems on the west coast and the most significant recreational fishery in all of Kamchatka, most of it easily accessed from the road system. All six species of salmon, rainbow trout (to 15 pounds), charr ("kundzha" and Dolly Varden to 10 pounds) and even grayling are found in abundance there. (There are even a few steelhead.) The Bolshaya enjoys special reputation among serious anglers throughout Russia, as THE PLACE to hook a big king salmon (to 50 lbs. in this river) and every year in early summer tourists from all over flock to the lower river for a chance at these coveted monarchs of the Pacific salmon clan.

The Bolshaya is wide, deep and multi-channeled, not ideally suited for fly fishing, especially early in the season, when it runs high with melt water. Though there are some better spots that can be accessed from the road system (mostly around the town of Ust-Bolsheretsk, which lies near the end of the highway linking Petropavlovsk to the west coast), a boat is almost a necessity to find water suitable for fly casting. Best bet is to hook up with an experienced guide/outfitter who knows the river; there are several (*Big River, Ltd.*) who run camps along the lower Bolshaya. (It is also possible to float fish the Bolshaya from road access points along the lower stretches of its tributaries, taking out at the bridge crossings or spots around Ust-Bolsheretsk.)

Fly anglers will find far more appealing water in the Bolshaya's fast, clear and rocky tributaries, the **Bystraya, Goltsovka,** and **Plotnikova rivers,** which join together not very far upstream from Ust-Bolsheretsk. All three offer good to outstanding fly fishing conditions for salmon, grayling, rainbow trout and charr. They can be accessed from the road system, with the Goltsovka limited to a single bridge crossing on the road from PK to Ust-Bolsheretsk.

Bystraya River

The fast-flowing **Bystraya River** ("bystraya" in Russian means swift) is one of the longest drainages in Kamchatka. It rises in a broad high valley between the southern peninsula's two major diverging mountain ranges, not far from the headwaters of the Kamchatka River. It flows some 150 miles south and west out onto the coastal plain before joining the other tributaries of the Bolshaya River, upstream from the town of Ust-Bolsheretsk. Crystal clear, broad and very scenic, the Bystraya is perhaps the most popular float fishing and rafting stream on the peninsula, known for its consistent fishing for salmon (six species), grayling, and rainbows (to 12 lbs.), along with Dolly Varden and white-spotted charr. It has abundant stretches of water offering outstanding fly fishing conditions, including excellent dry fly opportunities. It is also offers stretches of exciting floating, with several thrilling whitewater canyons along the lower river. Access to the Bystraya River is from multiple points along the road to Malki (and beyond) for bank fishing, boating or rafting (for trips of ½ to 5 days duration, using takeouts below). It has many fine tributaries offering good fly fishing conditions as well. Practically every tourist company on the peninsula offers some form of fishing and rafting adventure on this river, from day trips to week-long floats. Consider it a must-visit location if you have a day or two to kill in the Petropavlovsk-Yelizovo area.

Plotnikova River

Swift and rocky like the Bystraya, the **Plotnikova River** rises in the volcanic uplands along the eastern coast and flows west and south for some 80 miles before joining the other tributaries of the Bolshaya. Like the Bystraya, it shares its valley with a road for much of its length, providing multiple access points and abundant river recreation opportunities for Kamchatka's urban population.

Similar to the Bystraya, the Plotnikova offers good to excellent fly fishing conditions along much of its length for salmon, rainbows, grayling and charr, particularly in the lower reaches of its main stem and (at the mouths and along the lower stretches of) some of its better tributaries like the Karimchina River (accessed from the settlement of Apacha or by helicopter). With its abundant access, float fishing adventures of half a day to three days or more duration are easily done on the Plotnikova and, like on the Bystraya, there are numerous local outfitters (*Kamchatka Wild Nature*) providing a variety of fishing services there. Best fly fishing on the Plotnikova is from late summer into fall.

The Goltsovka River

The **Goltsovka River** rises in a small fan of highlands lying between the headwaters of the Bolshaya River's two other main tributaries, the Bystraya and Plotnikova rivers. Clear flowing, but much smaller and shallower than the other two, it offers good fly fishing conditions and is frequently worked for grayling and trout by some of the fishing camps along the lower Bolshaya River near the town of Ust-Bolsheretsk who access it by jet boat. It can also be fished and accessed for floating (with takeout below at Ust-Bolsheretsk) from the bridge crossing on the road from Petropavlovsk to the west coast.

SOUTHERN KAMCHATKA REMOTE

Zhupanova River

The **Zhupanova River**, lying just northeast of Petropavlovsk, on the other side of the group of volcanoes that dominates the skyline north of the city, is one of Kamchatka's most well- known and highly regarded fishing locations and is destined to be recognized as one of the world's great trout waters. A fair-sized drainage of about 1500 square miles, with extensive headwaters in the eastern edge of the coastal mountains, the Zhupanova flows south and east for close to 130 miles before emptying into the Pacific.

Because of its many fine qualities and proximity to Petropavlovsk, the Zhuponova has always been a popular river for outdoor recreation—camping, hiking, river rafting, fishing, and hunting—and was the first stream to receive serious attention from western anglers when Kamchatka was first opened to foreign tourism in the early 1990s. It quickly gained notoriety for its classic stretches of fly water and large rainbow trout (especially fond of hitting mouse patterns, they average well over 20 inches, with outsized specimens to 30+ inches and 12 pounds), very abundant charr (including some of Kamchatka's biggest kundzha, to 20 lbs.) and good runs of salmon (five species). The Zhupanova has some of the best dry fly fishing in all of Kamchatka, with big hatches possible from spring well into fall. The Zhupanova also has abundant waterfowl and mammal populations and is one of the peninsula's most scenic and interesting rivers, with stunning views of nearby active volcanoes (Karimsky and massive Zhupanovsky), whitewater canyons and hot springs along the river.

Visiting anglers have several options for fishing the Zhupanova. There are three sport lodges spread along the main river that use boats to ferry anglers to choice spots, and quite a few guides/outfitters running float trips down the different forks of the upper river. (The Zhupanova, though swift, does not present any great technical challenges other than some rocky stretches of Class II-III water, mostly in the main stem's middle section below the second lodge) Some companies also offer a combination of floating and short stays in semi-permanent camps set up along the way.

However you decide to go, plan on spending at least five days sampling the great fishing and other attractions there. (A side trip to nearby Valley of the Geysers is highly recommended.) Access to the river is usually by short (1/2 hour flight) helicopter ride from Petropavlovsk. The best time to fly fish the "Zhup" is from late summer into fall, but the river can be fished successfully from April to November usually.

Rainbow trout from the Opala and Zhupanova rivers on average run among the largest on the Kamchatka Peninsula

Opala River

Another stream within easy helicopter reach from Petropavlovsk that has become quite famous for big rainbows and great fly fishing is the **Opala River**, which flows swiftly south and west out of volcanic highlands in the lower peninsula and empties into the Sea of Okhotsk. About 80 miles long, it is comprised of two forks, one of them (main fork) flows through the remains of an ancient caldera before descending down to the western coastal plain. The other, shorter fork, the **Savan**, rises to the south. Both forks offer exciting whitewater, beautiful scenery, lots of wildlife (especially bears) and famous hot springs. The rainbows, never as abundant as you'd like them to be, are very robust, and the river offers some great mousing as well as good dry fly fishing opportunities. There is also good charr and salmon fishing in season. Nearly every outfitter in Kamchatka offers float fishing trips on this river, which is the best way to enjoy its great fishing and superlative wild country. There is also fishing from tent camps available. Access is usually by helicopter from Petropavlovsk.

Golygina River

The **Golygina River** rises in the southern tip of the peninsula not far from Kurile Lake, south of the Opala. It flows north out of a volcanic valley and then west across the coastal plain to the sea of Okhotsk, for a total of about 70 miles. Its major tributary, the **Kuzanek**, heads in a lake (Golginsky) to the northeast. There is a famous hot springs along the river near its confluence with the Kuzanek. A productive system that is underutilized by anglers, the Golygina offers good fly fishing possibilities for rainbows, charr, and salmon. Best way to fish it is by rafting down from the headwater lake, where there is a hunting lodge. A fly fishing jaunt of a few days on the Golygina and visit to nearby Kurile Lake to observe the abundant bears feeding on salmon would make an outstanding Kamchatka wilderness vacation. Access is usually by helicopter from Petropavlovsk.

Kihchik River

The **Kihchik River** is a multiforked, modest-size, but productive west side drainage of the lower Sredinny Range that empties into the Sea of Okhotsk about 90 miles west of Petropavlovsk. Known for its good runs of salmon (king and silver mostly), the shallow, clear Kihchik also has good fly fishing for charr and rainbow trout. (There is a small run of steelhead as well.) A few local companies fish it from rafts and tent camps. Access is usually by helicopter from Petropavlovsk, but the lower river can also be reached by the dirt road (used for local access and mineral exploration) leading north along the coast from the town of Ust-Bolsheretsk.

Pymta River

A well-known and very productive stream, the **Pymta River** drains the southern Sredinny Range just north of the Kihchik River. About 70 miles in length with two main forks, the Pymta, like most of its neighboring rivers, is swift, shallow, rocky and narrow in its upper reaches, but slows down and widens considerably as it flows out onto the western coastal plain. Crystal clear and perfect for fly fishing, with abundant spawning habitat in its middle and lower reaches, the Pymta has fishable numbers of all six species of Pacific salmon, in addition to plentiful, chunky rainbows and charr (including kundzha) and even a few fall steelhead. The upper river is accessed by helicopter from Petropavlovsk (45-minute flight); the lower river can be reached via the unpaved road that runs up the coast from Bolsheretsk. A great river for float fishing trips.

Kohl River

The **Kohl River** system flows swiftly just north of the Pymta along the edge of west-central Kamchatka. It is approximately 75 miles long from its headwaters to its terminus in the Sea of Okhotsk. Highly productive for its size, with no human settlement, it is now (along with neighboring river, the Kekhta) the site of a headwaters-to-ocean salmon refuge (540,000 acres), the Kol River Salmon Protected Area, which in 2015 was included in the UNESCO Volcanoes of Kamchatka World Heritage Site.

The river supports fishable numbers of all six species of salmon, as well as rainbow trout, steelhead, Dolly Varden and white-spotted (kundzha) charr. Like the Pymta, it has excellent fly-fishing conditions. Access is usually by helicopter from Petropavlovsk. There is a fishing camp near the mouth of the river, with jet boats to access prime water.

Note: Contact the Volcanoes of Kamchatka Visitors Center in Yelizovo for more information and necessary permits before visiting and fishing the Kohl River:

33 Zavoiko Street, Yelizovo, Kamchatka, Russia 684000
Phone: 7(41531)7-39-41; E-mail: park@mail.kamchatka.ru

Vakhil, Nalycheva and Ostrovnaya Rivers

The **Vakhil River** is one of several short streams that flow swiftly down beautiful volcanic mountain valleys along the Pacific coast between Avacha Bay and the Zhupanova River. Only about 45 miles long, it is floated and fished frequently, along with the nearby **Nalycheva** and **Ostrovnaya** rivers, by tour companies visiting the many spectacular attractions of Nalychevo Park. (There are also small lodges on these rivers.) The Vakhil has good wade and cast conditions and abundant charr and silver salmon. There are no rainbows there or on the Nalycheva, but the Ostrovnaya is reputed to have them. Access is usually by short helicopter flight from Petropavlovsk, but there is also a rough gravel road leading along the coast to the mouths of these rivers.

OTHER ATTRACTIONS

Yuzhno-Kamchatsky Nature Park

Located on the southern tip of the Kamchatka peninsula, with an area of approximately 900 square miles, Yuzhno-Kamchatsky Park (now included in the UNESCO World Heritage Site, Volcanoes of Kamchatka Park) was established in 1996 to protect the area's unique landscape features and wildlife. It is refuge for some 55-mammal species (including sea otters, for which the reserve was specially created to protect), 244 bird species, dozens of fish and one amphibian species, and 718 species of plants (16 of which are listed in the "Red Book" of endangered species of Russia, and 12 species endemic to the area).

Included in the reserve is spectacular Kurile Lake, the second largest in Kamchatka (948 feet deep and 30 square miles). Through its outlet, the Ozernaya River, passes the largest sockeye salmon run in Asia each summer, up to six million fish. A unique aggregation of brown bears, one of the densest in the world, gathers around the outlet during the spawning season to feed on salmon and provides one of Kamchatka's best opportunities for viewing. During winter, Kurile Lake is the site of one of the world's most unique gatherings of large raptors that come from near and far to feast on late-spawning salmon. It is possible to witness from 300 to 700 Steller's sea eagles, 100 to 150 white-tailed eagles, 50 golden eagles, and even, rarely a few bald eagles, roosting and vying for scraps along Kurile's snow and ice covered shoreline.

There are several active and extinct volcanoes in the park and reserve, including Zheltovsky, Mutnovsky (one of the most active volcanoes in Kamchatka), Ksudach (with a base diameter of 21 miles and a 4 mile wide caldera with two picturesque lakes), Kambalny (the most southern volcano in Kamchatka), Kosheleva and Ilyinsky. Within the park's border are also the peaks of Asachinsky and Vilyuchinsky volcanoes. In the area of Kosheleva and Kambalny volcanoes, there is abundant hydrothermal activity like the verkhnekoshelevskoye thermal field, with more than 40 hot springs and seething mud cauldrons.

The coast of the park and reserve abounds with more than 200 colonies of seabirds (murrelets, slaty-backed gulls, red-faced cormorants and tufted puffins) and marine mammals (whales, dolphins, sea lions and sea otters, which the preserve has brought back from near-extinction). Cape Lopatka is the southernmost point of the Kamchatka Peninsula, with extreme maritime climate and one of the largest fall seabird migrations in northern Asia. For more information and permits, contact the park office at:

33 Zavoiko Street, Yelizovo, Kamchatka, Russia 684000
Telephone/fax: 7 (415-31)-7-39-41, 7 (415-31) 7-24-00
www.wildkamchatka.ru; Email: park@mail.kamchatka.ru.

Nalychevo Nature Park

The Nalychevo Nature Park, established in 1995 (and shortly after included in UNESCO's World Heritage Site, Volcanoes of Kamchatka

Park), is situated along the southeast coast, just east of Petropavlovsk. Encompassing the scenic Nalychevo River valley with its numerous thermal and mineral spring sites and surrounding volcanoes, the protected area of Nalychevsky Nature Park is over 1100 square miles.

The park has many remarkable features. Among them are the mineral-rich hot spring sites, such as Goryacherechensky, Talovsky, and Kithoysky hot springs. There are 12 volcanoes including four active – Koryaksky, Avachinsky, Zhupanovsky and Dzenzur. A wide range of flora and fauna, including 561 plants (10 species listed in the Kamchatka Red Book), 53 species of mammals and 130 species of birds can be encountered here.

A ranger station and variety of accommodations are located at the center of the park (reached by a long trail from the village of Pinachevo or Avachinsky base camp, or short helicopter flight from Petropavlovsk), near the headwaters (and hot springs) of the Nalychevo River. Numerous hiking trails lead from there to area attractions like Vershinskoye Lake, Vershinskie and Aagskiye Narzany mineral springs, Talovskie hot springs, Avachinsky Pass and the active Dzensur Volcano.

For more information, including maps of the park showing trails and other features, contact the Nalychevo Nature Park Office at:

33 Zavoiko Street, Yelizovo, Kamchatka, Russia 684000
Tel/fax 7 (41531)7-24-00, 7-39-41
www.park.kamchatka.ru; Email: park@mail.kamchatka.ru

POPULAR VOLCANOES

Mutnovsky: A very famous and popular visitor destination about 50 miles south of Petropavlovsk, reached by rough road from the Paratunka valley, Mutnovsky (height 7546 ft.), is one of the most active volcanoes in Kamchatka. A hike up into its large crater (biggest in all of Kamchatka) from the extensive surrounding lava field takes one into another world of sulfurous gas vents, steaming geysers, bubbling mud cauldrons, boiling hot springs and hissing fumaroles. There is also a geothermal power site at its base. Many local (Petropavlovsk and Yelizovo) tourist companies offer treks there.

Gorely: Another very popular volcano trek for tourists because of its ease of climb, interesting features and proximity to Petropavlovsk, Gorely volcano (height 5944 ft.) is located some 50 miles south of Petropavlovsk, reached by rough gravel road leading beyond the Paratunka valley. It has several craters (including one with a turquoise lake), fumaroles, steam jets and impressive lava formations. Practically every Kamchatka tour company offers hikes up this volcano.

Hiking in the Mutnovsky volcano crater

Avachinsky and Koryaksky: At 8940 feet, Avachinsky is the lesser and easier climbed of the two very impressive active volcanoes that dominate the skyline of Kamchatka's major metropolitan area. Thousands of folks make the trek to its summit each year, mostly by access of a two-hour drive east from Petropavlovsk, then a relatively easy but long hike of 6-8 hours. With a history of many explosive eruptions, Avacha is one of the most active volcanoes in Kamchatka. It has numerous fumaroles and interesting lava formations in its horseshoe-shaped crater. Koryaksky volcano, located just to the north and west, at 11, 232 feet, is a much higher and more technically challenging climb.

Major Hot Springs

Malkinsky: The hot springs at Malki are some of the most famous and visited thermal pools in all of Kamchatka and the source of very well-known and popular mineral waters. They are located a few miles east of the settlement of Malki (on the road from Petropavlovsk to Milkovo) on the left bank of the Klyuchevka river (a tributary of the Bystraya), in a picturesque valley surrounded by thick birch forests. There is a public recreation center with outdoor pools and changing cabanas and nearby resort facilities. Many folks get to the hot springs by public bus from Yelizovo or Petropavlovsk

Paratunka: There are three hot springs sites spread out along the Paratunka River valley, a short drive south of Petropavlovsk, along southern Avacha Bay. The lower and most popular supplies the resorts, recreation centers, outdoor pools, sanitariums, hotels, etc. that make up much of the settlement of Paratunka. The upper springs are located about ten miles southwest of the village and are harder to get to. Below the village is located Utinoe (duck) lake, famous for its healing black mud. Paratunka can easily be reached by bus from Petropavlovsk or Yelizovo.

Vilyuchinsky: Vilyuchinsky hot springs are one of Kamchatka's more popular thermal sites, located not far south (2-hour drive) of Petropavlovsk along the scenic upper Vilyucha River. It can be reached by a rough spur road off the main thoroughfare to Mutnovsky and Gorely volcanoes. Actually a series of hot springs spread along the river, with an impressive waterfall and thermal pools for bathing below (with nearby primitive structures for changing clothes in), this is a highly-recommended attraction (and great place for campsites) if you are planning on a trek to the nearby volcanoes.

Apacha: Located about 9 miles south and east of the village of Apacha, along the banks of the Shikova River, this popular thermal site can be reached by a gravel spur road leading off the main highway from Petropavlovsk/Yelizovo to Ust-Bolsheretsk on the west coast. There is a public recreation center with pool and changing facilities.

CENTRAL KAMCHATKA

From the spurs of the lower Central (Sredinny) Range, beginning at about the 54 north parallel, to the southern fringes of the Koryak region (at roughly 58 degrees north latitude), lies the heart of Kamchatka. Dominated by the ancient range of mountains that forms the spine of the peninsula, this central region, ancestral home of the Itelman and Even native cultures, is a sparsely populated province of swift mountain rivers, colossal volcanoes and an immense valley drained by Kamchatka's largest river. The diversity of terrain, remoteness from major population centers and spectacular attractions make this a paradise for off-the-beaten path adventure—volcano trekking, river rafting, horse pack trips, hiking, and especially fly fishing, as most of its streams receive little or no pressure, yet contain Kamchatka's richest and most diverse populations of fish species.

THE COUNTRY OF CENTRAL KAMCHATKA

The western half of Kamchatka's central region is comprised of a wide arc of volcanic peaks and foothills (the Sredinny Range) gradually sloping westward into broad coastal plains along the Sea of Okhotsk. Numerous long, branched rivers dissect the terrain, swift and rocky in their headwaters, but slowing and meandering considerably as they pass through the swamps, broken forests and tundra of the lowlands. The mouths of many of the larger rivers terminate in estuaries and long parallel lagoons. There is only one active site among the dozens of extinct volcanoes scattered throughout the Sredinny Range, the impressive, glacier-capped Ichinsky, at 11,834 feet the highest peak in western Kamchatka.

Along the eastern, Pacific coast, similar to southern Kamchatka, a broad belt of younger, more active volcanic uplands, the Vostochny Range, defines the topography. Unlike the gradually sloped western side, with its extensive foothills and coastal flats, much of the eastern coastline is steep and rugged, with short river valleys and few estuaries.

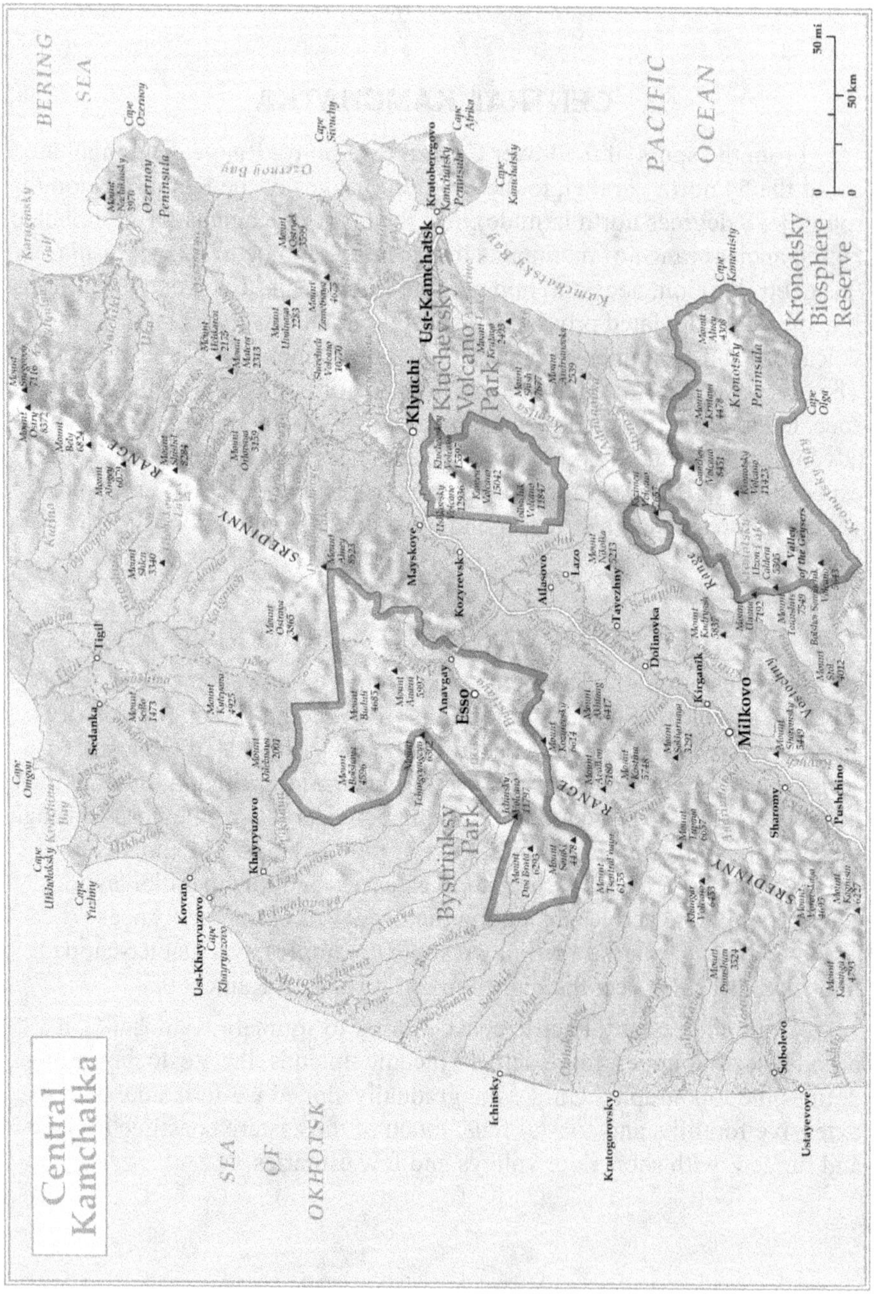
Central Kamchatka
BERING SEA
PACIFIC OCEAN
SEA OF OKHOTSK
Kluchevsky Volcano Park
Bystrinsky Park
Kronotsky Biosphere Reserve
SREDINNY RANGE
Klyuchi
Ust-Kamchatsk
Mayskoye
Kozyrevsk
Atlasovo
Lazo
Tayezhny
Dolinovka
Kirganik
Milkovo
Anavgay
Esso
Tigil
Sedanka
Khayryuzovo
Kovran
Ust-Khayryuzovo
Sharomy
Pushchino
Sobolevo
Ustyevoye
Krutogorovsky
Ichinsky
Kronotsky Peninsula
Ozernoy Peninsula
0 50 mi
0 50 km

Along this eastern side are Kamchatka's most impressive and largest active volcanoes, the Kluchevsky group, which includes the classic, cone-shaped Kluchevsky, at 15,584 feet the tallest in Eurasia, along with the Kaman (14,881 feet), Ushkovsky (13,351 feet), Krestovsky (12,814 feet), Tolbachik (11,966 feet) volcanoes and nine others. They make up the **Kluchevsky Volcano Nature Park**, a UNESCO listed World Heritage Site. This area also has the largest amount of glaciation in Kamchatka, with 47 glaciers and an ice-sculpted landscape, remnants from the extensive ice sheet formation that occurred there thousands of years ago.

South of the Kluchevsky group lies the **Kronotsky Biosphere Reserve**, one of the largest (and oldest) protected areas in Russia at 4200 square miles. Its main features are 12 active volcanoes —largest and most spectacular, the 11, 572 feet Kronotsky—fabulous Kronotsky Lake and the famous Valley of Geysers, a three-mile section of remarkable geothermal activity (40 geysers, numerous mud pots and dozens of gushing vents and hot springs) located along the Geysernaya River. The ancient caldera of the Uzon volcano is also located in the reserve, a vast volcanic bowl 5-7 miles in diameter, in which are concentrated numerous hot springs, mud pots, and thermal lakes.

In between these two impressive belts of mountains lies Kamchatka's great Central Valley, an immense lowland drained by the long, sprawling Kamchatka River and numerous swift, rocky tributaries that come off the steep slopes of the Central Range and volcanic uplands of the eastern ridge. With its sheltered, continental climate and rich soils, this area holds most of Kamchatka's agricultural land and forests, in addition to the fabulous fly fishing potential of the peninsula's largest and most productive river. Small isolated wildlife reserves provide sanctuary for less common animals like snow sheep, moose, sable and Kamchatka's only population of beavers.

Climate, Vegetation, and Conditions

Central Kamchatka's climate is varied. The western side has a much colder maritime influence (the Sea of Okhotsk, which is frozen for over six months of the year and never warms much above 50 degrees Fahrenheit), and so generally experiences cooler and more overcast summers, colder, drier winters and a later spring and earlier fall than the eastern, Pacific side. In the Central Valley, sheltered from maritime influences by two converging mountain ranges, the climate is more continental. Conditions there are generally drier (less than 20 inches total annual precipitation) and clearer, with colder winters and warmer summers than the rest of Kamchatka.

The vegetation in much of the region is similar to southern Kamchatka's, with extensive stands of stone birch (*Betula ermanii*) and meadows of tall grasses, ferns, wildflowers and briars in protected valleys and low elevation sites, along with poplar, alder, willow and Chosenia along the rivers and dwarf pine thickets on steep hillsides and in sub-alpine areas. But moist tundra becomes prevalent in the lowlands along the western coast, especially farther north, due to the more severe climate. In the central valley of the Kamchatka River, with its drier, warmer summers, are found the peninsula's only real conifer forests, of tall larch (*Larix dahurica*) and stately Yeddo spruce (*Picea ajanensis*) in the well-drained, sandy soils, along with the only pure stands of white birch (*Betula kamtschatica*) on the peninsula. There is also a rare, small grove of Sakhalin fir (*Abies sachalinensis*) in the Kronotsky Reserve, along the eastern coast.

Major Attractions

Central Kamchatka has barely tapped potential for serious world-class outdoor adventures. Its volcanoes are the most rugged and imposing on the continent; its remote nature parks and preserves encompass spectacular features and abundant wildlife, and its swift mountain rivers- utterly pristine and largely unexplored- arguably comprise the last remaining chunk of virgin trout water on the planet. On the cultural side, central Kamchatka's isolated and quaint villages provide visitors a glimpse of life in rural Russia and a chance to observe and interact with traditional native subsistence lifestyles.

But with little of the infrastructure and services available in southern Kamchatka, this vast and remote region is no place for casual outings. A safe and successful fly fishing trip or other outdoor adventure here requires nothing less than a carefully planned expedition, usually of more than a week total duration. (Many of the Europeans here on holiday during summer take two weeks or more to explore the major attractions of the region.) The guides and outfitters who service the heart of Kamchatka offer a surprising variety of options for fly fishing and other outdoor pursuits. There are whitewater and float fishing trips, "spike" camps with jet boat fishing, horseback and backpacking adventures, volcano and hot springs treks and helicopter drop-off camps for fishing, hiking and wildlife viewing.

Alexander Bichenko Photo

Serious adventurers the world over come to view and scale Central Kamchatka's impressive volcanoes.

Access, Infrastructure, and Services

A system of paved, gravel and rough dirt roads provides limited access to the central region. There is a main highway leading north from Yelizovo that connects various hubs along the central valley (Milkovo, Kozyrevsk, Klyuchi, and Esso) with Petropavlovsk. This road is paved only partially (for 70 miles or so north of Yelizovo, with plans to pave to Milkovo in the near future) and so for most of its length is a fairly well-maintained, though bumpy and dusty, gravel road. Public buses run regularly up and down this road providing daily service to and from Petropavlovsk-Yelizovo. There is also a primitive dirt road along the west coast that runs north from Bolsheretsk, used primarily for servicing the new gas line and mineral exploration and development in the Icha and Tigil districts, but also for recreation access by off-road vehicles. Numerous trails for hiking, horseback riding, and off-trail vehicles lead off into the hills from many of the hubs to popular area attractions like volcanoes, hot springs, lakes, waterfalls, and streams for rafting/fly fishing. Along the middle to lower reaches of the Kamchatka River, powerboats are used to access points along the main stem and numerous tributaries. Most of the villages in the region have airports, but not all are serviced by regular flights. Helicopter service is usually available from the settlements

139

of Esso, Tigil, Milkovo and Klyuchi to provide access to more remote locations throughout the region.

Major Hubs

Milkovo: Located 185 miles north of Petropavlovsk along the gravel road leading up the central valley, Milkovo (population 9000) is one of the oldest settlements in Kamchatka and the administrative center of the Milkovsky district, one of the peninsula's main agricultural and timber producing regions. Main local attractions are an ethnic cultural center (with a reconstructed fortress and Kamchatka native dwelling) and museum. The surrounding Milkovsky district is well known for its outstanding hiking trails, beautiful mountain lakes and famous hot and cold mineral springs like the Puschinsky, Shchapinsky, Belovsky, Krasniye Kascady etc. It is also a hub for access to the upper Kamchatka River and tributaries. Groceries, meals, lodging and fuel can be had in Milkovo, and there is even a sports complex. It is serviced several times daily by passenger bus from Petropavlovsk and has a small airport.

Esso: The village of Esso, population 2000, is the administrative center of the Bystrinsky district. ("Esso" in the native Even language means "larch.") Officially settled in 1932, it is located in the mountains, within Bsytrinsky Park, some 312 miles by road (via a spur off the main highway leading up the central valley) from Petropavlovsk. Esso is one of the prettiest and most interesting settlements on the peninsula, with magnificent surroundings (the "Switzerland of Kamchatka"), warm, dry summers and an abundant local geothermal site, the Uksichanskiye Hot Springs, which warms all the homes and greenhouses and also feeds a large outdoor pool in the center of town, open to all. A heliport on the outskirts of town provides access to important westside rivers, as do numerous hiking and horse trails (there are wranglers in the village for hire) and primitive 4WD roads leading into the mountains. Esso and nearby Anavgai are considered the cultural and ethnographic centers of the Kamchatka aborigines (Itelmans, Evens, Aleuts and Koryaks). Groceries, meals, B & B lodging, horse rentals, and local guided hiking, horseback riding, rafting, and fishing are available.

Kozyrevsk: Kozyrevsk, population 1500, is a small, rustic village on the right shore of the Kamchatka River about 300 miles north of Petropavlovsk, along the gravel road leading up the central valley. (A new bridge crossing on the Kamchatka River allows travelers easy, year-round access.) It was named in honor of Cossack Ivan Kozyrevsky, discoverer of the Kuril Islands in 1711 and creator of one of the first maps of Kamchatka. A jumping off point for trips to the nearby spectacular volcanoes of Kluchevsky Park, Kozyrevsk has limited services, supplies, and lodging. There is a small airfield outside of the settlement, but no regular flight service.

Klyuchi: The settlement of Klyuchi, population 6700, is located on the right shore of the Kamchatka River, approximately 385 miles north of Petropavlovsk, on the gravel road connecting all the settlements of the central valley. It was founded in the early 1740's by Cossacks from the Lena River in Siberia and derives its name from nearby hot springs that keep the river from freezing in winter ("klyuchi" is the Russian word for springs). It is a hub for ecotours to major volcanoes in the east-central region (Shiveluch and nearby Kluchevsky Park) and fishing and rafting expeditions on the lower Kamchatka River and many tributaries. There are key historic and cultural landmarks nearby, such as the "Nizhne-Kamchatsky ostrog" center and restored Memorial Cross on the left shore of Krestovaya River, originally erected in 1697 by Vladimir Atlasov and his Cossacks to mark Kamchatka as part of imperial Russia. Limited supplies, meals, and lodging are available there, and the settlement is serviced by regular public buses from Petropavlovsk. There is also an airport (with heliport capability) and nearby highly strategic military installation. (You may need special documentation to visit certain parts of the Klyuchi area. Check in advance with the Foreign Economic Relations & Tourism Department of the Kamchatka Regional Government in Petropavlovsk.) For travel on to Ust-Kamchatsk, it is necessary to use the ferry to cross the Kamchatka River.

Ust-Kamchatsk: The settlement of Ust-Kamchatsk, population 5000, located at the mouth of the Kamchatka River, is the administrative center of the Ust-Kamchatsky district. Founded in 1802 by Cossacks, Ust-Kamchatsk lies some 450 miles by (mostly) dirt road from Petropavlovsk. A historically important fishing village and seaport, Ust-Kamchatsk has an airport and regular passenger flight service to and from Petropavlovsk. It can also be accessed by public buses from Petropavlovsk and powerboat from hubs along the lower Kamchatka River. Limited services, supplies, and lodging are available there.

Fly fishing along the Tigil River system, west-central Kamchatka (photo courtesy The Fly Shop)

FLY FISHING KAMCHATKA'S WEST CENTRAL REGION

West-central Kamchatka has historically been an important fishing region, as it has some of the peninsula's most productive salmon and trout systems. (Commercial fishing sites are scattered along the coast at the mouths of the larger rivers there.) Because of the remoteness—access to the upper reaches of most of the rivers there during open water season is almost exclusively by helicopter —these streams receive minimal fishing pressure, despite their near-perfect fly fishing conditions and healthy runs of salmon (up to six species on many rivers), and abundant numbers of rainbow trout, Dolly Varden and white-spotted charr (kundzha). With their swift, rocky flows, beautiful scenery, and undisturbed wildlife, most of these west-central mountain rivers are ideal for wilderness rafting adventures of the highest quality, which more and more local tourist companies are keen to offer visitors. This is the most popular method of accessing and fishing these waters, but a few, semi-permanent sport fishing camps are springing up on the more popular rivers as well. The west-central region also contains Kamchatka's best steelhead water, on tundra

142

streams that flow into the Sea of Okhotsk between the 55th and 58th north parallel.

The following are some brief descriptions of some of the more notable and recommended west central Kamchatka rivers for fly fishing salmon, trout, and charr:

Vorovskaya River

North of the Kohl and Kekhta, the **Vorovskaya River** flows into the Sea of Okhotsk from the southern Sredinny Range. Multi-forked and fairly extensive (110 miles), it is swift, narrow and single-channeled in its upper reaches but slows, braids and meanders considerably in its course through the coastal plains. It has runs of all 6 species of Pacific salmon, plenty of Dolly Varden and kundzha charr and rainbows and even some fall steelhead. Because of its log jams and sweepers, this river doesn't receive a whole lot of fishing pressure from tourists. (The lower river does get fished for salmon by locals in powerboats from the nearby settlement of Sobolevo.) It can be accessed by helicopter (from Yelizovo or Milkovo) or by off-road vehicle from Bolsheretsk.

Kolpokova River

A well-known and very productive, swift water rafting and fly fishing stream, the rocky **Kolpokova River** flows west from deep within the Sredinny Range, just north of the Vorovskaya. A fair-sized stream about 110 miles long, the Kolpokova has beautiful mountain scenery, exciting floating and excellent fly fishing conditions for abundant rainbow trout and charr, plus fishable numbers of all six species of salmon (especially king, cherry, chum and silver salmon, best fished on the lower river near the mouth) plus a few fall steelhead too. It has been floated and fished over the years by many tour companies, a few offering fixed camps and jet boat access. (There is also a big commercial fish camp at the mouth). The headwaters are usually accessed by helicopter from Yelizovo-Petropavlovsk or Milkovo, but the lower river can also be reached by boat or rough road from Ust-Bolsheretsk. One of Kamchatka's best and most productive fly fishing rivers.

Krutogorova River

The **Krutogorova River** is a fast flowing, multi-forked stream that begins in steep mountain valleys lying between the headwaters of the Vorovskaya and Oblukovina rivers. It flows some 120 miles west into the sea of Okhotsk. All six species of salmon run in the Krutogorova, and there are rainbow trout (to 24+ inches), two species of charr, and even some steelhead. Because of its remoteness and proximity of other, more exciting and productive rivers, it is seldom float fished. Locals access and fish (for salmon and charr) the lower river by boat, from the small village ten miles up from the mouth. The upper river is usually accessed by helicopter from Yelizovo or Milkovo. The lower river can be reached by the new dirt road leading north from Bolsheretsk.

Oblukovina River

The Oblukovina is a beautiful, swift water rocky stream, 127 miles long, which flows into the Sea of Okhotsk from the heart of the Sredinny Range, between the valleys of the Icha and Krutogorova rivers. With rapids, waterfalls and sweepers, it makes for exciting but challenging rafting and has good to excellent fly fishing conditions and runs of all six salmon species, plus rainbow trout and Dolly Varden and white-spotted charr. (It also has a well-known run of steelhead late in the fall.) Accessed by helicopter from Petropavlovsk or Milkovo usually, sections of it have been float fished by tour companies (*Ouzel Expeditions*) over the years, but its remoteness and challenging rafting keep it from receiving much pressure.

Note: Before putting in on the headwaters of the Oblukovina for a float trip, scout the river by helicopter to check for log jams, sweepers, waterfalls and other obstructions.

Icha River

Remote, scenic and swift, the **Icha River** rises off the slopes of the immense Ichinsky Volcano and nearby highlands in the heart of the Central Range. An exciting and challenging wilderness river for rafting with outstanding fly fishing potential, the Icha has several rocky forks that flow spiritedly down steep mountain valleys to create a river of considerable size (approximately 140 miles in length, one of the west central peninsula's major drainages) once it emerges out of the foothills onto the coastal plain. Extremely productive, the Icha has strong runs of salmon (all six species, but especially chum, pink, late-running sockeye, and silver) and plenty of husky rainbow trout (to 28+ inches), with great stretches of wade and cast water. Dolly Varden charr and kundzha are plentiful also, and wildlife is everywhere (bears, ducks, foxes and eagles). Historically important for the Itelmen tribe, the Icha has primitive native camps and cabins scattered along the upper river and a small village farther down. Access to the headwater forks is by helicopter, usually from the town of Esso or Milkovo. One of central Kamchatka's most outstanding wilderness float fishing trips.

Note: Before putting in on the headwaters of the Icha for a float trip, scout the river by helicopter to check for log jams, sweepers, waterfalls and other obstructions.

Tikhaya River

With headwaters deep within the Sredinny Range in northwest Bystrinski Park, not too far from Esso, the multiforked, 160 mile long **Tikhaya** is a swift, rocky mountain river in its upper reaches, carving its way through ancient lava dikes and boulder-strewn canyons to join with the Khyryuosova River on the western Kamchatka lowlands not too far from the Sea of Okhotsk. Like the neighboring Tigil, the Tikhaya has abundant habitat for salmon spawning and great spring creek conditions for sight-fishing rainbows (especially fishing with the Mouse) and charr in its many headwaters. An excellent, seldom-visited float fishing river, the Tikhaya has numerous tributaries worthy of exploration. Best access is by helicopter from the town of Esso. (The headwaters can also be reached by horses and track vehicles along a rough trail from Esso.)

Tigil River

The 180-mile **Tigil River** is one of the largest and most productive systems in Kamchatka, with perhaps the greatest potential for wilderness fly fishing adventure. Historically used as a route from the Kamchatka River (by way of the Yelovka) to the Sea of Okhotsk, it has always been known for significant runs of salmon (all six species) and abundant populations of native rainbows and charr. Draining a vast area (almost 7000 square miles) of uplands and coastal plain just north of the Tikhaya, the Tigil has excellent fly fishing conditions in its upper reaches and many clear, swift, shallow mountain tributaries, which currently receive little or no pressure. Several outfitters (*The Fly Shop*) run float trips and primitive camps with motorboats along the mainstem and some of the better spring-fed tributaries (Sedanka, Kalgauch, Kemlayvayam, Rassoshina, Pirozhnikova, etc.). But for the most part, much of this vast but extremely promising system is yet to be fully explored by fly anglers. It is usually accessed during open water season by helicopter from the settlements of Esso, Milkovo or Tigil, or by boat from the village of Tigil. For someone wanting miles and miles of unfished streams to explore, way beyond the beaten path, the Tigil River system is it.

Kamchatka Steelhead Rivers

Kamchatka's west side holds almost all the known major fall steelhead runs on the peninsula, from the Kvachina River to the Bolshaya. These fish are found in a mix of rainbow life history variations that differs from watershed to watershed. Some rivers have mostly resident populations that never enter brackish or salt water, with only a minor component that leaves streams seasonally to feed in estuaries or the high seas; other streams have just the opposite—predominantly sea-run populations with only small numbers of resident rainbows. Generally, the swift mountain rivers that begin in the heart of the Central Range, streams like the Kolpokova, Pymta, Oblukovina, etc., have habitat that supports mostly resident fish, with only small runs of estuarine or high seas rainbows. These fish are encountered usually in the late summer or fall, as incidental catches by fishermen targeting rainbow trout or salmon.

A nice fall steelhead from one of Kamchatka's better west-central steelhead streams (Pete Soverel photo).

Farther north, the slower moving, tannic-stained rivers that begin in the modest foothills and meander through the broad coastal tundra hold the treasure of Kamchatka's largest runs and biggest specimens of true, "type A" steelhead that venture far out to sea. These systems do not have the complexity of habitat necessary to support a mix of trout life history variations but are better suited for spawning and rearing of fish that will quickly go to sea. Runs of up to several thousand steelhead move into some of the more productive rivers there (Kvachina, Snatolvayam, Utkholok, Sopochnaya, etc.), beginning in late summer and early fall (late August and early September) and continuing into November, with fish that average over 12 pounds and outsize specimens to 20 pounds or more.

Because they are still listed in Kamchatka's Red Book of endangered and protected species, anglers cannot legally target these elusive sea-run rainbows of the west side. For many years, a research program *(The Kamchatka Steelhead Project)* teamed fly fishermen with biologists, to measure, weigh, tag and take scale samples from captured fish, but its status at present is uncertain, due to politics and the limited number of anglers willing to take on the extreme challenge and expense of chasing these last truly wild runs of the North Pacific's most exalted game fish.

Major Steelhead Rivers of West-Central Kamchatka

Kekhta River

Vorovskaya River

Krutogorova River

Oblukovina River

Sopochnaya River

Kovran River

Utkholok River

Kvachina River

Snotolvayem River

Urgyvayem River

Rassoshina River

Voyampolka River

Belogolovaya River

Khayryayusova River

Moroshechnaya River

Saichik River

Pymta River

Kol River

Kolpokova River

Bolshaya River

Kihchik River

Utka River

Bolshaya River

FLY FISHING EAST CENTRAL KAMCHATKA

Kamchatka River

The immense **Kamchatka River** drainage, 460 miles long and 21, 500 square miles in area, is the peninsula's largest and most productive system and the centerpiece of the east central region for fly fishermen. Its numerous tributaries (7700 of them!), vast mainstem and associated lakes in the central Kamchatka lowlands support great runs of salmon (a major part of Kamchatka's total runs for each species, particularly coho, sockeye and king salmon) and abundant charr, rainbow trout (to 15 lbs.) and grayling populations. In its sheer size, diversity of water and the amount of high-quality stream fishing opportunity it holds (most of it unutilized), there are few other rivers in the world, save perhaps the Nushagak of southwest Alaska that can compare.

This vast, sprawling drainage rises from the southern crests of Kamchatka's two diverging mountain ranges, near the headwaters of the Bystraya River, not far north of the city of Petropavlovsk. It flows northeast some 300 miles or so, gaining size and speed from dozens of streams that drain both sides of the central valley, then veering directly east, skirts the edge of Kamchatka's most colossal volcanic massif (Kluchevsky), and, by now considerably widened, meanders through an immense, swampy, lake-dotted plain before breaching the Kumroch Range and spilling into Kamchatka Sound at the fishing village and seaport of Ust-Kamchatsk.

The Kamchatka is fed by various sources, predominantly springs, snowmelt, and glaciers. In its upper course, it is a swift, shallow mountain stream, with many sandbars and small rapids. As it flows through the Central Kamchatka Lowlands, it slows, deepens and develops numerous channels, sloughs, and tributary lakes. Highest water levels on the Kamchatka usually occur from June to early July; lowest in fall (September & October) and winter. The river usually freezes sometime in November (in places with hot springs, it may never freeze) and breaks up in late April or May. By mid-July, usually, all but the most turbid of its many tributaries have cleared. The river is considered navigable up to 300 miles from its mouth. Like most northern rivers its size, the Kamchatka can present a challenge to fly fishermen. Most of the lower mainstem (below Kozyrevsk) is too wide, deep and prone to turbidity for good fly fishing. Better conditions on this part of the river are found on some of its northern tributaries, particularly the **Yelovka River,** parts of which have been fished for years for salmon (king and silver) and its many productive, clear flowing western branches- **the Levaya, Shishey, Kunkhilok, Kinenin, Two Yurt** and others, draining the eastern slopes of the Central Range. These streams have achieved notoriety for their outstanding fly fishing conditions and healthy numbers of salmon, rainbows, grayling and charr. Other good fly fishing opportunities along the lower Kamchatka can be had on the **Raduga River** (salmon, rainbows, and charr) near the mouth of the Kamchatka, the outlet/inlet streams of **Lake Azhabachye** (rainbows and charr) and clear-flowing tributaries of the **Schapitsa River** (rainbows and grayling).

Access to the good water on the lower Kamchatka River is usually by boat from the villages of Klyuchi or Ust-Kamchatsk. Headwater access is also possible by helicopter from Klyuchi or Esso. There is also a very rough dirt road leading north from Klyuchi to the Yelovka River between the confluence of the Levaya and Starichok rivers. A small number of outfitters currently offer tent camps and float trips on some of the more outstanding tributary drainages.

Fly fishing the Elovka River, a clear tributary of the immense lower Kamchatka River (Eugeny Lukovnikov photo).

Along its mainstem, the middle Kamchatka River from Dolinovka to Kozyrevsk is much more amenable to fly fishing. However, fly anglers will still find the best opportunities at the mouths of (and along) the clear flowing tributaries that join the big river from the west. Many of these streams are too small and brushy to be accessed by anything other than foot, but a few of the larger ones can be navigated by boat or raft. The swift **Esso Bystraya**, a lovely river known primarily for its thrilling whitewater, also has some good fly fishing potential for rainbow trout, grayling, and charr. In its upper reaches above the settlement of Esso it is a classic mountain stream but takes on considerable water and gradient in its journey down to the Central Valley, making for challenging navigation (by raft) and fly fishing for much of its length below the village. The upper Bystraya (and its good fly fishing tributaries like the **Uksichan**) can be reached by horse and foot trail from Esso, and there are numerous points along the road connecting to the main highway up the central valley where the middle and lower river can be accessed. The lower **Kozyrevka River**, into which the Bystraya empties, is a much tamer (and larger) affair that meanders through the lowland forest and joins the Kamchatka River a short ways beyond where the Bystraya dumps in. Though not as clear as the Bystraya, the Kozyrevka and its main ally, the **Karakovaya River** both have worthwhile fly fishing potential for abundant Kamchatka grayling and rainbow trout, charr and silver salmon later in the season (August and September). These two rivers can be accessed from rough dirt roads leading west off the main highway north of Dolinovka or from the bridge crossing north of the spur road to the settlement of Atlasovo.

Not to be overlooked are some of the clear flowing drainages that rise in the volcanic headlands to the east and join the great river from the other side. Rivers like the **Shchapina** and **Kittilgina** and their many branches, which are fished by locals and some outfitters and by all reports have considerable fly fishing potential for grayling, rainbow trout, charr and some salmon. These streams are usually accessed by boat from Dolinovka or Lazo, off the spur road from the main highway. (There is also a very rough trail leading from the village of Kirganik to the headwaters of the Kittilgina.)

From Dolinovka to the Milkovo area, the Kamchatka River receives considerable attention from locals who access it by boat or by car from the villages (including Kirganik) or from numerous rough dirt roads leading off the main highway. Best bet for fly fishers would be to check out some of the larger, clear-flowing streams that come off the eastern slopes of the Sredinny and join the big river on the west side. Of these, the most promising (for rainbow trout, grayling, and charr) appear to be the **Andrianovka, Kirganik** and **Kimitina** rivers. These streams can be accessed at the bridge crossings and also by rough trails that lead upriver from the highway. According to locals, they can be floated with small raft or kayak, using extreme caution for sweepers and logjams. Worthy of note also is the **Kavitcha River** which flows out of a long valley in the eastern headlands and joins the Kamchatka near the mouth of the Andrianovka. It is said to have good fly fishing but extremely challenging rafting. Access would be by boat, helicopter or very rough trail from the headwaters of the Avacha River.

The upper stretches of the Kamchatka, above the villages of Sharomi and Puschino, present a different scenario, as there the river is more of a swift, shallow mountain stream, with small, brushy tributaries entering from both sides of the narrow valley. Many of these creeks can be accessed by foot from the highway for small grayling, trout, and charr and would be worth checking out while on the way to various attractions farther north. (Any salmon encountered this far upstream would not be good sport or decent fare for eating.)

Other Pacific Ocean/Bering Sea Streams

There are many other streams draining the eastern coast of central Kamchatka, some with great promise for fly fishing. Among them, the **Ozernaya River** is undoubtedly among the best. This fair-sized (over 100 miles long) drainage rises close to the headwaters of the Yelovka River on the eastern crest of the Sredinny Ridge, flowing directly east, about 75 miles north of the Kamchatka River. Clear, shallow and spring-fed, it has perfect fly fishing conditions and abundant salmon, rainbows, grayling and charr along its main stem and major tributaries like the **Maimlya**. A well-known, longtime Kamchatka outfitter (*Best of Kamchatka*) runs a semi-permanent fishing camp there. North of the Ozernaya, the **Naichiki** and **Uka** rivers, substantial drainages, flow off the eastern edge of the Central Ridge and empty into Karaginsky Sound. According to reports, these rivers have good fly fishing possibilities for salmon and charr, but no rainbows apparently. South of the Kamchatka River, along the Pacific Coast, the **Andrianovka, Storozh, Putaya** and **Bystraya** rivers beckon for exploration by fly anglers, with reports from locals of good fishing for salmon charr and even some rainbows.

OTHER ATTRACTIONS

Bystrinsky Nature Park

Over 5000 square miles in size, Bystrinsky Nature Park was created in 1996 to protect and showcase the many superb natural features (and traditional cultures) contained within the heart of the rugged Sredinny Range in central Kamchatka. Named after the largest of many swift rivers that sweep down its narrow, rocky valleys, Bystrinsky Park encompasses a wide range of physiography and vegetation, from sparse alpine tundra to lush evergreen forests, lofty ice-covered mountains and volcanoes to marshy lowlands, and bone-chilling rivers and lakes to steaming hot springs.

The Sredinny Ridge, the main feature of the park is the large, volcanic mountain spine that runs up the center of Kamchatka (more than 500 miles long). The remains and outpourings of dozens of ancient volcanoes are found throughout, along with numerous hot springs, among them: Anaun Volcano, Olengende Volcano, Oksinskiye Springs, Appapelskiye Springs, and Alney volcano. The largest active volcano in western Kamchatka, Ichinsky, at 11,834 feet, is also located in the park.

The rivers of the Nature Park are famous for their scenery and whitewater (including picturesque waterfalls): the Bystraya, Anavgay, Khairyuzova, Tikhaya, Icha and others. Most of the numerous lakes are small and located in the waterlogged Western Kamchatka Plain, but there are also many of glacier origin in the Sredinny Ridge (the biggest lakes of the park – Bolshoye Goltsovskoye and Ketachan, and the most visited, Ikar and Galyamaki).

34 species of mammals inhabit the park, including most of Kamchatka's terrestrial wildlife: squirrel, sable, mink, otter, ermine, wolverine, brown bear, reindeer, wolf, snow sheep, Kamchatka black-capped marmot and others, as well as introduced species such as beaver and moose. Birds are represented by 137 species, 106 of them nest in the park (osprey, white-tailed eagle, Steller's sea eagle, golden eagle, northern goshawk and others). Bystrinsky's flora contains more than 615 species, including four species of rare plants listed in the Red Book and 12 species entered into the list of Far-Eastern Rare Plants (*Epipogium alphyllum*, *Gentiana prostrate* and others).

Numerous trails (foot, horse, and all-terrain vehicle) lead from the park's center in Esso to various natural and cultural attractions near and far. With few developed roads, these trails serve as the main means other than helicopter to access most of the park's backcountry. Local outfitters provide horseback, hiking and river rafting adventures. More information, including maps and park registration, is available at the visitor's center in Esso or the administrative office (now part of the KGBU Volcanoes of Kamchatka Park headquarters in Yelizovo):

Bystrinsky Park Visitors Center
Lenin Street, Esso 684350
7-415-42-21461
www.bystrinsky–park.com

33 Zavoiko Street
Yelizovo 684000
7 (41531) 7-24-00
park@mail.kamchatka.ru

Kluchevsky Nature Park

Created in 1999 and recognized as a UNESCO World Heritage Site in 2001, Kluchevsky Nature Park, 300 miles north of Petropavlovsk, encompasses the most spectacular and active volcano group on the Asian continent, towering over the nearby Kamchatka River in an impressive massif with peaks soaring well over 15,000 feet. In addition to the famous volcanoes, the park contains seven natural monuments, protecting special features like colossal lava flows, basaltic canyons, domes from ancient eruptions and a meadow of rare edelweiss flowers. There are 418 plant species, 24 species of birds and 23 species of mammals inhabiting the park.

Access to the main attractions of Kluchevsky Nature Park is by off-road vehicle from the villages of Klyuchi and Kozyrevsk, which are reached by public bus or private vehicle along the main highway leading up the Central Valley from Petropavlovsk-Yelizovo. Ascent of Kluchevsky volcano is physically challenging, but not technically complicated, and with a good guide and luck in the weather, it can be accomplished without extreme hazards by folks in reasonably good shape. Would-be visitors to the wonders of Kluchevsky should contact the Kluchevsky Nature Park headquarters for a permit:

Kluchevsky Nature Park
33 Zavoiko Street
Yelizovo, Kamchatka, Russia 684000
7-41531-7-24-00
park@mail.kamchatka.ru

Kronotsky Preserve

Kronotsky State Nature Preserve, at more than 4000 square miles, is one of the largest and oldest nature preserves in Russia. It was created in 1934 to protect the wildlife and unique features of the area, such as the famous "Valley of Geysers," Kamchatka's Yellowstone, where some 40 large and small erupting steam springs and numerous hot, bubbling mud pots cover the floor of the Geysernaya River. Nearby Uzon Caldera is another area of immense geothermal activity within the preserve, with interestingly colored hot springs, thermal lakes, and mud cauldrons. The preserve also includes the incomparable Kronotsky Lake, the largest in Kamchatka, where populations of kokanee (landlocked red salmon) are found, along with resident charr. Some 26 volcanoes (12 of them active) are located within the preserve, among them the spectacular, perfectly-shaped Kronotsky at 10,584 feet. Also of great significance is a relict grove of fir trees (*Abies gracilis*), the only in Kamchatka, located along the valley of the Semyachik River. In 1996 the Kronotsky Preserve was entered in the UNESCO list of World Natural and Cultural Heritage Sites.

Kronotsky Preserve Visitor Center and Museum
48 Ryabikov Street
Yelizovo 684000
Telephone 7 (415 31) 7-39-05
www.kronoki.ru
E-mail: zapoved@mail.kamchatka.ru

The Valley of the Geysers in Kronotsky Preserve

Popular Area Hot Springs

Anavgai River Thermal Springs are a series of hot springs located along a major tributary of the Esso Bystraya River. The easiest accessed, Anavgaisky springs, is located by the mouth of the Anavgai, along the road that connects the main highway up the Central Valley with the town of Esso. There are three others (Oksinsky, Opalkinsky, Apapelsky), located much farther (24 to 30 miles) up the river valley.

Bystrinsky Thermal Springs are located in the middle of the Bystraya River, not far from the road to Esso, at the 47 Kilometer mark.

Uksichansky Hot Springs are located in the village of Esso along the right bank of the Uksichan River. The thermal waters of these springs warm all the homes and greenhouses in Esso, plus fill a large outdoor public pool in the center of town.

Puschino Hot Springs are located in the upper Kamchatka River valley, about nine miles north of the village of Pushino, located on the road leading up the Central Valley. They are accessed from the village via a rough off-road trail

NORTHERN KAMCHATKA

From about 58 degrees north latitude, beginning at the Voyampolka and Nachiki rivers, to Kamchatka's border with the northeast Asia mainland (and including Karaginsky Island), the northern, Koryak region encompasses a vast area—116,379 square miles, roughly the size of Arizona. With a population of fewer than 35,000 people and subarctic climate, it is the least settled and most inhospitable part of Kamchatka, sparse in amenities, but rich in possibilities for wilderness adventure and ethnographic tourism. Ancestral home of the Koryaks, nomadic reindeer herders, this is Kamchatka's "True North," with endless stretches of tundra and sparse forests, that very much resembles, in climate, lay of the land and vegetation, northwest Alaska. But even more than that remote corner of the 49th state, the Koryak region's potential is immense, particularly for fly fishing, as most of its rivers remain untouched and unexplored by anyone except locals.

The Country of Northern Kamchatka

The terrain of Northern Kamchatka is rugged and varied, dominated in the south by the core of mountains (Sredinny Range) that runs up the axis of the peninsula and, in the north, by the extensive Koryak plateau and Kolyma Mountains that run along the coast of the mainland. Elevations vary from sea level to over 9000 feet, with many small glaciers and the remains of ancient volcanoes spread throughout. Deeply cut river valleys dissect the uplands, the largest fanning out into extensive, lake-dotted, swampy lowlands, creating perfect habitat for waterfowl and slack water fishes like northern pike and whitefish. In their estuaries are large lagoons and coastal lakes. Most of the coast in the Koryak region is low-lying and flat, with the exception of the northeast, where the headlands front the sea in a rugged coastline containing many bays and fjords.

The main rivers draining the west side of Koryak into the Sea of Okhotsk are (from north to south) the lower Paren, the Penzhina (at 427 miles, the second largest river in Kamchatka), Talovka (274 miles), Pustaya, Shamanka, Lesnaya, Palana, Kakhtana, and the Voyampolka. On the eastern coast, flowing into the Bering Sea, the main rivers are the Ukzlyam, Ilpiveyem, Vatyna, Apuka (185 miles), Pakhacha (181 miles), Kultushnaya, Vivenka (245 miles), Anapka, Belaya, Karaga, Ivashka,

Kamchatka Fly Fishing and Visitors Guide

157

Rusakova and the Khulyulya. Major lakes of the Koryak region are the Talovsky and Palansky.

Climate, Vegetation, and Conditions

The climate of Kamchatka's northern region is subarctic, with seasonally varying influence from the adjacent Bering and Okhotsk seas and vast landmass of northeast Asia. Winters are long and cold, with freezing temperatures usually starting by the end of September and continuing into May. Average January temperatures usually are above zero along the eastern coast but can be much lower in inland valleys. Summers are short, cloudy and cool. During the warmest months, July and August, temperatures average in the 50's, with highs into the 70s or 80s possible. This region receives less precipitation than southern or central Kamchatka, with annual amounts ranging from 11 inches in the interior to 27 inches on the coast and as much as 35 inches at higher elevations. Most precipitation falls in summer, as winter snows average but a foot or so in depth.

The season for optimum enjoyment of outdoor activities is shorter in Koryak than in southern or central Kamchatka. Ice along rivers and in bays can linger into June in certain areas, and by late October or early November, most of the rivers and lakes are encased again. Prime conditions for fly fishing and river running occur from late June or early July, after the rivers settle, into September in most years.

The region's vegetation is characterized by the predominance of tundra and sparse forests, as one travels farther north. Stands of birch (stone and white) cover better sites in the south, giving way to shrub trees like the conifer *Pinus pumila* (Siberian stone pine*)*, and broad-leaved, Siberian alder, *Alnus fruticosa* in alpine areas and low elevations sites farther north. Significant stands of timber in the northern part of the region occur only along major river valleys (like the Penzhina), with willow (several species)*,* birch, Siberian poplar, Chosenia and scattered larch most common. In the most extreme parts of the region, on sites underlain by permafrost, shrubs like dwarf birch and willow and perennial plants provide meager cover above carpets of moss and lichens.

Major Attractions

Like northwest Alaska, Kamchatka's Koryak region attracts a special breed of adventurer. One who favors the most remote and primitive areas for the unique and high-quality outdoor and cultural experiences they offer, whether it be first-descent river rafting/kayaking, visiting isolated native villages and camps, trekking to seldom-visited hot springs and volcanoes, observing rare birds and other animals, or fly casting in virgin waters. The lack of any development and absence of amenities is all part of the adventure for those hardy folks who travel to places like Kamchatka's wild north in search of raw, undistilled interaction with nature and natives.

Protected areas comprise but 4 % of the Koryak region, set aside to preserve habitat for birds, plants and land and marine mammals—many of them rare or endangered—and the traditional lifestyles of Koryak's indigenous people. These reserves, preserves, parks and monuments are almost all totally undeveloped with no visitor facilities. The largest of the region's many protected areas are the **Koryak State Nature Reserve**, 1263 square miles, and **Karaginsky Island Wildlife Reserve** at 747 square miles.

Access, Infrastructure, and Services

Northern Kamchatka, a frontier in the truest sense, presently has little in the way of developed infrastructure and visitor services. There is no connecting road system. Access to and from this region is almost exclusively by airplane or boat. (Major hubs and larger villages are serviced by regular flights from Petropavlovsk-Yelizovo, and there is usually irregular, seasonal service from other southern hubs like Esso.) Helicopters, boats, all-terrain vehicles, snow machines and dogsleds are used to reach remote sites within the region. Limited accommodations and supplies are available in most of the larger settlements, but any visitors to the Koryak region should make all necessary arrangements well ahead of time, plan flexible itineraries and come fully prepared (with proper gear and provisions) for being totally on their own for extended periods of time and inclement weather.

Major Hubs

Palana: Palana, population 3928, is the administrative, cultural and political center of the Koryak Region. Located on Kamchatka's west coast, on the banks of the lovely Palana River, some 500 miles north of Petropavlovsk, it has an adjacent seaport linking it with other major coastal settlements in the Far East. A regional museum, famous local dance troupe and educational institute (children's art school) are some of the cultural attractions. Like many other major hubs in the Koryak region, it is serviced (almost daily) by flights to and from Petropavlovsk/Yelizovo. (It can also be reached by winter road along the coast.) Limited tourist services, supplies, meals, and lodging are available in Palana.

Ossora: The town of Ossora, population 6000, is the administrative center of the Karaginsky district of the Koryak region. It is located on Ossora Bay on the Bering Sea coast, some 488 miles north of

Petropavlovsk. A rough, unpaved road runs from Ossora to the nearby village of Karaga. Amenities, services, and supplies are very limited. There are regular flights twice a week connecting Ossora to Petropavlovsk-Yelizovo.

Tilichiki: Tilichiki, population 2000, is a small fishing village and administrative center of the Olyutorsky District of the Koryak region. It is located on the eastern coast at Korfa Bay, 662 miles north of Petropavlovsk. A rough road and ferry connect it to the nearby village of Korf. Amenities, services, and supplies are very limited. There are several flights a week linking Tilichiki to the metro Petropavlovsk-Yelizovo area.

Kamensky: A small village (population 675) located on the lower Penzhina River near its mouth, approximately 778 miles north of Petropavlovsk, Kamensky is the administrative center for the Penzhinsky district of the Koryak region. It has few amenities and visitor services. It is connected by rough road to nearby villages and serviced by regular flights from the Petropavlovsk-Yelizovo area.

The northernmost region of Kamchatka offers abundant virgin fishing opportunities for trophy grayling, northern pike, and charr.

FLY FISHING KAMCHATKA'S NORTHERN REGION

Aside from the easier accessed and more productive rivers of southern Koryak, Kamchatka's northernmost region presents some real challenges for fly anglers. For one, the variety of more desirable sport species (like salmon and rainbow trout) diminishes farther north, though it is compensated somewhat by the presence of other feisty fighters like northern pike and whitefish. Rainbow trout are found only as far north as the Palana River on the west coast and excepting for the larger rivers that empty into the Bering Sea, salmon runs become spotty along the coast. Kamchatka grayling (in rivers draining the mainland) and the ubiquitous Dolly Varden are widespread and common.

Complicating matters is the almost total lack of infrastructure and services and extreme remoteness of much of the region. Helicopter charters are expensive and available only from certain hubs (Palana, Tigil, and Ossora) at certain times of year. The most affordable option for access is to take advantage of the scheduled flights (both fixed wing and helicopter) that regularly service the major villages from Kamchatka's main hub of Petropavlovsk-Yelizovo. From the major settlements, transport by boat or all-terrain vehicle can be arranged to more remote sites along rivers and other waterways. Of course, the services of a local guide or tour company are most warranted for your safety and enjoyment in these far-flung locales.

Fly anglers not put off by all these daunting obstacles can enjoy exploring totally pristine drainages with virgin fishing conditions. Beyond the streams along the southern coasts- the Voyampolka, Palana, Lesnaya, Karaga, etc., the large and productive rivers flowing out of the highlands in the north hold the most promise, rivers like the Apuka, Vivenka, Pahacha, Penzhina, Apacha and Tolovka. Details of some of the better-known Koryak river locations are as follows:

Voyampolka River

Perhaps the most significant river in all of Koryak for fly fishing potential is the **Voyampolka** along the region's southwest coast. A classic Kamchatka mountain stream comprised of three main forks (the Zhilovaya, Kutina, and Materaya) and about 120 miles long, the Voyampolka flows swift and mostly clear (some of its headwaters are of glacial origin) down through the foothills and flat coastal plain before emptying into the Sea of Okhotsk at north latitude 58 degrees, 31 minutes. With five species of salmon (chum and silvers mostly) and abundant rainbows and charr and great fly fishing conditions, the Voyampolka is a highly coveted destination for float fishing, despite its remoteness and difficulty and expense of getting there. (It is also one of the last rivers this far north to hold a population of steelhead.) The south fork (Materaya Voyampolka) is the most frequently fished and is usually accessed by helicopter from the villages of Esso or Tigil. (There is also a fixed camp operation on the middle fork.) Take out is usually at the village at the mouth, where helicopters and fixed wing craft can transport fishermen back to main hubs farther south. Best fly fishing on the Voyampolka is from late summer into fall.

Palana River

Another one of Koryak's most notable streams in terms of productivity, relative ease of access and sport fishing potential is the lovely **Palana River**, on the west coast at roughly 59 degrees north latitude. A major sockeye salmon system, with a headwater nursery lake, the Palana also has a run of silvers, chums, pinks, a few kings and abundant charr (Dolly Varden and kundzha) and some rainbows (some of the most northerly occurring in Kamchatka.). About 84 miles long, winding through forested hills of stone birch, alder, and dwarf pine, the picturesque Palana can be accessed by boat from the village of Palana at its mouth or by the rough dirt road that follows the river to its headwaters above Palansky Lake and the popular hot springs there. A great river with many possibilities for exploration by foot, skiff or raft.

Penzhina River

The second largest drainage in Kamchatka (427 miles long), the **Penzhina River** rises from extensive headwaters in the Kolyma mountains and flows southeast and then west through immense, lake-dotted, marshy lowlands before emptying into Penzhina Bay on the Sea of Okhotsk. Its main tributaries are the Belaya, Oklun, Chernaya, Ayanka, Shaiboveem and the Kondyreva rivers. Significant for its fisheries and forests, the Penzhina has salmon (mostly chum, with rare numbers of silver, king, and reds) and abundant grayling, charr, whitefish and big northern pike. Of great importance for the subsistence of locals, the Penzhina has been fished by few foreign anglers, who have accessed it by boat or (in winter) by dogsled or track vehicle from the village of Kamensky at the mouth. Like other rivers its size, the best fly fishing on the Penzhina will be in its many smaller clear flowing tributaries and confluences.

Apuka River

Located along the Bering Sea coast of northeast Kamchatka, on Olyutorsky Gulf, the 185-mile long **Apuka River** is one of the most significant salmon streams in the Koryak region. A major producer of king and silver salmon, the Apuka also has chum, pink, sockeyes, and abundant Dolly Varden charr. With extensive headwaters in the eastern Koryak highlands, the Apuka is a sizeable stream, best accessed by boat from settlements along the river (like the village of Apuka on the bay). Best fly fishing conditions occur from late June or early July to September.

OTHER ATTRACTIONS

Koryaksky State Nature Reserve

Established in 1995, Koryaksky State Nature Reserve protects some 1263 square miles of territory in three separate areas of northern Koryak: the marshy, lake-filled lowlands of the Kuyul River and nearby rugged Cape Goven and Lavrov Bay along the Bering Sea coast. The unique wildlife habitat includes some of the most significant nesting sites for waterfowl and shorebirds in northeast Asia, including species like the whooper swan, yellow-billed loon, white-fronted goose, black brant, bean goose and the spoonbill sandpiper. Also protected are numerous important sites for marine birds like pelagic cormorants, slaty-backed gulls, black kittiwakes, puffins and guillemots and marine mammals like spotted seals, sea otters, and walruses. The reserve also is sanctuary for numerous birds of prey like Steller's, golden and white-tailed eagles and two rare species of falcons.

Koryaksky Reserve is virtually undeveloped, with no facilities for visitors and only a few short trails for hiking. Access to the Reserve from southern Kamchatka is almost exclusively by air, via scheduled flight to the nearby village of Tilichiki from Petropavlovsk/Yelizovo. From there, boats, helicopters, and all-terrain vehicles are used to reach different parts of the reserve. Visitors must obtain a permit to visit the Koryaksky Reserve, available from the office at:

Koryaksky Reserve
Naberezhnaya Street, # D 8
Tilichiki, Olyutorsky District
Kamchatka, Russia 688800
Phone/fax: 7 (41544)-52-074; 7 (41544)-52-338
Email: koryak1@rambler.ru

Karaginsky Island Wildlife Preserve

Karaginsky Island and the surrounding marine waters and adjacent Kamchatka coast comprise Karaginsky Island Wildlife Preserve, 774 square miles, one of the most significant areas for breeding waterfowl and seabirds in the Far East. The island has mountains, meadows, and marshes, with numerous lakes and streams. Dominant vegetation is sparse forests and tundra. Over 500 species of plants occur here, including stone birch, Siberian dwarf-pine, willow, and aspen.

The area supports large breeding populations of diving ducks, gulls, terns, cormorants and hundreds of thousands of migrating and breeding waterfowl, including some of the largest breeding densities of harlequin ducks in the Russian Far East. The streams of the island and adjacent coastline support runs of five Pacific salmon species. Surrounding marine waters provide important habitat for groundfish like yellowfin sole and herring and are the major spawning area for walleye pollock in the western Bering Sea. The island is also breeding grounds for the southernmost population of Pacific walrus (*Odobenus rosmarus*) in the western Bering Sea, and the surrounding Karaginsky Gulf is an important walrus feeding area. Other important marine mammals found within Karaginsky Gulf are spotted, ringed, ribbon and bearded seals, gray, humpback, and fin whales and Steller sea lions.

Major Area Hot Springs

Rosakovsky: Rosakovsky springs are located in the scenic upper Rosakova River valley, on the eastern slope of the Sredinny Ridge in the Karaginsky district, not far from the ancient Tylele volcano. They are usually reached via a rough dirt road (approximately 40 miles) that runs from the settlement of Ivashka on the Bering Sea coast.

Palansky Hot Springs: A very popular site with locals and visitors, the Palansky Hot Springs are located at the headwaters of the Palana River above Palana Lake. They are reached by dirt road (approximately 55 miles) from the village of Palana near the western coast.

TECHNIQUES AND GEAR FOR KAMCHATKA FLY FISHERS

WET FLY FISHING

Using a forage pattern and simple wet fly swing to work a small canyon on the Tikhaya River in west-central Kamchatka

The fly angler's stock-in-trade for handling the majority of situations encountered when fishing trout and salmon in Kamchatka is the basic wet fly presentation and its many variations. To do well there requires mastery of but a few of these: traditional wet fly swings for fishing attractors (salmon, trout and charr); modified fly swings and drifts for working forage patterns (trout, charr and grayling); the dead-drift for working egg/flesh flies and steelhead patterns (trout and charr); and nymphing (for trout, charr and grayling). The techniques and rigging used in some of these presentation methods (drifting and nymphing, for instance) are very similar, with only slight differences. The following are brief descriptions.

Wet Fly Swing

When fishing attractors (flies that do not imitate a food item but provoke response with certain colors and pattern) for salmon, trout and charr, it is essential to have the fly presented at proper depth. This is particularly true for salmon, which are generally not inclined to notice or pursue enticements that are not at eye level, which is not far off bottom. Use the proper line, along with sufficient leader and additional weight if necessary, to present your fly in the "strike zone"

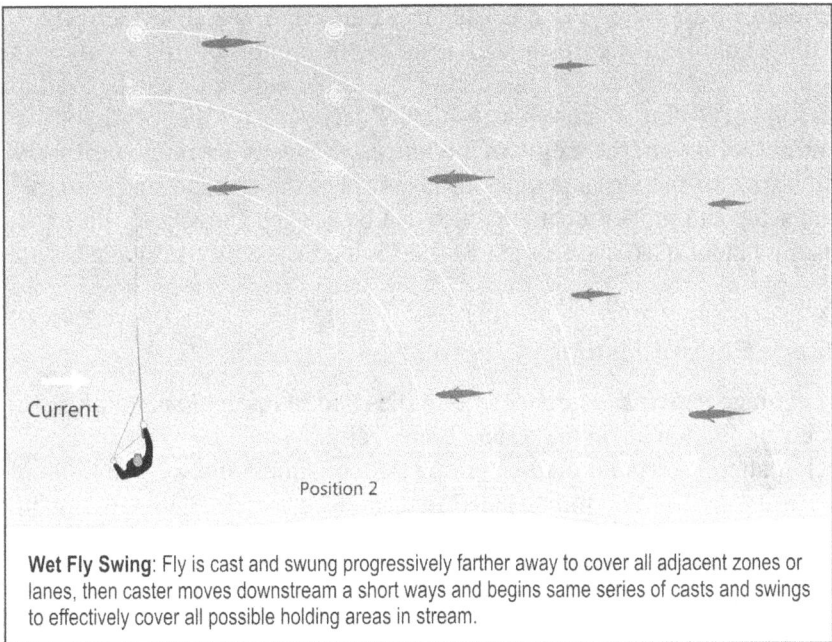

Current

Position 2

Wet Fly Swing: Fly is cast and swung progressively farther away to cover all adjacent zones or lanes, then caster moves downstream a short ways and begins same series of casts and swings to effectively cover all possible holding areas in stream.

Generally, for headwaters and most stream conditions in Kamchatka, this means floating lines, with 7 to 10 foot (depending on depth and current) tapered leaders and weighted flies or split shot, if needed. Special sinking leaders are most useful for these situations. For the bigger water encountered in the lower sections of larger streams or rivers (when fishing salmon, for instance), you can use short (3 to 7 foot) medium-density sink tip lines to get your fly down, along with shorter (7 foot) leaders. (When fishing estuaries, river mouths or the lower sections of giant rivers like the Kamchatka, some anglers may opt for longer sink tips, shooting heads or even full sink lines.) It is important to "fine tune" your setup for the conditions and species. Too much weight and/or too much drag and you will hinder your drift and hang up on bottom. Too little weight and you will be swinging your fly above the heads of your quarry, wasting your effort.

The basic wet fly swing technique involves a short cast (usually 20 feet or less), perpendicular to shore or slightly upstream, to place the fly at proper depth through most of an arc encompassing roughly 90 degrees (from slightly above the angler to near the bank below, depending on water depth and velocity). The fly fisher keeps the line taut and his strike reflex on the ready by following the fly with his rod and using short fast line strips for more control if needed. Generally, the take will not be as aggressive from salmon as it is from trout and charr, which are actively feeding, but in either case, a quick response from the angler is necessary to set the hook before the fish rejects the fly. Strike indicators can be used for this kind of fishing, but are not absolutely necessary. Proper depth, line control (because of the length of the line used, mends are rarely necessary in this kind of fishing) and quick reflexes are of the essence, and with the right setup and proper technique, fish can be hooked anywhere within the quadrant mentioned above, not just the 45 degree arc that most anglers are effective in.

Forage Pattern Fishing

Forage patterns are basically any flies tied to resemble naturally occurring food items in the water. Technically this includes just about every pattern except attractors. For the sake of simplicity, we will limit this discussion to flies that mimic small fish and leeches—live prey that swims below the surface. Egg and flesh patterns, nymphs, dry flies, and rodents will be treated separately

Small fish comprise a significant part of the diet of all large trout in Kamchatka. Indeed, at certain times of year, the rainbows (and charr) there feed exclusively on the young of salmon and other species and would probably not reach the robust sizes seen without the abundant fish life available. It's no surprise then that an amazing variety of baitfish and small salmon patterns can be fished with great effect in many situations on Kamchatka's streams, throughout the open water season. Sculpin patterns of all imaginable variety, along with numerous baitfish and smolt and fry imitation streamers are among the most popular and productive forage flies used.

To this, of course, must be added the venerable Leech, perhaps the most universally fished trout pattern (along with the Muddler) in the world. No matter what the conditions or time of year, it seems, a properly fished Leech will get a response from trout anywhere, and the waters of Russia are no exception. (If we include the egg-sucking variety and all its permutations, then the Leech is arguably the most productive wet fly in Alaska and Kamchatka.) Purple, black, pink, olive, brown; chenille, hackle, fur or Mylar; it doesn't seem to matter what the color or material, as it is undoubtedly that tantalizing swimming action that prompts such certain response from hungry trout.

Depending on the situation and fly used, Leeches and small fish patterns are best fished by either drifting or using a wet fly swing, enhanced by short strips and/or twitches of the rod tip to impart lifelike action. Small fry and alevin patterns are usually fished with a drift. Areas of fast current like rapids and tailouts are also more commonly fished by merely drifting the fly through. In more calm waters like big pools and lakes, when fishing larger flies like Muddlers, Smolt, and Leeches, a short, fast, irregular strip (sometimes with a slight twitch of the rod tip) can prompt more strikes. When fish are actively and visibly feeding on smolt or baitfish (as they frequently do during spring and early summer), practically any kind of presentation will produce results.

Whether drifting or using a modified wet fly swing on forage patterns, the angler must keep his fly at proper depth and avoid the drag of a slack line. The idea is to present the most naturally appearing bait, one that mimics the most likely movement of forage in various kinds of water. (Remember to think like a fish! Where are the places that small minnows or leeches are found, and how do they move through these areas? It certainly helps to spend time observing the various types of forage moving through different kinds of water.) Floating lines or short sink tips and standard length (7 to 9 foot) wet fly leaders will cover nearly all the forage pattern fishing situations one might encounter in Kamchatka. Specialty sinking leaders, small BB shot, wrap lead and weighted flies provide additional weight for fine tuning depth presentation. If you fish strike indicators, a standard nymph rig (see illustration further on) will work fine when drifting forage patterns, as the techniques are quite similar.

Drifting

The drift technique is used primarily for trout and steelhead fishing, with egg/flesh or certain attractor patterns usually, for drag-free presentations through holding areas to entice takes. This method is similar to wet-fly swinging in that the angler, using similar rigging, usually begins with a short cast slightly upstream and follows the downstream movement of the fly with his rod (usually) as it passes through the holding water. The difference is in the greater finesse involved in keeping the line drag free and the fly drifting, not swinging through the holding water. Diligent mending of the line (to keep it drifting <u>above</u> the fly) is necessary to avoid as much drag as possible, and, as in fishing attractors (and even more so), the angler must hone his senses to detect the slightest variation in the drift that may signal a take and have swift reflexes to set the hook before the fish spits the fly. Most fly anglers these days use buoyant strike indicators for this kind of fishing, especially in deeper or off-color waters where it is difficult to sight fish. These indicators are attached at or slightly below the end of the fly line (depending on depth), and act very much like bobbers (see illustration of standard nymph/drift rig). Plastic egg-imitation beads of various sizes and colors, so productive on the trout rivers of Alaska when fished this way, will also work very well on the rainbows (and charr and grayling) of Kamchatka.

Floating lines and standard length leaders (7 to 9 foot) are most commonly used for drifting flies in Russia, but low density, short sink tips can also be effective in certain conditions (deep, fast water). It is important to keep the fly drifting along bottom, especially when fishing egg/flesh patterns and a small, BB-sized shot attached 8 to 12 inches above the fly usually does the trick. (If you are fishing with indicators, check your drift after adding weight to make sure your rig has enough buoyancy.)

For late fall steelhead fishing, good drift technique can make the difference between success and failure, as these fish become notoriously unresponsive when water temperatures plummet. The fly must be slowed way down and presented right in front of the mouths of these finicky fighters, without the slightest bit of drag. Line control is of the utmost in this kind of fishing, and the best and most successful steelhead anglers are masters at managing their lines to get that perfect drift. They also use strike indicators, specially rigged leaders, "zone" fishing, and long rods to get an edge when pursuing these elusive, late season sea-run rainbows. (See the chapter on Kamchatka steelhead for additional tips on late season presentation for these conditions.)

Nymphing

"Nymphing" refers to the technique of fishing subsurface larval insect patterns for trout (and in a broader sense can also include fishing other forage patterns). It is very popular among fly anglers, especially effective at certain times of year, such as in spring, when water temperatures are cold, and there is little forage available, or in situations later in the season where fish are feeding heavily on subsurface aquatic insect life. Also, certain species like grayling seem more prone to respond to nymphing at any time of year, due to their predominantly insectivorous diet. Along with fishing tried-and-true forage patterns like leeches, sculpins, and smolt, nymphing can be one of the most productive "searching" techniques when fish are scattered, and no feeding can be observed. Kamchatka's abundant aquatic insects are an important part of the diet of all resident species, and the peninsula's trout, charr, and grayling, in varying degrees will instinctively respond to properly presented artificials that mimic the many larval forms of this forage, no matter almost what the conditions.

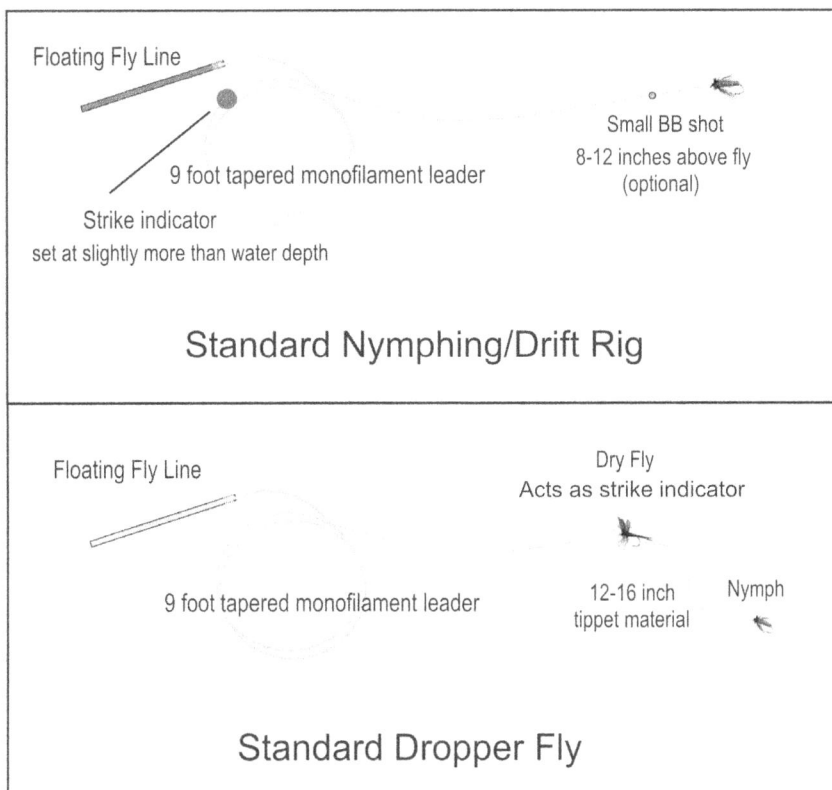

Floating Fly Line

Small BB shot
8-12 inches above fly
(optional)

9 foot tapered monofilament leader

Strike indicator
set at slightly more than water depth

Standard Nymphing/Drift Rig

Floating Fly Line

Dry Fly
Acts as strike indicator

9 foot tapered monofilament leader

12-16 inch
tippet material

Nymph

Standard Dropper Fly

Doing consistently well with nymphs requires perception and diligence. It helps to know what kinds of insects are available in the stream. In the old days, you would cut open a trout's belly and see what it had been feeding on. Now you have to work a little harder and poke around the stream to see what kinds of bugs live there. Look carefully in the water, stir up the bottom, turn over some rocks, inspect vegetation (in and out of the stream), check the banks, etc., for any clues to the insect biota that the river supports. (A fine mesh net is a tremendous aid if you have one available.) Kamchatka's streams support a rich assortment of bugs, so it is highly unlikely you won't find something there that the fish can eat. The accepted strategy is to try to match your fly to the insect forage you've found, but lacking that, you can use universal nymph patterns like the Hare's Ear, Brassie, Emerger, etc., to search for hungry fish.

Like other fly fishing techniques, nymphing has evolved into different variations to handle the complexity of conditions encountered on trout streams. In its simplest form (perfect for Kamchatka), it is nothing more than drifting, using rigging similar to what would be used to float eggs or flesh flies (see illustration). Strike indicators have become a big part of nymphing nowadays, and practically every angler in Alaska and Kamchatka nymphs with them. As a good drift at proper depth is essential, anglers will make use of sinking leaders, split shot and/or weighted flies (bead heads and/or tungsten wire wraps), if needed, and fine tune their indicator rigs accordingly.

Most casts are made upstream, with a quick mend, if needed, to throw any excess line above the fly. The angler, holding the rod up, follows the drifting fly as it sweeps down river, mending as needed (the fly will almost always be drifting slower than the line and indicator) to keep a natural drift. If the line is properly managed (no slack), the fish will hook itself on the take in water of any current, with only a slight rise on the rod required of the angler to set the hook (remember that trout do not have hard mouths like salmon).

Not all situations require deep nymphing, however, as there are times, such as when fish are feeding on emergers right below the surface when a more buoyant fly is called for (see the dropper rig illustration for a common and very productive variation for these situations). There are also situations when a less stringent technique, such as a simple wet fly swing, will be more than adequate to take trout feeding heavily on nymphs. As in all fishing, the highly successful nymph angler creatively adapts his technique and rigging to the conditions encountered.

Wet Fly Gear

You do not need an extensive array of gear to equip yourself for the different kinds of wet fly fishing you will be doing in Kamchatka. For rainbow trout and charr, a 5 or 6-weight, medium-action, 8 ½ to 9-foot graphite rod will handle most of the presentations called for in headwaters and smaller streams, with a 7-weight for the bigger water encountered in the lower sections of Kamchatka's larger streams and rivers. (If you fish the fall steelhead runs along the west side of the peninsula, you will need a sturdy 8-weight.) The dainty Kamchatka grayling ideally should be pursued with a small rod, 4-weight or less, but you certainly can fish them with your larger trout rod.

If you are planning on swinging flies for salmon, you will need stouter gear, with a 7 to 8- weight recommended for Kamchatka's silver, chum and red salmon and a sturdy 9 or even 10-weight for Kamchatka's king salmon. The smaller pink and cherry salmon can be taken quite easily with the same setup used for rainbows. Casting and pulling the big, bulky flies needed for Kamchatka's pike will require an 8 or 9-weight.

As noted regarding fly lines, most of the conditions encountered in Kamchatka can be successfully fished using weight forward, performance-tapered floaters, with the more extreme situations (like those when fishing salmon in the larger rivers right above tidewater) calling for sink tips. A tapered monofilament nylon leader of 7 to 9 feet, with varying tippets, will handle practically any type of wet fly presentation needed in Kamchatka.

KAMCHATKA DRY FLY FISHING

Fishing a hatch on the Zhupanova River in southern Kamchatka

One of the most exciting discoveries made early on by the first western fly anglers to explore Kamchatka's productive stream fisheries was the surprising abundance of hatching insects and superb dry fly fishing conditions. The diversity and number of caddis, stone, dragon, damsel, crane and mayflies, along with numerous midges, gnats and mosquitoes was quite unexpected, given the experiences in neighboring Alaska. This smorgasbord of insect life provides a rich food source for the peninsula's trout, charr and grayling populations, augmenting the considerable energy stores they derive from the prodigious runs of spawning salmon. And with Kamchatka's superabundance of clear, swift, shallow waters, it creates a dream come true during open water season for those who pursue trout for the thrill of the surface take.

Granted, Kamchatka's hatches don't match the variety and size seen on some of the more productive, large trout rivers of the American West and Southern Hemisphere. There are no salmon flies, for instance, and nowhere near the number of mayflies you'll encounter on rivers down south (Kamchatka has probably two dozen species, including several Baetis and Red Quills) but there are quite a few caddis (at least 47 species) and stoneflies (about 30 species, including yellow sallies, goldens, blacks and browns) that, along with abundant midges, gnats (black flies) and mosquitoes, can thicken the air and cover the water along river stretches.

The timing of the various hatches in Kamchatka is not as precise as on many western U.S. rivers. The onset of summer and warmest days (in June) bring the first big hatches of mayflies (along with abundant mosquitoes), then later, the various caddis and stones emerge throughout July and August and into fall on many rivers, augmented by thick clouds of midges and gnats. (Terrestrials like beetles, ants, hoppers, caterpillars, bees, etc. are present in Kamchatka and certainly comprise a significant part of the hapless mix that falls in rivers and gets slurped up by Kamchatka's voracious resident fish species, but currently, few anglers exploit their presence.)

Another thing about Kamchatka's dry fly fishing, which might disappoint some anglers, is that given these fish are perhaps the wildest, most robust and opportunistic of their kind, this is not a technical fishery requiring extreme finesse or specialized gear. (Certainly nothing like is seen on many waters down south.) As in Alaska, in Kamchatka, you can forgo the super long leaders, wispy tippets, fluorocarbon, trick rigging and hero casts and still do fabulously well with the native fish population.

This is not to say, of course, that fly anglers won't encounter situations on the rivers of Kamchatka that try their skills and judgment. Rainbows and rarely even Dolly Varden will, under certain conditions, become quite selective as to size and pattern, requiring considerable effort to "match the hatch." (For anyone who has fished Alaska and experienced its hordes of greedy Dolly Vardens gobbling up practically anything thrown into the water, it will come as a mind-blowing shock to encounter schools of these feisty charr in Kamchatka feeding only on tiny midges and flatly refusing any other enticement that the angler throws in front of them, short of fresh salmon roe!) Kamchatka's grayling seem less inclined toward this snootiness and are usually kindly tolerant of offerings that bear only slight resemblance to what they are feeding on, but even they will have their moments. Suffice to say that if you are reasonably competent in the basic fly fishing skills and have some experience fishing hatches elsewhere, you will most likely do great on the rivers of Kamchatka. (And even if you are a rank beginner, not to worry; you'll pick it up quickly over there with the help of your guide and take plenty of fish.)

Dry Fly Techniques

Most of the dry fly patterns you'll fish in Kamchatka, at least the more traditional flies, will be drifted along the surface, with no drag, through holding areas, to create as natural a presentation as possible. (Observe a hatch to get an idea of how winged insects emerge and are taken by the fish.) Skating or twitching bushy patterns along the top of the water can be very effective at times on large rainbows, steelhead and some salmon; this technique is covered separately in our section on Mousing and in the trout and salmon chapters. For standard dry fly presentations in Kamchatka, you'll be making simple casts of 20 to 40 feet most of the time, in a variety of water. As elsewhere, managing your line to avoid drag and slack, while maintaining visual contact with your fly is paramount, as are quick reflexes to respond to the take before the fish spits the fly.

To begin, you need to locate a hatch somewhere and then determine what kind of insects the fish are feeding on so you can select an appropriate matching fly to present to the surface feeders. (Once you find a hatch, it should be very easy to identify the kind of bug the fish are keen on.) It is not necessary to present an identical match to the natural; just try to use something that resembles it as much as possible in size, color, and form. (Also take note, if possible, of any larvae or emergers in the water, if you can't find anything in your fly arsenal to reasonably match the adults.)

Some anglers will position themselves downstream of the action to facilitate better presentation, others will fish above, but there is no hard fast rule for the best position to cast to surface feeding trout. Either way, you will drift your fly into feeding fish, and work your line so that it does not pull the leader and fly in an unnatural way across the water and spook the fish. This is where the finesse and mastery of technique comes in, to hone your casting and management of the line so that your fly has the most natural presentation and greatest chance of being noticed.

To start, use wider loops and "snake casts" to place the fly gently on the water with a little slack to delay the inevitable drag as it begins to float downstream, while you reposition the rod for the drift. As a belly in the line develops and starts to pull the fly, you can use a flip of your rod to gently lift the slack up and over without disturbing the fly. (This is called "mending," and takes practice; the idea being to get the end of the line upstream from the fly without too much effort and disturbance.)

It is most important to know where your fly is at all times. You can increase its visibility by wearing polarized sunglasses and using larger or more prominent patterns, if possible (Bivisible, Humpy, Stimulator, etc.). You can also use a very small, bright slip indicator on the end of your fly line to help locate your fly. The "take" on a dry fly is, of course, hard to miss visually, but easy to miss with a timely response if you are not paying attention or cannot see your fly. (The fish will only have the fly in its mouth for an instant before rejecting it.) Most anglers set the hook by quickly raising the rod with their casting arm while pulling the line in the opposite direction with their other hand. (Remember that trout, charr, and grayling, in contrast to salmon, have soft mouths and do not require stout hook sets.) If you miss the take, try extending the drift by feeding line out, moving the rod or repositioning the fly upstream with a short roll cast. This will give the fish additional opportunity to hit the fly again. If you do connect with a fish only briefly, you can cast to it again, and if it doesn't respond, wait a few minutes, then recast. Many times, the fish will take the fly again after a short while if it has not been stung too hard by the hook.

Sampling emergent insect life helps "match the hatch"

You can certainly fish dries without any signs of surface feeding in Kamchatka, prompting takes from opportunistic trout, charr, and grayling that will seldom refuse any available food. This works best during summer when hatches occur with enough frequency that the fish are constantly primed for surface feeding. Look around first for any signs of insect life— on the surface, in the water, in the air, along the banks, and on streamside vegetation. This may give you a fix on a suitable imitation to rouse the local stream inhabitants. If you can't locate any clues to what types of hatches have been occurring along the stretch of river you are fishing, use generic patterns with universal appeal like the Elk Hair Caddis, Black Gnat, Adams, Humpy, Royal Coachman, etc., in sizes 10 to 18, to search for top-feeders. Likely areas to cast your searching patterns are shallow to medium depth runs, pools and tailouts, current seams, shelves, drop-offs, under cut banks, in pocket water around structure, etc. If you don't have any luck initially drifting various searching patterns through likely holding water, you can keep trying different dry patterns, to maybe spark some action on the surface, or try something a little different, say a dropper fly (a nymph fished off a short piece of tippet attached to your dry fly or to the leader above the fly—see section on nymphing and wet fly fishing) or maybe even skating a bushy Caddis, Muddler, Bomber or Mouse across the surface to tempt them with a high protein snack. This sometimes can do the trick, to jolt them into feeding when they seem apathetic to the floating fly. If you don't have any luck with that, it's time to find some other fish or switch to a totally different fishing strategy, like nymphing or fishing attractors or egg/flesh flies.

Dry Fly Gear

If you're dry fly fishing rainbows and charr, you'll probably want a medium-fast action, average length, 5 or 6-weight graphite rod for headwater stream conditions, switching to a solid 6 or even 7-weight for the larger stream and river conditions frequently encountered on the middle and lower sections of drainages. (For fishing the Mouse and other surface rodent imitations, see our separate recommendations for proper gear and techniques.) For grayling, a 3 or 4- weight is ideal. A performance-tapered or weight forward floating line and tapered, 9-foot nylon monofilament leader are all you'll need (along with a good selection of patterns) to complete your dry fly fishing setup for Kamchatka.

Tippets are a personal matter, and many trout anglers, out of habit, will rig super light, but as stated, you certainly don't need spider web thinness (or long length) to fool the fish in Kamchatka. A tippet much lighter than 5X (4 lb.) is not recommended, given the size of the fish, you may encounter and frequent challenging conditions. Fluorocarbon or other trick materials are not necessary, as Kamchatka's trout are not the least bit leader shy. A medium-hard, abrasion and shock resistant nylon monofilament tippet will do the trick.

KAMCHATKA MOUSING

One of the most thrilling ways of fishing Kamchatka's big rainbows is to skitter a fake rodent across the water to induce savage surface strikes. There's just something about a giant trout coming up to whack a top water fly that sets an angler's pulse racing, especially in clear water where you can see all the action. Fishing mouse and other rodent imitations is arguably the ultimate "dry fly" angling for trout. It is usually done in tamer places only at night or more rarely, during very special conditions in daylight. But in the Far North—especially Alaska and Kamchatka, where the rainbows come big, bold and unsophisticated— an angler can consistently lure them to the surface with faux rodents practically any time of day. And though Alaska has some really great mousing water, Kamchatka, for reasons not entirely clear, has far and away the most abundant opportunities for taking big rainbows in this unique and exciting way. In fact, at times on certain rivers, you can fish a Mouse exclusively and take all the rainbows your arms can handle, all day long, day after day. It can be that good.

In addition to traditional mouse, rat and lemming patterns, many other large, top water creations like bass poppers, pike frogs, diver flies, hopper patterns, pollywogs, steelhead waking flies, etc. will take Kamchatka's rainbows. Anything of size that's not too ridiculous looking and creates some kind of topwater disturbance will get the attention of these marauding, opportunistic feeders (shy trout don't make it in this part of the world), and it's not uncommon for them to pursue your fly until they hook themselves, quite often literally right at your feet, so focused and determined they are on getting big food morsels! Like any other pattern, however, a Mouse, when well presented, will have the greatest chance of enticing every trout within striking distance, including the largest and best fed.

Fishing the Mouse

The theory and techniques behind fishing rodent imitations are the same, regardless of the fly used. These topwater creations mimic small mammals (mice, voles, shrews and lemmings) found in cyclically varying numbers along trout streams in the Far North. During times of great abundance, these little critters are prone to fall or leap off banks into streams, where they become prime fare for hungry rainbow trout, charr, and even grayling. This creates a common enough food source for the trout to be constantly alert for any large surface commotion, particularly in areas near shore.

Kamchatka's streams have physical characteristics that make them ideal for mousing. Though they can be successfully fished just about anywhere along their length with rodent imitations, the best water on most rivers is usually found from the midsection down to the mouth, where there is less gradient and the kind of cover conducive to holding good rodent numbers. Best areas to tempt these large surface-feeding rainbows are in the backwaters of sloughs and meandering side channels, around brush piles, log jams and in back eddies. In the main channel, look for moderately shallow pools, drop-offs, cut banks, and rocky riffle sections of moderate depth. (Avoid very swift water with no structure or water that is too deep or too shallow.) Some of the best and most enjoyable mousing can be had in canyons with boulders large enough to break up the current and create spots where trout can hide and ambush prey. There an angler may even be able to hop (very carefully!) from rock to rock and lob a Mouse out into the small pockets of holding water, often with spectacular results. There is also great mousing to be had along Kamchatka's countless spring creeks, with their abundant aquatic vegetation that creates perfect ambush sites for hunky rainbows that explode out of the thick green cover to annihilate drifting rodent imitations.

Experience has shown that Kamchatka's rainbows can be taken on rodent imitations throughout the season, and at any time during the day, but are most prone to succumb to fake mice in late spring/early summer and late fall when the rich and easy fare of summer salmon spawn is not as readily available and during low light conditions such as in early morning, late evening and on cloudy days, when trout are more reckless in feeding. On rivers where rodent populations are at peak levels, however, the Mouse and similar patterns seem to fish well even during the height of salmon spawning and in bright midday conditions.

It should be said that mousing, compared to just about any other technique for rousing rainbows, involves significantly more effort and time to work productive stretches of water, so that, albeit the results are more dramatic and exciting, you won't cover the ground and take the numbers of fish that your comrades will using other, more traditional methods like swinging attractors or drifting egg/flesh flies. This is especially true during the height of the season when a wide variety of food sources is available. For those determined to have the indescribable experience of a big trout thrashing the surface in pursuit of their little mouse fly, the tradeoff seems of little concern.

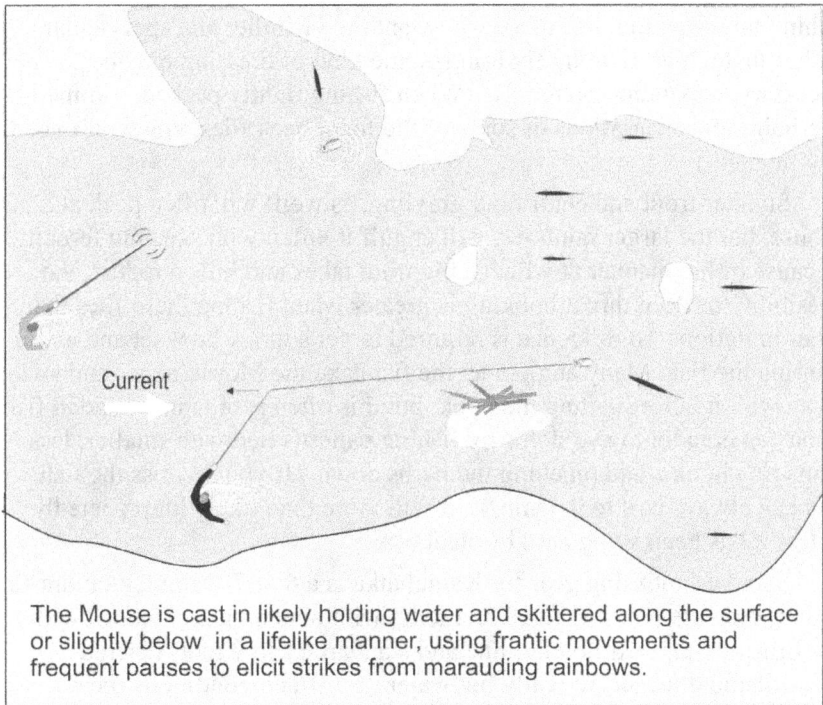

The Mouse is cast in likely holding water and skittered along the surface or slightly below in a lifelike manner, using frantic movements and frequent pauses to elicit strikes from marauding rainbows.

Technique

As far as basic mousing technique goes, the idea is to mimic the frantic movements of a small rodent adrift or drowning in the stream. Your fly should be presented as cleanly as possible in a promising area, and then allowed to sit for a moment or two before you begin your retrieve. Some anglers use a passive style, mostly drifting the fly, with maybe a twitch every now and then to create a slight wake. But most fishermen like to work the Mouse more, using twitches of the rod tip, held high, to jerk it in small hops along the surface, the idea being to create a noticeable wake and splash to sound the dinner bell for all nearby trout. You can vary the hopping motion with occasional side quivers of the rod to impart a nervous shake to the Mouse, for more realism. Most successful mousers do not work the fly too fast; slow retrieves seem to take more fish. And don't forget to pause every few hops; many strikes will come when the Mouse is at rest. If a fish follows it but doesn't take or only nibbles at the Mouse, kick up the action a bit to incite a strike, and if that doesn't work, wait a bit and then cast to it again.

Should these flies be dressed? Some guides and anglers prefer to fish mouse patterns, especially those made of rabbit fur, as drowning mice, working them at or slightly below the surface. They have great success fishing this way, too. For those who want the visibility and spectacular strikes that a high floating fly bring, some kind of dressing may be necessary, depending on the fly. (When fishing tightly packed, trimmed deerhair mouse variations or some of the foam back flies, you won't need any floatant.)

Smaller trout and charr (and grayling, as well) will often peck at a big Mouse, but the larger rainbows will engulf it, often with startling ferocity. Because of the manner at which a big trout takes and kills a rodent, the possibility of deep throat hooking is greater when fishing these flies than other imitations, so diligence is required to get a quick hookset and avoid injuring the fish. Many anglers let the fish take the Mouse under and swim away with it before setting the hook, but this often results in wounded fish. (You can do a lot to avoid this by fishing patterns tied with smaller, less damaging hooks, and pinching the barbs down.) If you do miss the fish, you can always cast to it again, as it will more than likely hit repeatedly unless it has been stung hard by steel.

Standard mousing gear for Kamchatka is a 6 or 7-weight, medium-fast action, graphite rod, 8 ½ to 10 feet long, with matching reel loaded with performance-tapered floating line and standard (7 to 9 foot) tapered monofilament leader. In really big water or difficult conditions (heavy wind), you can bump up to an 8-weight. Tippets used are usually in the 0X to 2X (8 to 10 lb.) range.

Choosing the Right Pattern

Selecting appropriate patterns for a Kamchatka mousing expedition is complicated considerably by the plethora of rodent patterns currently available in shops and catalogs. Many are extremely lifelike and hard to resist, with cute little whiskers, tails, ear tufts and beady eyes that implore you to take them home. While the fly tiers have certainly achieved their goal of making them irresistible to fishermen, catching trout with these imitations is another matter. Some of the most likely looking ones fish horribly, while the least lifelike creations turn out to be stellar performers on stream. What are some of the characteristics of a great performing pattern that you should look for in a prospective mouse fly?

If you think about, little of the external adornment on these patterns is of any real consequence to a hungry, wild northern rainbow responding reflexively to a noisy disturbance and rodent profile on the stream's surface (quite often in diminished light). For the serious mouse angler, the concern should be more with a fly's potential performance than how well it mimics all the physical details of a rodent. How well will the fly cast? How will it float (buoyancy and staying upright)? Is it durable? And, of course, will the trout fall for it?

The materials and design used in these patterns is everything as far as performance goes. Spun deer hair, the original material used in mouse patterns (Whitlock's MouseRat) is still one of the best for creating flies that have buoyancy, realism, durability and are easy to cast. Fur, usually rabbit, certainly is tops for realism, but absorbs water and tends to sink and is more difficult to cast. Foam, a great material used in some of the more innovative patterns, is light, easily shaped and has unexcelled buoyancy and durability.

Most of the traditional patterns have a natural profile (i.e. Deerhair Mouse/Shrew and Fur Lemming) for realism that also makes them easier to cast and creates a good wake and splash. Sculpin and popper heads, foam backs and other nonconventional features may make the fly not as lifelike and/or easy to cast, but they add buoyancy and fish appeal with more surface wake, splash and quiver, so that many of these newer patterns, surprisingly, fish just as well, if not better, under most conditions than the old standards most folks are familiar with.

TOP PATTERNS FOR MOUSING IN KAMCHATKA

The following are the most widely used big top water patterns for rainbow trout in Kamchatka, for reasons noted. They are available in nearly all the shops that cater to Alaska and Russia anglers. Keep in mind that you can select (or tie) many other similar patterns that will perform just as well, based on some of the criteria mentioned. Generally, rodent imitations are tied on a size 2 to 4 specialty hook.

Deerhair Mouse/Rat The original bass/pike mouse pattern (Whitlock's MouseRat being one of the most famous, in existence since 1965) of tightly wound, trimmed/untrimmed deer hair on a stinger hook now comes in many variations, all of them deadly on rainbow trout. I prefer the smaller, simpler versions that simulate a mouse/shrew (leather tail and ears, bead eyes and tiny whiskers optional!). Other common variations have long, bushy fur/deer hair tails or untrimmed deer hair bodies. This fly can't be beat for its performance. It's a great floater, easy to cast, unmatched for durability and the trout can't leave it alone. It comes in natural brown and black, both great colors for Kamchatka rainbows. (Many versions come with a weed guard on the hook, which is unnecessary for most of the trout fishing in Kamchatka and should be removed.)

Morrish Mouse This is one of the more innovative and successful mouse patterns in recent years (since 2001), that incorporates foam into the body for superior performance (great buoyancy and easy to cast). Compared to more traditional mouse patterns in the fly shop, this creation from famed fly tier Ken Morrish may at first not impress you for its lack of lifelike frills, but out on the streams of Kamchatka, it consistently fishes among the best, in nearly all conditions. Don't go to Russia without some of these in your fly box!

Fur Mouse/Lemming Another common, long-used rodent pattern for big Alaska/Russia trout, this is basically the fur version of the MouseRat and has unexcelled realism when tied with brown, gray or black rabbit fur. Unlike deer hair, fur absorbs water, and the performance (floating and casting) of this fly is markedly different than that of spun hair creations, and so it is usually fished as a drowning mouse or rat, with good results. Variations include deer hair sculpin heads with long tails and articulated bodies. Many have foam incorporated into them, adding buoyancy. Another essential fly to include in your mousing arsenal.

Mercer's Lemming This is another extremely popular and productive pattern used all over Alaska and Kamchatka, created by the Fly Shop's Mike Mercer over a decade ago. Somewhat different from other traditional mouse flies, Mercer's Lemming combines a bushy fur (rabbit and possum) and Deerhair body with a foam popper head that adds flotation and splash. This fly really rousts the big ones! Another essential pattern for the serious Russia trout mouser.

Babine Foam Back This is one of the best, newer "non-traditional" top water flies seeing more use in Alaska and Russia. Actually created as a top water silver salmon pattern, this foam backed, highly buoyant, takeoff from the foam 'Wog is tied by Rainy Flies and features a long tail of rabbit fur mixed with some rubber legs. It has great action, and the rainbows just go nuts over it, though you do get some tail strikes. (The tail can be shortened somewhat to compensate.) Best colors are natural brown, though, like the 'Wog, you can fish bright colors for both trout and fall silver salmon. You can have a lot of fun with this one, as it really gets the trout worked up, and they annihilate it with great vigor.

Bomber This classic Atlantic salmon/steelhead pattern, very similar to a small deer hair Mouse in design and profile, will take rainbows on the surface when fished the same way. Quite a few of the larger (#2-4 hook) and fatter variations of this fly (Bulkley Mouse, Waller Waker, Moose Turd, etc.) offered by the shops and catalogs will work great to simulate a plump shrew or small vole. Natural colors work best.

Popper Bass/pike and salmon/trout popper flies will also take big, surface marauding Russia rainbows. There are many styles to choose from these days, fashioned from wood, foam, fur and hair. I like the hard foam and wood poppers (if you can find them), festooned with fur/leather tails and rubber legs. They fish best late in the evening, early in the morning or on cloudy days and are lots of fun, bringing savage surface strikes. Be sure to bring a few on your trip to Russia.

Wog A fast becoming classic Northwest top water Deerhair creation, the Pollywog was originally designed for Pacific Northwest silver salmon and steelhead trout. It has received quite a bit of subsequent notoriety here in Alaska, with spin-off variations like the Foam 'Wog, which is a great trout fly, also seeing a lot of use. For big rainbows, use either a natural color in the Deerhair versions or darker colors in the foam back 'Wogs. Another great fly for spectacular surface strikes.

GEARING UP FOR FLY FISHING KAMCHATKA

Breaking camp on the lower Pymta River, southern Kamchatka. Note the mountain of personal gear and fishing equipment.

Guides/outfitters in Alaska and Kamchatka are frequently asked by prospective clients about the amount of fishing gear they will need to bring to successfully pursue the variety of species available in the timeframe they have in mind, with the common misconception being that a mountain of rods and reels is required, making a fishing vacation to these regions a daunting and expensive proposition. The truth is you can get by quite nicely with a minimum of two to three rods and a couple of reels and perhaps a spare spool or two for some different lines.

Just about every angler who visits Kamchatka goes there primarily for the superlative rainbow trout fishing, so you should definitely bring a good trout stick, which for most of the waters would be a five or six weight. You'll want a spare rod, of course, so take your favorite seven along, to double as a bigger stick for the more challenging trout water you'll encounter and to serve as a suitable, if somewhat sporty rod for Kamchatka's silver, chum, and red salmon. If you're fishing early in the season and wanting to tussle with the king of salmon, you'll need to bring something much stouter, say a nine or even a ten weight. (Same goes if you are planning on an expedition to Kamchatka's northernmost waters for fearsome giant pike.) Going after grayling and cherry and pink salmon would fit in the category of light tackle angling in Kamchatka, providing the most fun on smaller rods. If you had something like a 4 or 5-weight, that would be a good compromise for all three species. If not, these fish would still be a kick on your trout rod, albeit not as challenging.

Multi-piece rods, if you have them, are the way to go, as they are easily stowed as carry-ons when flying (saving baggage fees) and don't seem get in the way when traveling in boats and rafts like longer rods do. (And as a safety rule, it's a good idea never to have more than one rod set up when fishing out of a boat or raft; too many rods are lost overboard or damaged that way.) If you are travelling to Russia from far away, with connecting flights, you might want to pack all your fishing gear— rods, reels, lines and flies—into your carry-on, in the event that some of your luggage gets misrouted or lost, suitable substitutes for your personal gear could always be rounded up by your hosts, but nothing can take the place of your prized rods and reels.

You'll probably need at least two reels, though you certainly could get by in a pinch with just one and some spare spools. The two main types of lines you'll need to bring are floaters and sink tips. For trout, you should take your favorite reel and a spare spool, for both types of line. (Unless you opt for an interchangeable tip line system, which frees you from the burden of carrying spare spools.) Now, if you want to fish salmon, a larger reel, say something in the 7 or 8- weight range (to go with the larger backup rod you are bringing) and perhaps a spare spool (if you don't have interchangeable tips) would be the way to go. For the smaller species, you could bring another 4 or 5-weight reel or use your trout reel with a different spool. For king and pike fishing, you'll want a special heavy duty reel with spare spool and appropriate line

If you're fishing with a guide or staying at a lodge, you should naturally follow all their recommendations for fishing equipment and flies (and personal gear as well). Keep in mind that many conveniences you may take for granted in your country are not yet available in Russia, one of them being large department stores with ample sporting goods sections. (There are scant shops in Kamchatka that sell any fly fishing gear, and they are located in Petropavlovsk.) So you must come fully prepared with all the necessary gear, including enough flies, split shot, leaders, etc. to get you through all the inevitable break-offs, lost fish and wear and tear that occurs during a weeklong fishing safari on some of the wildest rivers on the planet. (Check out the trip planning section for tips on preparing your personal gear for Kamchatka.)

CATCH AND RELEASE TECHNIQUES FOR KAMCHATKA

Kamchatka is still in its infancy as far as ethics for sport fishing are concerned, with most Russians just barely aware of the importance of minimizing their personal impact on the fragile fishery resources. Hopefully, as things progress, people will change their attitudes and behavior. As a visiting angler, you can do your part, of course, to set an example and possibly even educate others on some of the principles and techniques of low impact sport fishing. The following are some of the main guidelines for "catch and release" fishing.

Gear

- Use strong enough tippet material to bring your catch in quickly. If you should accidentally hook a much larger fish than you are geared for, break it off as soon as possible.

- Use the right size hook for the species you are targeting. Overly large hooks can damage mouthparts, eyes, and gills. Likewise, hooks that are too small can hurt fish, as they may be taken deeply, damaging gills and gullet and even causing death.

- Microbarb and barbless hooks allow for quicker, less painless and less damaging releases of fish. Buy or tie flies with these kinds of hooks or pinch the barbs down on regular hooks with a set of pliers.

Landing Your Catch

- Land your fish as carefully and quickly as possible.
- Avoid removing any fish that you intend to release from the water.
- Do not let fish flop in shallow water, over rocks, or up on to the riverbank
- If you use a net, make sure it is of soft or knotless mesh (rubber).

Handling Your Catch

- Keep the fish in shallow, calm water. Cradle it gently with both hands, one under its belly, one under the tail wrist.
- Use wet cloth gloves or wet your hands before handling the fish. Keep your fingers out of and away from the gills and never squeeze the fish.
- If someone is taking your photo with the fish, cradle it in both hands and lift it up just enough to get a good shot of its size.

Removing the Hook

- Using pliers or forceps, remove the hook quickly and gently by backing it out, keeping the fish in the water.
- Use forceps to remove hooks from trout, charr or grayling; for salmon use a stout pair of fishermen's pliers.
- If the fish is hooked deeply, do not attempt to pull or wrest the hook free; instead, cut the line near the hook.

Reviving & Releasing Your Catch

- Be aware of the condition of your catch before releasing! Some fish, particularly rainbow trout, can fight so hard, they totally exhaust themselves and need sufficient time to recuperate and gain strength before they can swim in the strong river currents.
- Pick a calm back eddy, slough or shallow pool to release your fish in.

- If the fish is totally exhausted, gently move it back and forth in the shallows until its gills are working properly and it maintains its balance.

- When the fish recovers and attempts to swim out of your hands, let it go.

- Fish that are large or have fought very hard or gotten injured may take some time to revive.

- Any fish bleeding heavily or that does not show signs of reviving after a few minutes should be kept.

KAMCHATKA TRIP PLANNING

OVERVIEW: PLANNING YOUR TRIP TO KAMCHATKA

Compared to almost any other tourist destination, Kamchatka is a true frontier, with barely developed infrastructure, and a language and culture unlike any that most folks are used to. To have a safe and enjoyable vacation there will require significantly more planning and preparation than for most anywhere else. To begin with, of course, for any other than citizens of the Russian Federation, Kamchatka is a foreign country, with strict requirements for foreign visitors that include necessary documentation (passports, invitations, visas, custom declarations, etc.), inspection at entry and registration upon arrival. (Check section on requirements for foreign visitors.)

Unless you have familiarity with the Russian language and their way of doing things and possess the time and gumption to take on the daunting prospect of a do-it-yourself adventure in a strange land that is quite often not very accommodating to foreigners, we strongly urge you to seek the services of a reputable Kamchatka tourism company or outfitter. (In any event, you will need a sponsor host in the way of a tourist company, hotel, or individual to get your entry Visa.) These organizations have the experience, connections, and wherewithal to take care of all the essential arrangements and preparations necessary for your adventure once you arrive in Kamchatka. Most are operated as joint ventures with European or American partners, to utilize the considerable marketing expertise, reputation and other advantages of long established, free market enterprises. No matter whom you book with or what kind of tour you sign up for, however, your hosts and guides in the field will undoubtedly be local Russians, who know the country like no other and want nothing more than to give you the adventure of a lifetime.

There are a surprising number of options available for guided adventure recreation on the peninsula, given how new tourism is in Kamchatka. Depending on what your main interests are and how much time and money you want to spend, you can arrange for "soft," "hard," or even extreme adventures that focus solely on your favorite activity or combine it with another (or even two or more) for more interest and variety. And generally, most of the more established tour companies can make all the arrangements for you, no matter what kind of hybrid adventure you come up with.

Because of all there is to see and do in Kamchatka, and the expense and time involved in getting there, most folks, especially Europeans, will plan vacations there of two weeks or more duration. (Americans are usually more limited in their time and travel options, and so most opt for one-week trips.) More time obviously allows you to see and do more things in Kamchatka, but just as important, it creates a more leisurely pace and flexibility in the itinerary, so there's less stress. However much time you decide on for your Kamchatka adventure, it's a good idea to plan and make arrangements well ahead, by late fall or early winter prior to your target date at the latest.

GETTING THERE AND GETTING AROUND

Aside from the few big cruise ships that visit Petropavlovsk in summer, the only legitimate international tourist access to the peninsula comes through the airport complex at Yelizovo. It receives regular direct flight service from surrounding countries in the Far East (Japan, China, and Korea) and the rest of Russia. There are two terminals, one international, and the other domestic. Moscow, Vladivostok, Khabarovsk and other major hubs are linked by flights from regional carriers almost daily. There are charters and seasonal service as well. (At the time this book went to press, there were still direct weekly flights from Anchorage, Alaska during summer.) International travelers can usually reach Kamchatka year-round by connecting through Moscow, Seoul, Beijing, or Tokyo.

Once you get to Yelizovo and nearby Petropavlovsk, your options for surface transportation are limited mostly to the public bus system and taxis. The metropolitan area is serviced rather effectively by a fleet of buses that run regularly, every 10 minutes or less, down the main thoroughfares. Fare is very reasonable, something like the equivalent of 50 cents. (Be sure to carry some roubles with you for bus fare!) Taxis seem everywhere as well and can be hailed along busy streets or summoned by phone. (Don't be too shy to ask clerks in the shops, restaurants or hotels you are patronizing to call you a taxi; it is called by the same name in both languages.) Their fares are very modest compared to the States, and you can go quite a ways for the equivalent of five dollars.

There are also public buses that run regularly along the entire road system, connecting all the major hubs. (You will notice all along the roads strategically placed bus stops with crude shelters.) From the station in downtown Petropavlovsk or Yelizovo, it is possible to ride across Kamchatka to the west coast at Ust-Bolsheretsk or north to Milkovo and Esso and even Ust-Kamchatsk at the mouth of the Kamchatka River. The fares vary but are very affordable. Tickets usually must be purchased (only with roubles!) in advance at the ticket offices located at every bus station. Don't forget to tip the driver if you have more than one bag.

Currently, there are scant car rentals available in Kamchatka, but you can charter buses, vans, SUVs and even off-road vehicles from private organizations in the major hubs like PK, Yelizovo, Milkovo, etc. Prices vary widely depending on the vehicle and length of the charter, but usually include the services of a driver. (Be sure to make arrangements for these charters well in advance and confirm your reservation before you arrive in Kamchatka.)

Practically all major hubs and villages lying off the road system are linked by regular scheduled flight service from Petropavlovsk-Yelizovo (fixed wing or helicopter). As with other public transportation, fares are very reasonable. Information on schedules and prices can be had at most local airports or the domestic terminal at Yelizovo.

As far as hitchhiking goes, most Russians will discourage you from trying it. But people will stop to give you rides along the road, a lot more than they do in the U.S. and other countries, so it's certainly an option to consider if you find yourself stranded somewhere with no bus or taxi available. Obviously, it helps to know a little Russian so you can communicate to the driver where you are going!

FLY FISHING OPTIONS

Zenzhur Lodge on the Zhupanova River in southern Kamchatka is an example of the more upscale accommodations for fly-out sport fishing on the peninsula (Fly Shop photo)

Kamchatka's wealth of unexploited productive rivers with near-perfect conditions is a paradise of opportunity for adventurous fly fishermen. How you choose to enjoy this bounty of great fishing depends on your taste for adventure, time and budget. At the top of the list for those wanting the ultimate fly angling experiences are the remote lodges/camps and float fishing expeditions on the wildest rivers, far removed from Kamchatka's roads and people. These entail daily guided fishing (from jet boats or rafts) comfortable, but rustic accommodations and transportation to and from the river, usually by helicopter. The rafting trips offer access to miles and miles of unfished headwaters; the fixed camps, while nothing like some of their counterparts across the Pacific, provide a much greater modicum of creature comforts for guests. There are hybrid programs that combine the best of both with stays at small cabins or semi-permanent tent camps while on float safari. Prices for Kamchatka's remote lodges, camps and float fishing expeditions vary widely depending on river location, accommodations, services provided, etc., but expect to pay anywhere from $500 to $900 U.S. or more per day per person for the more established, reputable operations.

Fishing less remote streams that can be accessed from Kamchatka's road system is a hugely popular option which offers great flexibility and economy. You can hire local guides and camp and fish or take short float trips by raft along popular roadside streams. (Combined with visits to nearby volcanoes and hot spring sites, if you like.) Or stay at established fish camps on some of Kamchatka's most popular rivers. And if you are hankering for more adventure, there are outfitters/guides that use off-road vehicles, boats and even horses from points along the road system to access more remote streams, where you can camp and fish (and float) without seeing other anglers. Prices vary with the kind of services, accommodations, and location, but these options that don't involve expensive helicopter transport generally run much less than fly-in operations, anywhere from 200 to 500 U.S. dollars per person per day of fishing. Just about every tour operator in Kamchatka offers these lower priced trips, with a variety of options that can be arranged to suit your desires, time constraints and budget.

At present, Kamchatka lacks the necessary infrastructure and services to facilitate do-it- yourself fly fishing adventures by anyone lacking connections and a working knowledge of the language and how things are done over there. (There are of yet virtually no car or gear rentals available, for instance.) It will no doubt take years before anything close to what we have here in Alaska for unguided ventures is available in Kamchatka. For this reason (and many others), it makes total sense for anglers to seek the services of established guides/outfitters to make their great Kamchatka adventure a reality.

CHOOSING A REPUTABLE GUIDE/OUTFITTER OR LODGE IN KAMCHATKA

Enlisting the services of an experienced and reputable tourist business when vacationing in a foreign land is more than just a good idea, it's almost essential for your safety and enjoyment. This is especially true for fly fishermen wishing to sample some of the legendary waters of the last frontier of cold water stream angling. There is too much at stake and your time is too valuable to try and take on a fishing trip to Kamchatka on your own. Get a good guide who knows the country, the conditions and where the best fishing is so you can concentrate on having a great time.

But how does one go about selecting a good guide/outfitter or other tourist organization in a foreign land still relatively new to international travel? The horror stories abound of the "Russia Trip from Hell" where tourists get soaked or stranded by shady, inexperienced or ill-prepared operators whose prime motive, it seems, is to make some quick roubles from trusting and gullible visitors. In their rush to adapt and make good in a totally new economic system, some otherwise decent and well-meaning

Russian entrepreneurs get in over their heads with start-up tourist businesses, lacking the experience and/or wherewithal to deliver the kinds of service and accommodations that modern world travelers have come to expect. It is important, therefore, to select businesses with a proven track record and good references.

Nowadays, the internet will probably be your first and main source of information for selecting appropriate Kamchatka tour businesses for the vacation you have in mind. Accessing search engines, paid ads, forums, magazine articles, travel blogs, social media networks like Facebook and Twitter and travel rating sites like Trip Advisor, Expedia, Virtual Tourist, etc. should provide plenty of leads and other useful information to narrow down your search. Print publications (like this book—see the tourist businesses and individuals cited in the Acknowledgements), sports shows, television and radio broadcasts, travel and sports groups (like fly fishing clubs), fly shops, and word-of-mouth are some of the other avenues to come by the necessary information to select a reputable service for your Kamchatka vacation. Don't forget to allow enough time for your research and interaction with the various organizations you'll be contacting. Do most of your homework the fall and winter before your vacation time so you can book reservations well ahead of the start of the busy season in Kamchatka. (And also factor in the time necessary to apply for a passport, if you don't already have one.)

And finally, a word about appropriate expectations and attitude for expeditions into a foreign frontier. Having seen my share of otherwise worldly travelers come unglued when things don't go the way they expect in the travel itinerary, for a variety of reasons associated with doing trips in Russia, I would caution prospective visitors to keep in mind at all times that a trip to the Kamchatka Peninsula, especially its hinterlands, is high adventure. There are not too many places left in the world where you can have such a raw and undistilled experience of wild nature, native cultures, and magnificent landscapes. Tourism and the associated infrastructure is in its infancy in Kamchatka, along with a market economy, so you can't expect the same kind of service and treatment you would find in more established destinations, like those in Europe and the Americas. Keep an open mind, a friendly, positive attitude and a willingness to make the best of whatever the situation, and you'll have a wonderful time and make some great friends in Kamchatka.

ACCESSING WATERS

The versatile and powerful MI-8 helicopter remains the workhorse of Russia's remote air transport fleet

Getting to the best fishing is the crux of the challenge for fly anglers in Kamchatka. The peninsula's limited road network provides a surprising amount of access to many good streams and rivers. Streams like the Bystraya, Plotnikova, Paratunka, Avacha and dozens of tributaries of the fabulous Kamchatka River can all be reached from the road for bank fishing and launching of watercraft. And there are literally hundreds of rough roads and trails leading into the taiga to waters more off the beaten path. Just about every Russian of modest means is the proud owner of some kind of off-road capable vehicle, whether it be an all-wheel-drive, diesel Mitsubishi van, Toyota Road Runner, Land Cruiser or even an old, beat-up, green Soviet era, Russian style "jeep," still in use all over the country. They will not hesitate to take these rigs, loaded to the max, into country so rugged and trails so marginal, it would make an American off-roader shudder. The Ruskies also use all manner of power boats and inflatable rafts to extend their access wherever they can, and some even wrangle horses to carry gear and people far into the wilderness for good fishing.

Public taxis are available for transportation within the greater Petropavlovsk-Yelizovo area. And a fairly reliable public transportation system provides regular scheduled bus service along the entire road system, with a few companies even that will rent out small vans, buses, and SUVs for groups. For serious cross-country expeditions, there are large 6-wheel drive trucks, mostly old military rigs (called "vakhtovka") , and giant track vehicles for hire that can ferry a sizeable group with gear across big rivers, breach impossible snow fields and plow through the muckiest swamps. Some of the fancier of these machines, with drivers, rent out for considerable fees per day.

A. Bichenko

But to reach the most remote and unexploited streams, those in the west-central region and beyond, will most certainly involve air transport. Currently, there are no fixed-wing air taxi services available in Kamchatka, only helicopters. The twin turbine MI-8, the most versatile and widely used helicopter in the world, is the workhorse of the charter fleet throughout the peninsula, providing safe, reliable remote access for all sectors of the tourist trade, mineral exploration and scientific research, in addition to linking the most isolated villages with the main hubs of the province. These amazing craft are capable of carrying remarkable payloads and can land in the most otherwise inaccessible places, and so open up many opportunities for exploration of rivers and streams that would not be possible by any other means, similar to the access afforded by small, fixed-wing planes equipped with floats or big "tundra" tires throughout Alaska. The helicopters used for tourists are all well maintained and crewed by extremely competent pilots and flight engineers, despite what you may have heard or be inclined to believe. The only downside to using the MI-8 helicopter transport is the cost, as rates have risen sharply due to changes in the economy and other factors in recent years (from $3300/hour and up, at time of press). As in Alaska, you are charged for the backhaul time for any drop-off or pick-up flight.

Most of Kamchatka's charter helicopters operate out of the Petropavlovsk-Yelizovo area and other regional hubs like Esso, Milkovo, and Palana. Occasionally they are available for tourists in other locations like Tigil, Klyuchi, Sobolevo, etc., when deployed for major projects of construction, mineral exploration, and scientific research. (Keep in mind that most helicopter companies only take payment in roubles and that the exchange rate for U.S. dollars has varied quite a bit in recent years.)

Standard procedure when accessing remote waters by helicopters is for the pilots to fly up the river a ways to scout for any potential hazards like log jams, sweepers, waterfalls and high water. This becomes most important on seldom visited or unexplored streams, and for this, the expedition leaders are allowed access to the cockpit for a better view of the river. No rivers are attempted, of course, without getting reliable firsthand information on current conditions from local pilots, guides, hunters, trappers, etc. to determine suitability for river running and fishing, and no reputable organization would consider any river that presented too much of a risk or challenge or lacked the potential for a great float fishing trip. Before the pilots leave you with a mountain of gear on some gravel bar far removed from civilization, rest assured that they have discussed the possible pickup points with the trip leaders, who have marked them on their maps, and will faithfully locate them by GPS and reconfirm with a call by satellite phone.

OTHER ACTIVITIES

Tours that feature interaction with Kamchatka's indigenous culture are enriching, interesting and increasingly popular (Irina Kruglykova photo).

Kamchatka offers many world-class adventure recreation opportunities besides fly fishing. Many of these activities are done at the same time and even in the same areas as fly fishing, and so lend themselves well to hybrid adventures that combine some fishing with wildlife viewing, volcano trekking, hot springs visits, etc. Most of the larger tour companies in Kamchatka offer a variety of popular tourist activities in their programs, things like wildlife viewing, volcano trekking, visits to hot springs and rafting/fishing. If you are interested in doing some of these activities in addition to sampling Kamchatka's great fly fishing, be sure to ask the tour company you are negotiating with what they have to offer in the way of special combination tours. Here is a brief description of the most popular tourist activities besides angling that are done during the warm weather season in Kamchatka.

Whitewater Rafting: Kamchatka's abundant swift, rocky rivers lend themselves well to whitewater rafting adventures. Most tour companies offer rafting options in addition to fly fishing and other popular activities and will be happy to accommodate your desire to include some whitewater thrills in your vacation experience. Everything from half day to full week rafting trips is available, on rivers along the road system and those more remote.

Wildlife Viewing: Kamchatka is world famous for its abundant wildlife, with many unique opportunities for close-up viewing of bears, eagles, waterfowl and marine mammals. A fly fishing adventure usually puts you right in the heart of the action, as all kinds of wildlife vie for some of the abundant salmon that fill the rivers. But you may want to visit special areas like Kurile Lake or other sanctuaries for concentrated viewing opportunities and/or to see certain species. Most of the tour companies that offer fly fishing will also have some wildlife viewing options, and the two activities are easily combined.

Volcano Trekking: With numerous active volcanoes, many within easy reach of the Petropavlovsk-Yelizovo area, hiking up into craters to witness the various associated phenomena like steam vents, fumaroles, lava flows, mud pots, calderas, etc. is extremely popular. Everything from half day to multi-day treks is available, often in combination with visits to nearby hot springs. Most of these treks are not technical, though they require a certain level of fitness. Almost every tour company in Kamchatka offers some kind of volcano trekking experience.

Geysers and Hot Springs: No one should leave Kamchatka without visiting and soaking in one of its many therapeutic thermal pools which are scattered along its volcanic mountains, some within sight of the Petropavlovsk-Yelizovo area. And the incomparable Valley of the Geysers in Kronotsky Preserve is but a short helicopter flight away from Kamchatka's largest city. Be sure to let your guide/outfitter know you want to include a visit to a hot spring in your fly fishing adventure. (See our hot springs recommendations in the regional sections of the book.)

Horseback Riding: Growing in popularity every year are tours that include some horseback riding, exploring Kamchatka's picturesque backcountry, visiting lakes, rivers, hot springs, native villages, etc. Presently these options are based mainly out of Bystrinsky Park (Esso), the central valley (Milkovo area) and the Avacha River valley (Yelizovo). Everything from half day rides to multiday pack trips is available, including horseback fishing adventures.

Sport Hunting: Kamchatka is world famous for its hunting opportunities and attracts elite trophy seekers who come in fall to bag big bear, moose, and mountain sheep. Many hunters also fish while on safari, as many of the camps are located along productive streams and lakes. If you come to Kamchatka to hunt, but also have a secret passion for fly fishing, be sure to inquire with your outfitter about a combination hunting/fishing expedition.

Cultural Tours: Many Kamchatka tour companies offer programs built around interaction with Kamchatka's indigenous culture- the Evens, Itelmen, and Koryaks. On these tours, you visit native villages, ethnographic museums, and reindeer herding camps, attend festivals and folk ensemble performances, see and buy native art, sample traditional dishes, etc. Everything from half day to week long or more cultural tours are available from local operators.

Marine Excursions: For tourists wanting to see Kamchatka's impressive, rugged coastline and view some of its abundant seabirds and marine mammals, there are sailboat, yacht and kayak tours of lovely Avacha Bay and surrounding environs. Crab pots and fishing rods are available (for crabs, urchins, halibut, cod and rockfish), with tasty seafood soup made from your catch always an option. Enjoy fantastic views of coastal volcanoes and visit seabird rookeries, sea lion haul outs, secluded beaches and other attractions. Whale watching, special dive tours and even surfing are also available in the clear Pacific waters.

Mountaineering/Rock Climbing: Kamchatka's abundant volcanic peaks attract climbers from the world over to pit their skills against her mountains. Accommodating all levels of technical skill, rock and mountain climbing tours offered by local companies are led by the most experienced Russian mountain guides. They offer everything from day trips to local peaks to multi-day assaults of Kamchatka's most forbidding mountains, like those of Kluchevsky Park.

Hiking/Backpacking: a very popular option, especially among European tourists, is the hiking tour. Kamchatka has literally thousands of miles of trails leading off into the mountains and taiga, to take you to special places like hot springs, volcanoes, lakes and waterfalls. Many of the best of these are located in parks, preserves, and other protected areas. Every tourist company in Kamchatka offers hiking and backpacking tour options of some kind. A great way to see the country and very economical, too.

Ecotours: Local companies offer programs specifically focused on Kamchatka's superlative nature parks and preserves, with interpretive tours to acquaint visitors with the ecology of the region and the major features that have been set aside for protection. Many of these trips use a combination of hiking, off-road vehicles, rafts, helicopters and even horses for access to and within the special protected areas. Special programs also include ethnographic tourism.

Scientific Tours: For folks with a professional or intense personal interest in earth science and biology, Kamchatka provides a living laboratory for study of the various processes at work shaping the earth and affecting ecosystems. Likewise, the peninsula offers unparalleled opportunities for hands-on archeological and ethnographic research. Many organizations, government and private, conduct ongoing research programs throughout the peninsula, some offering cooperative participation from scientists and other interested persons abroad. Information on available opportunities can be had through professional scientific organizations, government agencies and private entities that support research (WWF).

WINTER RECREATION

A. Bichenko

Kamchatka is a year-round adventure recreation destination, with numerous winter sports and other activities available during the long "off-season" (November to May). Alpine and Nordic skiing, snowboarding, dog mushing, sledding, snowmobiling, snowshoeing and skating come instantly to mind as some of the most popular activities available in abundance during Kamchatka's long snowy winters. But many of the things folks enjoy during the warmer months can also be done, in somewhat different form perhaps, during the rest of the year. There is fabulous ice fishing to be had on Kamchatka's many frozen rivers and lakes, for a variety of feisty species. And the peninsula's many wild animals are easily detected and observed in a stark and snowy landscape with fewer, more concentrated food sources (the late spawning salmon of Kurile Lake and the gathering of eagles it attracts, for instance). Visits to native villages this time of year can provide unique opportunities to witness and take part in traditional winter activities like reindeer/dog sledding, fur trapping, seasonal festivals, dance performances, races, etc. And at the end of a day spent in the brisk outdoors, Kamchatka's numerous hot springs take on special appeal to visitors seeking to warm their bones with a relaxing soak.

Most of the major local tour companies stay busy during winter offering all manner of activities for visitors, no matter what their persuasion or budget. For the super adventurous, there is heli-skiing and Heli-snowboarding down steep volcanic slopes; for the less bold, local ski-runs, ski bases and ski resorts catering to a wide range of skill levels and activities. (Gear rentals are available, as well.) Custom tours that combine a wide range of winter activities— from skiing to dog sledding to visiting native reindeer herding camps— can be arranged through these local operators. And for those who like competitive winter sports, Kamchatka hosts annual international winter sporting events like dog sled races, biathlons, and ski marathons.

TIMING-WHEN TO GO

With proper preparation and mindset, Kamchatka, like Alaska, can be fly fished successfully throughout the open water season. If you have certain species in mind, however, your timeframe may be more limited (see chart below). While most folks elect to visit during the months of summer and early fall (June into September) because of the pleasant temperatures and generally more stable conditions that allow for maximum enjoyment of warm weather activities , the "shoulder seasons" can be just as productive, though potentially more challenging. And Kamchatka in the winter is, of course, a whole 'nother story, a bracing but beautiful wonderland of unique and exciting outdoor adventure. Here's a brief rundown on Kamchatka's seasons and their advantages and disadvantages for fly fishermen and other tourists:

Spring: April to mid-June

Advantages: Trout (and charr) are concentrated around stream mouths, lake outlets and in deep pools. They are ravenously hungry and attack just about any enticement. Little competition for visitor services. Almost no biting bugs.

Disadvantages: Vagary weather, often raw and tough stream conditions, with cold, high water and turbidity from snow melt. Salmon runs are spotty until June. Usually too early for many other warm weather activities. Access to Kamchatka from U.S. limited and expensive.

Summer: Mid-June to mid-September

Advantages: Salmon are running up rivers. Trout and charr are positioning themselves for the big feed and easily provoked. Stream conditions become stable. Air and water temperatures reach their peak. There are abundant insect hatches. Lots of other fun activities-river rafting, volcano trekking, wildlife tours, etc., are available.

Disadvantages: Biting bugs reach their peak; long stretches of rainy weather possible in August. Keen competition for visitor services.

Fall: Mid-September to mid-October

Advantages: Trout and charr are in peak condition and hungry. Beautiful fall colors and Indian summer weather predominates. Bugs disappear. Less competition for visitor services.

Disadvantages: Salmon runs wane; frosty nights; fall storms possible. Insect hatches fall off. Snow line creeps down toward end of season.

Winter: November-April

Advantages: Increased access (you can walk on water); best rates and almost no competition for visitor services; no bugs; your catch is instantly frozen; variety of exciting winter activities available

Disadvantages: Cold, snowy weather; thick ice covers almost all waters; reduced variety of species available and fish tend to be sluggish and not easily enticed; tough camping; more limited and expensive access to Kamchatka from U.S.

Kamchatka Freshwater Run Timing

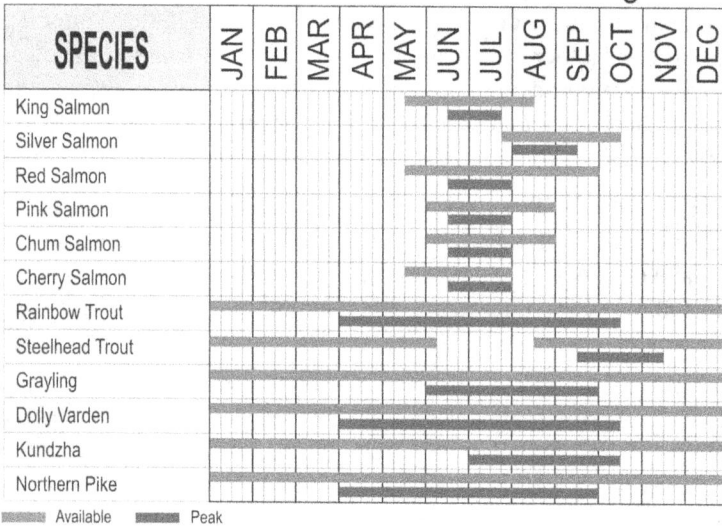

SPECIES	JAN	FEB	MAR	APR	MAY	JUN	JUL	AUG	SEP	OCT	NOV	DEC
King Salmon												
Silver Salmon												
Red Salmon												
Pink Salmon												
Chum Salmon												
Cherry Salmon												
Rainbow Trout												
Steelhead Trout												
Grayling												
Dolly Varden												
Kundzha												
Northern Pike												

▬▬▬ Available   ▬▬▬ Peak

Time periods shown in blue are for bright fish in the case of salmon entering rivers, or for general availability for resident species. Peak sportfishing periods are shown in red. Run timing can vary with location. Check with your outfitter/guide or other local contacts for run timing specifics for waters and dates you intend to fish.

KAMCHATKA ACCOMMODATIONS

Visitors arriving at a comfortable B & B homestay in Esso

Travelers should not come to Kamchatka expecting the same level of accommodations they are accustomed to at other more developed destinations. There are few establishments in this part of Russia that could even begin to qualify for what passes for a luxury stay in other parts of the world. But if you set your sights on getting a clean, if somewhat Spartan room at reasonable rates, where you can sort your gear, dry your clothes, take a hot shower and collapse in a comfortable bed to get a good night's sleep for your next day's adventure, then you won't be disappointed. Actually, things have improved quite a bit in recent years, with noticeable upgrades in quality and availability of lodging throughout Kamchatka, not just in the Petropavlovsk-Yelizovo metropolitan area. As in most of Russia these days, you will find three basic types of accommodations available in Kamchatka: hotels, resorts, and homestays (the Russian equivalent of B & B's).

Hotels There are usually several (or at least one) hotel buildings in most of the larger settlements and major hubs. They have come a long way from the grim Soviet-era, state-run establishments, where hot water and decent customer service were precious commodities, and nowadays, most of Kamchatka's hotels have modern décor, rooms with good beds and showers and personable staff. The bigger and fancier ones will usually have a restaurant or café where meals are served and many offer room and laundry service. Prices vary depending on time of year but expect to pay from $75–150/night for a no-frills double in most locations.

Resorts Certain establishments located in special areas like Paratunka, Malki, Esso, etc., have upgraded accommodations and services to cater to more exclusive clientele. In addition to fancier rooms and better food, they offer things like heated outdoor pools, spas, gaming rooms, discos, etc., in true resort style. Prices vary widely, from around $150 to $300 or more a night for a room.

Homestays In Russia, the equivalent of the Bed and Breakfast facility is the "homestay." This is usually a spare bedroom rented in someone's home but can be a separate dwelling like a small cabin or guest house. Meals are included, as is the use of the banya (sauna) and any other simple features on site. In many of the smaller villages, the homestay is the only accommodation available, and it affords an excellent opportunity to get to know the locals and experience true Russian hospitality (your hosts will never let you go hungry). Most of the better homestays become well known and are not hard to find. Prices for these accommodations vary, from $30–75/night, with an additional fee for meals sometimes.

About Camping Other than in Kamchatka's parks and preserves, there are few, if any officially designated campgrounds. This does not mean that camping is not allowed nor done anywhere else. You can camp just about anywhere on public lands in the countryside, and many people do, as you'll see vehicles parked off the road by streams, hot springs, volcanoes, etc., with tents set up nearby, especially on weekends. Russians love to camp! Just use common sense and good manners, the same as you would anywhere else, especially around others. (Remember that you are guests in a foreign land!) Avoid crowded campsites, as they tend to encourage rowdiness and excessive drinking, and camp only out in the countryside, not within the limits of town, for the same reason. If you plan on camping within one of Kamchatka's parks or preserves, be sure to secure the necessary permits from the park office beforehand.

PERSONAL GEAR FOR KAMCHATKA

All the effort put into meticulous planning and arrangements for your vacation in Kamchatka will be for naught if you do not bring the proper personal gear necessary for your safety and enjoyment in the challenging conditions you will possibly encounter there. The trick here, as in outfitting for Alaska, is to dress in layers, making heavy use of synthetics or wool, for their superior wicking qualities and warmth. (For colder weather activities, outer layers of down provide additional lightweight warmth.) A breathable waterproof shell provides a final barrier against the elements.

Do not make the mistake of taking too much personal gear! You can easily outfit yourself for an expedition of 7 days duration (or more), with no more than 40 pounds of gear (this includes your fishing outfit). Your adventure within and travel to and from Kamchatka will go much smoother (and cheaper!) with streamlined baggage. A high quality, large waterproof gear bag with straps should be used to transport all your personal gear. Here's a sample list of recommended items for a summer float fishing trip:

- High quality, breathable chest waders, wading belt & boots
- Full-body, expedition-quality rain suit with hood
- Wool or synthetic knit cap
- Brimmed, water repellant fishing hat
- Fingerless wool, polypro or neoprene gloves
- Set (top & bottom) lightweight, synthetic long underwear
- Lightweight flannel, canvas or wool long-sleeve shirt
- 3 pairs t-shirts (synthetic or cotton)
- 4 pairs underwear briefs (cotton OK)
- Shorts or swim trunks (synthetic, wool or cotton)
- Medium-weight, synthetic pile pants
- 4 pairs light to medium-weight wool boot socks
- Leather or nylon hiking boots

- Spray bottle of insect repellant (30 % DEET)
- Small knife/lighter/waterproof matches
- Medium-weight synthetic fleece jacket
- Lightweight, water-resistant, down, wool or synthetic overcoat
- Digital camera with extra batteries and memory cards
- Polarized sunglasses
- Handkerchief
- Sunscreen lotion
- Small LED flashlight & extra batteries
- Pair field binoculars
- Synthetic sleeping bag (warm to 30 degrees F) with compression sack & sleeping pad
- Small, water-resistant pack for day-use items (can also be used for carry-on)
- Toiletries (washcloth, soap, toothbrush, razors, small towel, medications, etc.)
- 2 sets disposable ear plugs for noise suppression
- 1 quart Nalgene or similar plastic water bottle
- 1 roll toilet paper in small Ziploc bag

For your Time in and Around Town

Dress casual for all your activities in town. Even if you go out to eat at the fanciest restaurants in Petropavlovsk, conservative attire is appropriate, especially since you're a tourist and don't want to attract any undue attention to yourself. A decent pair of slacks or nice jeans, a cotton dress shirt and/or sweater and you should be good to go. Be aware that in Russia, most folks remove their hats when they enter homes and business establishments.

Forbidden Items

Do not, under any circumstances, try to bring the following items into Russia: Religious or government propaganda, pornography of any kind, illegal drugs, contraband, weapons of any kind or excessive amounts of cash. Also, do not pack glass bottles of any kind in your luggage, as they will probably break and spill their contents in your gear.

If you are booking with an established Kamchatka tour operator (highly recommended), they, of course, will provide you with their own detailed lists of recommended personal gear for the expedition. Follow their lists faithfully when doing your trip preparations, and don't hesitate to contact them if you cannot get a specific item of gear or have any questions. As the Russians say, "There is no such thing as bad weather, only bad gear (and not enough vodka)!"

OTHER IMPORTANT INFORMATION FOR VISITORS

Communications

Foreign travelers to Kamchatka can expect a fairly modern level of communications efficiency, though probably not comparable to what they are used to back home. International cell phone service is available through most networks by arrangement with your carrier or through purchase of special (SIMS) phone cards. Reception is quite good in and around larger towns like Petropavlovsk, Yelizovo, Milkovo and Esso, but spotty in some of the smaller villages and non-existent in the vast wilderness surrounding. Private landline phones in homes and businesses give much more reliable service, and you can use phone cards with them. (The international dialing code for Russia is 007; U.S. country code is 001; Kamchatka's area code is 415.) Internet is available in many of the hotels, restaurants, cafes, businesses and government offices in the major hubs. The postal service in Kamchatka and the rest of Russia is fairly reliable but notoriously slow. It can take weeks for a letter to reach a foreign country, so don't bother sending postcards to the folks back home.

Money

The only official way to do business in Russia is with roubles. You can trade dollars or Euros for them at just about any bank in Kamchatka. The exchange rate varies, from 31 to over 60 in recent years, due to economic unrest. Traveler's checks are nearly worthless in Kamchatka, and credit cards are accepted only at banks and major restaurants, hotels, businesses and supermarkets in the Petropavlovsk-Yelizovo area. You can use an ATM to get roubles at banks, certain businesses, and supermarkets in the Petropavlovsk-Yelizovo area, but beyond that, you will have to carry sufficient cash with you. (Don't forget to notify your bank before leaving the country that you plan on using an ATM in Russia; otherwise, they will put a hold on your card.)

Tips

Russia is still really just catching on to the idea of a market economy, so gratuities are not anywhere near as expected among staff people as they are in other parts of the world. So if you like the service somewhere at a restaurant or hotel, by all means, let them know it with a tip and some kind words ("Bolshoi Speciba!"). It will go a long way to improving customer service in that particular business and elsewhere in Kamchatka.

Food and Drink

Russian cuisine is wholesome and tasty and consists of hearty soups (borscht, shchi, ukha), special raviolis, spiced pork cutlets, baked and fried salmon and roast chicken and beef dishes. The main course is almost always preceded by tasty salads made from fresh local vegetables (cabbage, cucumbers, tomatoes, peas, beets and dill). Plates of dense Russian bread (light and dark) are always served with meals and a bottle of vodka (and caviar) seems to magically appear at every lunch and supper. Kamchatka's local beer, like the vodka, is pretty darn good (it's the water!), and cheap too and is available in bottles and by the liter in most of the grocery stores. Mass market regional and national brands of beer are sold in cans in most of the shops as well. The tap water throughout Kamchatka is perfectly OK to drink, as could be expected in a country with so much pristine surface water. If you like the bottled variety, be sure to get the big liters of great tasting water and carbonated mineral water from the springs at Malki, which are sold all over the peninsula. If you do tire of Russian food, there are some really good restaurants in the Petropavlovsk-Yelizovo area serving Oriental and Asian cuisine.

Electricity

Kamchatka's public utility electric network, like in the rest of Russia and Europe, produces 220 volts and 50 HZ. The standard outlets are two pin prong.

Time Zone

Before you call your buddies back in the States to brag and send pictures of those big rainbows you've been catching, remember that Kamchatka is hours behind (or ahead of) the rest of world. It is located nine hours ahead of Moscow and four hours behind (and a day later than) Alaska.

Insurance

Travel insurance is a great idea to protect your vacation investment and is available for a nominal fee from many companies these days (check with your travel agent or look on the internet— travelinsurance.com, worldnomads.com, insuremytrip.com, etc.) Check to see if your health insurance covers international travel and if not, you can purchase this additional coverage for a small fee. If you have any serious health issues, it might also be a good idea to get some medivac insurance, available for a relatively nominal sum. Should you find yourself in need of local care, the Russian hospitals and other medical facilities in Kamchatka are surprisingly good and, unlike the U.S., very affordable.

Markets & Shopping

Shopping in an open air market in Petropavlovsk

The large markets in Petropavlovsk and Yelizovo will amaze you with their amount of goods and sophistication, similar to supermarkets in the U.S. and Europe. In the smaller hubs and villages across the peninsula, there are still hundreds of "mom and pop" grocery stores, where you can get staples like local produce, meat, cheese, milk, bread, eggs, beer, etc. They are the only source of supplies once you leave the populous southeast Kamchatka area. Open air markets are a big deal in Russia, and nearly every town of size has one. Petropavlovsk and Yelizovo have large open-air markets located in their town centers, where you can easily spend a morning or afternoon cruising the stalls and marveling at all the things that can be had, everything from smoked fish to fur hats to flowers. (If you are interested in something, you can haggle the price with the vendor.)

Museums and Souvenirs

Kamchatka has some excellent museums and souvenir shops located in the major hubs like Petropavlovsk, Yelizovo, Esso and Milkovo. In them, you can learn quite a bit about Kamchatka's history, native culture, and art and even take a small piece of it home with you. Most tours in Kamchatka will schedule a visit to a museum and at least one souvenir shop in the itinerary, usually at the end of the trip. (Be sure to let your tour operator know you would like to see a museum and do some souvenir shopping .) Be aware that certain items, like ivory and animal fur, may create problems with Customs back at home, so choose your souvenirs carefully.

Permits & Licenses

If you intend to do activities in any of Kamchatka's nature parks & preserves, you will need special permits. These can be acquired through the offices of each individual park. (If you are part of a group hosted by one of the local tour companies, they will normally handle all these arrangements. Permits for the preserves are more exclusive and can be quite spendy. Also, if your itinerary is going to take you into one of the restricted zones, you will need a special permit. (See section on requirements for foreign travelers for more info on that.) Sport fishing and hunting will require special licenses as well. See appendix for the government offices to contact for additional information on permits for nature parks, preserves and restricted areas; sport fishing and hunting licenses.

Kamchatka Sport Fishing Regulations

Visitors are required to have special sport fishing licenses if they fish in almost all Kamchatka waters. These licenses are specific to certain waters, with varying fees and are usually purchased by your host tourist organization. In addition, certain waters have special regulations and restrictions such as catch and release angling. For more information about Kamchatka's sport fishing regulations and licenses, contact:

Kamchatka Ministry of Fisheries
1 Lenin Square
Petropavlovsk, Kamchatsky
Russia 683040
fish@kamgov.ru
Phone/fax: (4152) 42-10-37; (4152) 42-09-55

REQUIREMENTS FOR FOREIGN TOURISTS

The Russian Federation requires all foreign nationals to obtain a Russian Visa prior to entry, except for those covered under International Agreements. This visa must be obtained prior to entering the Russian Federation. It is attached directly to your foreign travel document and has the following information: Last name, First name (in both Russian and English lettering), date of birth, sex, citizenship, passport number, date of visa issuance along with permitted duration of stay in the Russian Federation, invitation number or a Telex number, Visa period, purpose of travel, and the information of the inviting agency or the inviting person, and the Visa multiplicity.

Reciprocal agreements between the U.S. and Russia have made it much easier for travel between the two countries, with creation of new, more efficient Visas and processing. In addition to the standard single entry authorization, tourists will now be able to acquire multi-entry visas, valid for up to 36 months. To apply for a tourist Visa for entry into Russia, the following items are required:

1. A current, signed national passport valid for six months beyond the visa expiration date.

2. A confirmation of the hotel reservation, contract for provision of tourist services or confirmation of reception of the tourist, with register number from the Uniform Federal Register of the Tour Operators of the Russian Federal Tourism Agency and the seal of the host organization.

3. A completed and signed Visa application (available online at http://visa.kdmid.ru).

4. A passport size photo (1 3/8 by 1 ¾ inches) of the applicant.

5. A cover letter specifying itinerary, dates of entry and departure, purpose of your trip, cities to be visited in Russia.

6. Money order or certified bank check for visa processing fees.

Visas are processed by the Russian Consulate through a visa services company, Invisa Logistics Services LLC, www.ils-usa.com, with processing centers in Washington, D.C., San Francisco, New York, Houston, and Seattle. Applicants can apply through the mail or in person.

Check online with the visa processing company or with your local Russian Consulate for further details and latest developments.

When You Arrive in Russia

After you de-board your flight, you'll pick up your luggage and pass through Russian Immigration Control and Customs, which will require you to fill out a couple of forms. The whole process can take anywhere from twenty minutes to one hour, depending on the number of passengers. Once you clear Customs with your bags, you will leave the secure area and be met by your Russian hosts in the terminal building.

Registration

In accordance with legislation of the Russian Federation, any foreign citizen staying in Kamchatka must register with either the Passport Office or at the hotel they are staying within 3 calendar days of entry. If a foreign citizen travels to another community, he must register there again within 3 working days. If you are using the services of a tourist company, it is the responsibility and obligation of that company to make an official registration and follow all necessary procedures.

Other Requirements & Recommendations

Tourists should be aware that Kamchatka for a very long time has been a closed territory for the visits of Russian and foreign tourists. There are still many restricted zones for foreign visitors, with entry only by permission of the proper authorities and usually only to Russian organizations taking responsibility for your stay in Kamchatka. Adherence to the rules of travel within these restricted areas is directly connected to your safety. You can obtain all necessary information and forms from the Foreign Economic Relations and Tourism Division of the Kamchatka Regional Government (Phone/Fax: 11-23-55, 12-08-22) or from local tourist firms.

Most tourist routes within Kamchatka will take you into totally wild surroundings, completely isolated from civilization, with considerable potential risk. The best guarantee for your safety and enjoyment is to enlist the services of a licensed local tour operator, who will provide you with professional and reliable guides. If you are a tourist committed to independent travel and willing to take all the inherent risks, we strongly recommend you register your route with the Search and Rescue Service of the Kamchatka Department of Emergencies, located in Petropavlovsk, (415-2) 11-03-95; (415-22) 7-65- 60. If you plan on visiting one of

Kamchatka's Nature Parks, you must get permission from the Nature Parks Management Office.

Karl Marks Prospect, 29/1, Office 310
Petropavlovsk, 7(4152) 25-19-70
or www.wildkamchatka.ru.

Regulations for Foreign Hunters

If you plan on hunting Kamchatka, you must complete an agreement with a receiving hunting tour operator for services rendered, no later than a month before the scheduled beginning of your tour. You must also inform your tour operator of the kind and caliber of the weapon and the amount of cartridges you intend to bring. This information is necessary to obtain permission for taking weapons into Russia.

If you intend to take a hunting trophy out of Russian territory, you will need a veterinarian certificate issued by the Customs Veterinarian Office and a special certificate for endangered species (CITES) for the following Kamchatka animals: brown bear, lynx, and wolf. All these papers can be obtained from your receiving tour firm.

Special Regulations Concerning Items of Cultural Value

For certain items of cultural value that you have acquired during your stay in Kamchatka, a Customs certificate for taking them out of the Russian Federation is required. These certificates are issued by the authorized representative of the Cultural Ministry in Petropavlovsk (#1 Lenin square, Tel/fax (4152) 11-21-63). Contact the agency for details on the types of items requiring certification and necessary documents.

ABOUT KAMCHATKA'S BEARS

Kamchatka, like Alaska, is definitely world class bear country, and you should be aware of and concerned (but not fearful) about your safety at all times when you are out in the wilds there fishing, camping, hiking or doing any other activity that might put you in contact with the big bruins of this province. Always keep in mind that bears are wild animals and essentially unpredictable. As a foreigner, you will most likely not be able to take any kind of bear protection with you (but your hosts undoubtedly will), so give yourself a wide margin of safety by observing these common sense rules:

1. There is statistical safety in numbers. Never fish, hike, camp or do any other outdoor activity alone in bear country. Go as a group and stay together, do not get separated!

2. Be extremely cautious when moving through heavy brush, forest or wading along rivers; especially on windy days, or early in the morning or late in the evening. Stay alert, make plenty of noise and stop frequently to

look around for any bear sign. If you come upon signs of recent bear activity, leave the area immediately!

3. If you are wading in a river or hiking along the banks and see a bear in the water or along shore, it is best not to stress the animal in any way. Leave the river immediately! You can cut a wide swath around the bear and continue your fishing up or down the river.

4. Keep a very clean camp. Put your sleeping tents well away from your cooking area and <u>never</u> bring food of any kind near your tent. (Do not store clothing or other items that may smell of food or fish near your tent, either.) Throw all your biodegradable food waste (food scraps and fish entrails) in the river or burn it completely in the fire. Bury all human waste a good distance from camp. Put all your food in a cooler and if you cannot secure it in any way (by hanging it in a tree or locking in a vehicle), set it out in the open, well away from your sleeping area. Never clean fish in the boat/raft, in camp, or on the river bank, do it in the water and be sure to thoroughly clean all traces of fish smell from your body, clothing and utensils.

5. Never approach a bear. If you see one at a distance, give it a wide berth, especially if it is with cubs. If you should come on a bear at close range, try not to panic. Depending on the bear's initial reaction, it is usually best to back away from the animal, slowly at first, talking to it softly. You cannot outrun a bear and shouldn't try in most situations.

6. Be cautious, use common sense, don't travel alone and keep a clean camp and you should have no problems in bear country. Report all incidents to local authorities.

APPENDIX

FLY PATTERNS FOR KAMCHATKA

Green Butt Skunk

Most of the fly patterns used in Kamchatka, with few exceptions, are basically the same as those which have proven so successful in Alaska waters over the years. These flies can be grouped in six basic categories: attractor patterns, dry flies, forage patterns, nymphs, egg/flesh flies and specialty patterns (rodent imitations, large surface/diving flies for northern pike, large attractors and egg/flesh flies for king salmon). Many of these traditional patterns (like the Leech and Flesh Fly) have evolved into countless variations that can be very productive in Kamchatka waters. Fly anglers should use this list as a starting point to assemble a wide assortment of patterns (including those recommended by their guide/outfitter, of course) to bring with them and be creative in their selection out on the river when the need arises. Keep in mind that many of the patterns shown come in a variety of colors, many of which will work well in Kamchatka.

Attractors

Alaskabou
Popsicle
Candy Cane
Supervisor
Fall Favorite
Comet
Boss
Green Butt Skunk
Practitioner
Purple Peril
Deceiver

Coho Fly
Polar Shrimp
Clouser Minnow
Freight Train
Montana Brassie
Outrageous
Sockeye Charlie
Skykomish Sunrise
Pink Sparkler

Kamchatka Special
Egg Sucking Leech
Starlite Leech
Zonker
Egg Sucking Zonker
Copper & Orange
Everglow
Intruder
Sparkle Shrimp

Krystal Bullet
Mickey Finn
Krazy Charlie
Sockeye Orange
Rajah
Woolly Bugger
Matuka
Yarn Fly
Russian River
Dolly Lama
Wiggletail

228

Nymph

Brassie
Hare's Ear
Black Gnat
Pheasant Tail Nymph
Zug Bug

Bitch Creek
Stonefly
Caddis Case
Mosquito Emerger

Bead Head Emerger
Chironomid
Brown Caddis Nymph

Dragonfly Nymph
Caddis Larva
Brown Emerger
March Brown

Forage

Leech
Smolt
Alevin
Fry
Muddler

Marabou Muddler
McCune's Sculpin
Parr

Scud (pink)
Minnow
Thunder Creek
San Juan Worm (green)

Shrimp

Egg/Flesh

Glo Bug
Bead Egg

Flesh Fly
Carcass Fly

Cluster Fly
Babine Special

Two-Egg Sperm
Battle Creek

Dry Fly

Adams
Mosquito
Black Gnat
Wulff
Elk Hair Caddis
Cahill

Midge
Humpy
Bivisible
Bomber
Irresistible

Parachute Adams
Royal Coachman
Stimulator
Blue Wing Olive

Yellow Sallie
Red Quill
Golden Stone
Griffith Gnat
Clark's Stonefly
Spinner

Specialty

Mouse
Lemming
Pike Fly
Waterdog
Wog

Popper
King Caviar
Clown
D's Minnow
Slider

Seaducer
Whistler
Baitfish
Slider

Pike
McMurderer
King Flash Fly

FAUNA OF KAMCHATKA

Utgard photo

The Fauna of Kamchatka is rich and varied, with some 918 species of vertebrates, including 500 species of fish (sturgeons, sharks, skates, whitefish, salmon, greenling, rockfish, flounders, codfish and sculpins, with 30 species found in freshwater); 322 species of birds (accipitridae, falconidae, anatidae, laridae, alcidae, passeridae and others); 88 species of mammals (including 23 species of cetaceans and 9 species of pinnipeds) 3 species of lampreys; no reptiles and only two amphibians (Siberian salamander & marsh frog).

The best places to observe and photograph Kamchatka's abundant wildlife are along its numerous rivers, lakes, seashores and bays, and in open meadows and alpine tundra. Many of these best areas lie within Kamchatka's many state and federal protected nature parks, preserves, reserves, monuments, etc. Be sure to bring a good pair of binoculars with you and adequate telephoto lenses and tripod for your camera.

Common Kamchatka Birds & Mammals

1. Brown Bear, *Ursus arctos*
2. Caribou/Reindeer, *Rangifer tarandus*
3. Red Fox, *Vulpes vulpes*
4. East Siberian Lynx, *Lynx lynx*
5. Wolf, *Canis lupus*
6. Steller's Sea Eagle, *Haliaetus pelagicus*
7. Arctic Ground Squirrel, *Spermophillus parryi*
8. Kamchatka Sable, Martes *zibellina*
9. Cuckoo, *Cuculus canorus*
10. Orca, *Orcinus Orca*
11. Steller Sea Lion, *Eumotopias jubatus*
12. Ptarmigan, *Lagopus lagopus*
13. Northern Bat, *Eptesicus nilssoni*
14. Mountain Hare, *Lepus timidus*
15. Kamchatka Shrew, *Sorex camtchatica*
16. Capercaillie (Wood Grouse), *Tetrao parvirostris*
17. Mink, *Mustela vison*
18. Moose, *Alces alces*
19. Kamchatka Black-Capped Marmot, *Marmota camtschatica*
20. Northern Fur seal, *Callorhinus ursinus*
21. Walrus, *Odebenus rosmarus*
22. Homed Puffin, *Fratercula comiculata*
23. Sea Otter, *Enhydra lutris*
24. Wolverine, *Gulo gulo*
25. East Siberian Ermine, *Mustela ermina*
26. Magpie, *Pica pica*
27. Seal, *Phoca vitulina*
28. River otter, *Lutra lutra*
29. Raven, *Corvus corax*
30. Common Merganser, *Mergus merganser*

THE FLORA OF KAMCHATKA

Irina Kruglykova

As with its fauna, the size and diversity of Kamchatka's vegetable world has been greatly shaped by the powerful forces of glaciation, volcanism, extreme weather and isolation. Its vascular plants number some 1170 species, comprising 89 families and 411 genera. Similar to Alaska, the various vegetation zones and their inclusive species are easily visited by traversing altitude. Kamchatka's wildflowers, in particular, offer a spectacular pageant of color, beginning in the lowlands with the melting of snows in May-June and continuing up the mountains in July and August.

Visitors are often amazed by the density and height of the summer foliage in Kamchatka's forest and meadows, with herbs, grasses, and ferns growing as tall as Iowa corn in the luxuriant excess of light and moisture. Tall jungles of meadowsweet, fireweed, cow parsnips and spirea cover shorelines and meadows; on slopes and ridges, up into the subalpine zone (and beyond) are dense, often impenetrable thickets of dwarf pine and shrub alder. And throughout most of the peninsula's forest zones, the gnarled and twisted Erman's (stone) birch rises up in defiance of Kamchatka's crushing winter snows.

The following are brief descriptions of Kamchatka's most common flowers, trees, herbs, and berries. Readers wanting more complete information on the flora of Kamchatka are encouraged to consult some of the authoritative texts on the subject listed in the reference section of the appendix.

Common Wildflowers of Kamchatka

1. NORTHERN GERANIUM, *Geranium erianthum*

Common Kamchatka perennial wildflower of fields, forests and subalpine meadows. To 1 ½ feet, with upright stems, splayed leaves and copious lovely, blue five-petal flowers. Blooms in early summer; called "Geran" by the Russians.

2. VIOLET, Viola selkirkii

Common Kamchatka perennial wildflower to 5 inches high, found in damp forest areas. Has heart shaped leaves and dainty violet-blue flowers. Blooms in early summer. Russians call it "Fialka".

3. KAMCHATKA FRITILLARY (Chocolate Lilly), *Fritillaria camschatcensis*

Common perennial wildflower of Kamchatka's beaches, meadows and woods, to fifteen inches tall. Has spherical root bulb, whorls of long, petal-like leaves along thick upright stalk and black or chocolate brown lily flowers. A plant of traditional food and medicinal value all across the North Pacific, called "Rabchik" by the Russians. It blooms in early summer.

4. LOBELIA, *Lobelia sessilifolia*

Showy perennial wildflower common to swampy margins of rivers, ponds and thermal pools in Kamchatka, to three feet in height. Grows upright with thick stems sprouting many lanceolate leaves and adorned at end with irregular blue, draping blossoms. Blooms in mid-summer.

5. FIREWEED, *Chamerion angustifolium*

A very common, widely distributed perennial wild flower of the North Pacific. Found in meadows, clearings, burns and stream sides. Upright leaf and flower stalk, to six feet tall, adorned with alternate, lanceolate leaves and long crown of abundant magenta/pink flowers that bear minute cottony seeds easily air born in fall. Blooms continuously from early summer to early fall; called "Ivan Chai" by the Russians.

6. SLENDER LILY, *Lilium debile*

Very lovely perennial wild lily found in meadows and woods of Kamchatka. Has upright stem, to 2 feet, with long, lanceolate leaves and large, showy orange lily blossoms. Blooms in mid-summer.

7. ALPINE SWEETVETCH, *Hedysarum hedysaroides*

A very common and widespread perennial plant of the northern latitudes, found in meadows, woods, riversides and scree slopes of Kamchatka. Semi-upright stems to 15 inches with paired elliptical leaflets and separate stalks bearing tight groups of irregular purple-blue flowers. Blooms in early summer; called "Koleechnik" by the Russians.

8. FISCHER MONKSHOOD, *Aconitum fischeri*

A common perennial wildflower occurring in meadows and forests of Sakhalin, Primorye and Kamchatka. Straight stems to four feet tall, with alternating wide jagged leaves and loose crown of blue-violet hooded flowers. A poisonous plant, blooms in mid-summer.

9. WILD FLAG, *Iris setosa*

A common wild iris of the north Pacific, found in the damp woods, swamps and meadows of Kamchatka. Straight-stemmed, to 1 ½ feet tall, with long, spiky leaves and striking blue-violet blossom. Blooms in early summer. Frequently found in great numbers; called "Iris" by the Russians.

10. YATABE LADY'S SLIPPER, *Cypripedium guttatum yatabeanum*

A delicately beautiful wild orchid of the North Pacific, found in the meadows, woods and swamps of Kamchatka. To 24 inches, with long, wide elliptic leaves and single large, yellow-brown, spotted blossom. Blooms in early summer.

11. NORTHERN TANSY, *Tanacetum boreale*

Common wildflower of Asia and North America, found on drier, marginal sites in Kamchatka: rocky slopes, gravel bars, roadsides, etc. Has upright stems to 30 inches, with marigold- like leaves and yellow blossoms. Blooms in mid-summer.

12. SIBERIAN ASTER, *Aster sibiricus*

A common wildflower in Kamchatka, found in rocky, marginal sites like beaches, lake and stream shores, bare slopes and roadsides. Has long thin stems to 12 inches with long elliptic leaves and narrow blue petal rays on yellow disk heads. Russians call this plant "Astra". It blooms in mid-summer.

13. GOATSBEARD, *Aruncus dioicus*

Common perennial wildflower of Northern Hemisphere, found in forests and meadows of Kamchatka. Has stems to 4 feet with pinnate, serrated leaves and spike like groups of small white flowers at head.

14. SPIREA-LEAVED GOLDENROD, *Solidago spiraeifolia*

A common Far East wildflower of fields, meadows, forests and slopes of Kamchatka. Has upright stems to 20 inches, with alternating lanceolate leaves with serrated edges and dense yellow ray flower clusters. Blooms in mid-summer.

15. WILD CHIVE, *Allium schoenoprasum*

A common, widely distributed perennial herb, found in Kamchatka's woods and meadows. Has one to several oblong bulbs sprouting stems to 16 inches, with very long, thin leaves and spherical, multi-blossomed, pink or rose-violet flower heads. A plant of traditional food and medicinal value, called "Luke" by the Russians. Blooms in mid-July.

16. AMUR ANEMONE, *Anemone amurensis*

Very common perennial wildflower of Kamchatka's forests and meadows. Upright stems to 10 inches, with broad, three-part, jagged leaves and multi-petalled, 1 to 1 ½ inch diameter, star-shaped white flowers. Blooms in mid-summer.

17. KEYFLOWER, *Dactylorhiza aristata*

Common and widespread ornamental wildflower, found in Kamchatka's forests, meadows and swamp margins. Has thick upright stem to 16 inches with spotted oval leaves and dense, spike like crown of small, exquisitely-shaped, purple or pink flowers. Blooms in early summer.

18. KAMCHATKA TRILLIUM, *Trillium camtschatcense*

Common ornamental wildflower of the Far East, frequently found in Kamchatka's woods, meadows and swamp margins. Straight-stemmed to 16 inches, with thick roots and whorl of 3 oval, sharp pointed leaves and terminal, star-shaped blossom of three green sheath and three white flower petals. Called "Trilliyam" by the Russians. Blooms in early summer.

19. UPSIDE DOWN LOUSEWORT, *Pedicularis resupinata*

A common perennial plant of Kamchatka's meadows, woods and swamp margins. Single straight stems to 20 inches with alternate, lanceolate leaves and pink flowers, grouped in a dense crown and inverted separately along upper stem. Blooms early to mid-summer.

20. TALL COTTONGRASS, *Eriophorum polystachion*

A very common and widespread perennial plant, found in dense swards in Kamchatka's swamps, damp meadows and tundras. To 30 inches, with long stout stems, grass like leaves and easily recognizable, densely tufted flower heads. The Russians call this plant "Pushitsa".

21. LAPLAND CORNEL, *Chamaepericlymenum suecicum*

Common and very widespread dwarf plant (also identical to the dwarf dogwood of North America) of the forest understory in Kamchatka. Straight stemmed, to 10 inches, with large, oval opposing leaves and terminal, small white and black flowers. Fruit is bright red, globular. Blooms in early summer.

22. MARSH LABRADOR TEA, *Ledum palustre*

Very common and widespread evergreen shrub of the northern latitudes, to three feet tall. Found in Kamchatka's forests, meadows and tundras. Has long, green, leather like leaves and numerous heads of small fragrant white blossoms. An aromatic, medicinal plant. Blooms in early summer.

23. NARCISSUS ANEMONE, *Anemone narcissiflora* ssp. *villosissima*

Perennial wildflower of Kamchatka's eastern coastline, found in meadows and beach terraces. Has broad, complex, five-part basal leaves, straight stems to 15 inches and white or creamy-white, open flowers with yellow stamens. Blooms in early summer.

24. YELLOW MARSH MARIGOLD, *Caltha palustris*

Common and widely distributed perennial flower of Kamchatka's river banks, lakes and swamps. Has hollow, variable stem, usually upright to 12 inches, (but sometimes decumbent) with rounded, irregular-edged leaves and bright yellow, 5 petal flowers. Blooms in early summer.

25. NORTHERN GRASS OF PARNASSUS, *Parnassia palustris*

Common perennial wildflower of Kamchatka's moist meadows, swamps and thermal pool margins. Has numerous straight stems to 15 inches, with basal oval leaves (and single leaf at midstem) and solitary, five-petal (or more) white flowers with shorter green calyx lobes. Blooms in early summer.

26. ARCTIC STARFLOWER, *Trientalis europaea* ssp. *arctica*

Common perennial wildflower of Kamchatka's woods, meadows and swamps. Has upright stems to 10 inches, with whorl of shiny oval leaves topped with 1-3 delicate white flowers on short, thin stems. Blooms in early summer.

27. ARCTIC DAISY, *Arctanthemum arcticum*

Common perennial wildflower found along Kamchatka's rocky sea coasts and in meadows. Has thin stems to 15 inches, thick, oblong pinnately-lobed leaves and trademark daisy flowers, with white-petals and yellow disks.

28. FALSE-TILESII SAWWORT, *Saussurea pseudotilesii*

Widely distributed, perennial flower of Kamchatka's meadows, forests, swamp margins and tundras. Has straight stems to 2 feet or more, large, tooth-edged, lanceolate leaves and numerous small, purple-violet flower heads. Blooms in mid-summer.

29. BLUE MOUNTAINHEATH, *Phyllodoce caerulea*

Common and widespread, evergreen dwarf shrub found in Kamchatka's alpine areas. Has dense whorls of short, rigid, spiky leaves like a crowberry and numerous light pink, drooping bell flowers. Blooms in early summer.

30. WHITE MOUNTAIN AVENS, *Dryas punctata*

A widespread and common dwarf shrub, found on rocky slopes and alpine tundras. Grows prostrate woody stems with oblong, rough tooth-edged leaves and short (5 inches or less), upright flower stalks supporting single white, poppy like blossoms with profuse yellow stamens. Blooms in mid-summer; called "Dryada" by the Russians.

31. WEASELSNOUT, *Lagotis glauca*

Common perennial wildflower of Kamchatka's alpine slopes, tundras and stream sides. Has single upright stem to 12 inches with thick oval leaves, culminating in a spike of small, purple-blue flower bracts. Blooms mid to late summer.

32. VOLCANIC CINQUEFOIL, *Potentilla vulcanicola*

Common perennial wildflower of Kamchatka's rocky high slopes, screes, lava fields and tundras. Has long thin stems, three part, tooth-edged basal leaves and solitary (or two) yellow flowers. Blooms in mid-summer.

33. MICROCARPUS POPPY, *Papaver microcarpum*

Common perennial wildflower of Kamchatka's alpine slopes, slag fields and gravel bars, where it forms dense swards. Has hairy, pinnately sectioned leaves and separate thin flower stems to 8 inches, crowned with broad yellow flowers. Blooms early to mid-summer; called "Mak" in Russian.

34. THUNBERG'S FLEABANE, *Erigeron thunbergii*

Common perennial of Kamchatka's alpine meadows and stony slopes. Has upright stems to 8 inches, with oblong leaves and single ray flower with blue petals and yellow disks. Blooms in late summer.

35. KAMCHATKA ERITRICHIUM, *Eritrichium kamtschaticum*

Common perennial wildflower of Kamchatka's rocky alpine slopes and tundras, to six inches usually. Has short, hairy, spatula shaped leaves and profusions of bright sky blue flowers. Blooms in mid-summer.

36. SHRUBBY BEARDTONGUE, *Pennellianthus frutescens*

A perennial wildflower of the mountains of the Far East, occurring mostly in southern Kamchatka on rocky alpine slopes, screes and lava fields. Stems to 6 inches tall, with oblong, leathery leaves and densely packed, bell-shaped, five petal lilac flowers. Blooms in mid-summer.

37. NORTHERN PARRYA, *Parrya nudicaulis*

Common perennial wildflower of Kamchatka's rocky slopes and tundras. Has stout root with basal oblong leaves and upright stem to 8 inches, bearing big, evenly clustered flowers, usually purple or pink, rarely white. Blooms in mid to late summer.

38. SNOW BUTTERCUP, *Ranunculus nivalis*

Common perennial flower of Kamchatka's moist alpine areas. Has several, cleft basal leaves and single thick, upright stem to six inches with long petal leaves and solitary, poppy-like yellow flower. Blooms mid-summer.

39. CLUBMOSS MOUNTAIN HEATHER, *Cassiope lycopodioides*

Creeping matted dwarf shrub of Kamchatka's alpine stony slopes, meadows and tundras. Has long, thin prostrate branches with small, tightly grouped leaves and short, thin stems supporting tiny white, drooping bell flowers. Blooms in early to mid-summer.

40. MOUNTAIN HAREBELL, *Campanula lasiocarpa*

A common perennial alpine flower found on Kamchatka's rocky slopes and tundra, especially volcanic areas (lava flows). Usually six inches in height or less with striking blue, bell-shaped flower, 1 ½ inches long. Blooms in late summer.

41. THICK VIOLET, *Viola crassa*

Perennial alpine wildflower common to rocky slopes in certain areas of Kamchatka. Has thick, heart-shaped leaves, stems to 6 inches and dark yellow flowers. Blooms in early summer.

42. CREEPING PINK, *Dianthus repens*

Perennial wildflower common to the rocky alpine slopes and meadows of Kamchatka. Usually grows with stems and flowers branching prostrate from taproot. Has five petal, finely toothed flowers, pink or magenta. Blooms in mid-summer.

43. KAMCHATKA OXYTROPE, *Oxytropis kamtschatica*

Perennial wildflower of Kamchatka's high volcanic slopes and alpine tundra, to six inches tall. Has short, purple-blue flowers grouped at top of upright, hairy stems, with squat, lanceolate leaves arranged in pairs on separate stems. Blooms in mid-summer.

44. WHITE GENTIAN, *Gentiana algida*

Perennial circumpolar alpine wildflower found on rocky mountain slopes and meadows of Kamchatka. Has upright stem to 9 inches, oblong leaves and beautiful, creamy-white, violet-streaked bell shaped flowers. Blooms in mid-summer.

45. GOLD RHODODENDRON, *Rhododendron aureum*

A familiar evergreen shrub of Kamchatka's alpine tundra, slopes and meadows, to three feet in height. Has a fan of stiff smooth, elliptic, leathery leaves surrounding broad, bell-shaped yellow blossoms. An impressive plant of ornamental and medicinal value. Blooms in early summer.

46. KAMCHATKA RHODODENDRON, *Rhododendron camtschaticum*

Creeping dwarf shrub, to 1 ½ feet, of Kamchatka's high meadows, slopes and tundra, bearing beautiful purple-magenta flowers. Has upright stems, short, thin oval leaves and 1 ½ -2 inch blossoms. Blooms in mid-summer.

47. NORTHERN JACOB'S LADDER, *Polemonium boreale*

Widely distributed, familiar perennial plant of rocky alpine slopes, meadows and river bars, common to Kamchatka. Has pinnate leaves with 5-10 pairs of elliptic leaflets, short hairy flower stems and light blue, broad, bell-shaped flowers with yellow centers. Blooms in mid-summer.

48. CUTLEAF ANEMONE, *Pulsatilla nuttalliana*

A common and widely distributed northern subalpine/alpine perennial wildflower, found on the sandy slopes, meadows and lava fields of Kamchatka. Has late developing, multi-segmented basal leaves and upright, hairy stem to 10 inches, with large, blue-violet flowers above hairy, multifrond leaf collars. One of the first alpine flowers to bloom in spring and early summer.

49. PALLID PAINTBRUSH, *Castilleja pallida*

A common and widespread subalpine/alpine perennial of Asia, found in meadows, tundras, stream sides and high forest margins. Has upright stems to 16 inches, bearing long, lanceolate leaves and dense bracts of upright, oblong pale yellow and green flowers. Blooms in early summer.

50. LARGEFLOWER SPEEDWELL, *Veronica grandiflora*

A perennial alpine wildflower of Kamchatka's rocky slopes and tundras. Has upright hairy stems to 5 inches, with dense, large, hairy-edged, elliptic leaves and open, pansy-like, bright blue flowers. Blooms in mid-summer.

51. ALPINE AZALEA, *Loiseleuria procumbens*

A very widespread and common, dwarf, evergreen creeping shrub that decorates many alpine/arctic areas, found on Kamchatka's rocky slopes, lava flows and tundras. Has thick stems adorned with small, elliptic leathery leaves and many small, bell-shaped pink flowers. Blooms in mid-summer.

52. WEDGELEAF PRIMROSE, *Primula cuneifolia*

Ornamental perennial wildflower of Kamchatka's rocky slopes, meadows and tundras. Has spatulate, sharp-tipped, basal leaves and upright, leafless stems to five inches, adorned with large, long-lobed pink to lilac flowers. Blooms in mid-summer.

53. MOSS CAMPION, *Silene acaulis*

Common low-growing alpine perennial of Kamchatka's rocky slopes and tundras, forming short but dense cushion-like mats (the plant is often called cushion-pink) with its numerous shoots. Has short, lanceolate leaves and abundant, star-shaped, pink (rarely white) flowers. Blooms in mid to late summer.

54. DIAPENSIA, *Diapensia obovata*

Common, creeping, dwarf evergreen shrub of Kamchatka's rocky alpine slopes and tundras, often forming dense, cushiony swards. Has oblong, lustrous, leathery leaves and five-lobed white flowers with yellow sepals. The Russians call this plant, "Diapensiya". It Blooms in mid-summer.

55. STONECROP, *Rhodiola integrifolia*

Widely distributed, small shrub of rocky slopes and seashores, tundra and high meadows, common to Kamchatka. Has thick, straight, short stems (to 10 inches), rosettes of thick oval leaves and dense, deep purple flowers. Blooms in mid-summer.

56. LESSING'S ARNICA/NODDING ARNICA, *Arnica lessingii*

A perennial wildflower of Kamchatka's windswept high meadows and tundras. Has deep-rooted, thin upright stem to 16 inches, narrow oblong basal leaves and large, solitary, drooping yellow ray flowers. Like other members of this large genus, this plant may have certain medicinal qualities; blooms in late summer.

Common Tall Plants of Kamchatka's Meadows

1. OSTRICH FERN, Matteuccia struthiopteris

A common and widely distributed large fern of the Northern Hemisphere, one of Kamchatka's 22 native ferns; edible, found in damp, lowland forests. Grows to 3 feet.

2. KAMCHATKA MEADOWSWEET, Filipendula camtschatica

An extremely common, widespread, fast-growing perennial herb of Kamchatka's forests, meadows, and riversides, usually occurring in dense swards. Reaches up to 10 feet in height, with hollow stems supporting evenly spaced, large, broad, multilobed leaves and dense heads of small white flowers. Important forage for wildlife, called "Shelomaynik" by the Russians. Blooms in mid-summer; leaves turn yellow in fall.

3. COMMON COW PARSNIP, *Heracleum lanatum*

A very common, tall perennial herb of Kamchatka's meadows and forest margins. Has a thick, hollow, tall stem to 7 feet, with sheath-stemmed branches supporting large, trisected leaves with toothed edges. It bears large, broad crowns of small white flowers that later in season produce a thick crop of flat seeds that is forage for bears. The sap is highly irritating and blistering to skin in bright sun. A medicinal and food plant.

4. KAMCHATKA THISTLE, *Cirsium kamtschaticum*

Common tall herb of Kamchatka's forests and meadows. Has straight, thick stem to 5 feet, with oblong, pinnately sected, spiny-edged leaves and large, dense pink or violet flower heads. Blooms in late summer. Russians call this plant "Vodyak".

5. HEMP-LEAVED RAGWORT, *Senecio cannabifolius*

Common Kamchatka wild perennial herb of meadows and forests. Has stout, upright stem, 3-6 feet, with long-lobed, palmate leaves and numerous small, dense yellow flower heads. Blooms in mid-summer. Called "Krestobnik" by the Russians.

6. WHITE FALSE HELLEBORE, *Veratrum oxy*sepalum

A very common and widespread perennial wildflower, found in the forests and meadows of Kamchatka. Has stout upright stem to 5 feet, with large oblong leaves angling off stem and spike like crown and short branches of small, yellowish or whitish green flowers. Poisonous blooms in early to mid-summer.

7. COW PARSLEY, *Anthriscus sylvestris*

Common perennial herb of Kamchatka's meadows and riversides. Has straight, thin stem to five feet, with branches of pinnate triangular leaves and loose crown of small, white flower clusters.

8. FALSE SPIRAEA, *Sorbaria sorbifolia*

Common and widespread shrub of northern Asia found in swards along Kamchatka's forest margins, streamsides and in meadows. To six feet, with lanceolate, tooth-edged leaves and dense, branching bracts of small white flowers at stem apex. Called "Ryabinik" by the Russians.

9. COWBANE, *Cicuta virosa*

A widely distributed and common perennial herb of Kamchatka's swampy meadows and stream sides. Has hollow upright, branching stem to 4 feet or more, with narrow, pinnately sected leaves and spherical, compound head of small white flower umbels. A very poisonous plant.

10. URALS EDGEPISTIL, *Pleurospermum uralense*

Common perennial herb of Kamchatka's tall herb meadows. Has thick, upright hollow stem, 3-6 feet, with pinnately sected leaves and dense crown of small white flowers.

11. GREATER BURNET, *Sanguisorba officinalis*

Common, widespread perennial flower, found in Kamchatka's meadows and forest margins. Grows to three feet, with oblong, tooth-edged leaves and spherical red, black or purple flowers at the end of long, thin stalks. Blooms in early summer.

Common Wild Berries of Kamchatka

1. RED CURRANT, *Ribes triste*

A common shrub berry found across the moderate zone of northeast Siberia, including Kamchatka, in forests, hillsides, meadows, and along river valleys. Grows in bushes to three feet, with dark brown, woody stems and three-lobed, green leaves that turn bright yellow-orange in autumn. Small red flowers develop into drooping fruit clusters of small, round, clear bright red berries with intense tart flavor, prized for juice, jams, and pies.

2. HONEYSUCKLE, *Lonicera caerulea*

A very common and important large berry shrub found in the meadows, forests, tundras and swamps of Kamchatka. A dense, upright bush, to six feet in certain areas, with elongate leaves and brown stems, bell-shaped, yellow-white flowers and small, oblong, pale blue berries very similar in taste to blueberry. Prized for intense flavor, the berries are used for juice, pies, and jams.

3. BOG BLUEBERRY, *Vaccinium uliginosum*

Small berry shrub, to three feet tall, common in tundras, swamps and wood margins across Kamchatka. A plant of considerable food and medicinal value. Has waxy, small oblong leaves on stiff brown stems, with dainty, pink-white bell flowers that develop into familiar small, round, powder-blue fruits of exceptional flavor, prized by bears and humans. (The Russians call this berry, "Golubika.")

4. LINGONBERRY, Vaccinium vitis-idaea

A common, dwarf evergreen berry shrub found across the northern hemisphere, including Kamchatka, where it occurs on tundras, ridges, and slopes all across the peninsula. It grows as a thick prostrate shrub, with creeping rootstock. The leaves are small, waxy and elliptical, with dainty bell- shaped pink flowers that develop into dark red, round berries of tart, earthy flavor best enjoyed after the first heavy frost. A plant of significant medicinal and food value, utilized by man for centuries. (Called "Brusnika" by the Russians.)

5. BOG CRANBERRY, Oxycoccus palustris

An evergreen, dwarf berry-bearing shrub found on bog mosses throughout Kamchatka. Grows in long, spindly stalks, with elliptical waxy leaves and shooting star-like pink flowers. Bears sparse, purple-red berries of bright flavor. Best in late fall.

6. RED RASPBERRY, Rubus idaeus

A prickly, berry-bearing small shrub common to Kamchatka. Grows in clearings, meadows, forest margins and along rivers, to 4 feet. Has green, thorny stems with tear-shaped leaves with serrated edges and whitish bottoms. Flowers are small, round, white; bears familiar, juicy, red multiglobular fruit, prized for jams, pies, and liquors. ("Malina" is raspberry in Russian.)

7. CROWBERRY, *Empetrum nigrum*

A prostrate, berry-bearing, dwarf shrub that grows on tundras and swamps throughout the North, including Kamchatka. Dense, ground-hugging growth creates immense patches. Has thin stems bearing evergreen, whorled, short spiky leaves and tiny pink flowers. Of significant food and medicinal value. Bears abundant fruit- juicy, small, hard black spheres of non-descript flavor, usually dried and used in a variety of traditional ways by natives. (The Russians call this berry, "Shiksha.")

8. BEARBERRY, *Arctous alpina*

A common, creeping dwarf, berry-bearing shrub found on the dry tundras and rocky alpine slopes of the North, including most of Kamchatka. Has thick oblong leaves that turn bright red in fall, small green and white flowers that become plump, round black berries that ripen with the first heavy frosts.

9. WILD ROSE, *Rosa spp.*

Common, thorny, medium-size (to six feet) shrub with large, edible seed pods (called rosehips) found throughout Kamchatka, from seaside meadows to interior forests to subalpine slopes. Three very similar species occur, all with thorns along stems, pinnate leaves, large, delicate pink flowers, and oblong or spherical, bright orange-red fruits with high nutritive value. (Best picked after the first heavy frost.)

10. SIBERIAN JUNIPER, *Juniperus sibirica*

A medicinal, aromatic perennial bush, member of the Cypress family, found mostly on rocky slopes, terraces, and edges of clearings across Kamchatka. Grows as a prostrate shrub or upright bush to 2 feet in height, with short, bent, prickly needles on woody stems, and small, round black berries of pungent flavor and smell. Occurs all across Siberia.

Common Trees of Kamchatka

1. ERMAN (STONE) BIRCH, *Betula ermanii*

An extremely common large tree, found across entire peninsula (occupying 30% of forest area), often in pure sparse stands among tall herb meadows. Height to 60 feet, diameter to four feet, with wide, low crown on gnarled, bent trunk and thick, rough, flaky gray-white bark; wood creamy to yellow-white. Lives to 800 years. (The Russian word for birch is "Bereza.")

2. WHITE BIRCH, *Betula kamtschatica*

A much less common birch than stone birch, occurring mostly in the Kamchatka River valley. Found in pure groves, with slender, graceful trunk to 60 feet height and 2 feet diameter. Bark is smooth, white, wood white to creamy white. Short-lived, to 120 years.

3. DWARF BIRCH, *Betula exilis*

Common, widespread small shrub of alpine tundras, swamps and meadows throughout the North (occurs as *B. nana* in America). To 2 feet in height or more, with densely branching, heavily blistered woody stems and small roundish, tooth-edge, veined leaves that turn reddish-orange in the fall. Produces small birch catkins. Grows often in immense, impenetrable thickets.

4. POPLAR, *Populus suaveolens*

A common large, furrow-barked tree found along river valleys across most of Kamchatka. Fast growing, to 120 feet and over 4 feet diameter. Has large, palmate leaves that develop from sticky, resinous buds and fluffy cotton covered seed cones. Wood yellowish-white to orange white. Lives to 300 years. (The Russian word for poplar is "Topol.")

5. ASPEN, *Populis tremula*

Found mostly in the Kamchatka River basin, in pure stands, usually on well-drained terraces and hillsides. Slender trunk with smooth, greenish bark with black splotches, to 60 feet tall and 1 ½ feet diameter. Oval leaves turn brilliant yellow-gold in autumn. Wood is soft, creamy-white. Lives 200-300 years.

6. CHOSENIA, *Chosenia arbutifolia*

Unique and important tree of the Far East, member of the Willow family, found across much of Kamchatka in dense stands along swift mountain rivers. A large, stately tree with furrowed bark, extremely fast growing, to 120 feet and 4 feet diameter. Leaves willow-like, wood yellow-white, used for firewood, lumber, and poles. Lives to 200 years.

7. LARCH, *Larix dahurica*

A deciduous conifer found across most of northeast Siberia, occurring in Kamchatka in the Kamchatka and Penzhina river valleys. Tallest tree in Kamchatka, to 150 feet and 3 feet diameter. Has red-brown, fissured bark and soft, flat green needles in large bunches that turn yellow in fall, small cones and yellow-orange wood. Lives to 400 years.

8. AYAN SPRUCE, *Picea ajanensis*

A fairly common spruce of the Far East montane forests, occurring in Kamchatka extensively along the Kamchatka River basin. A very stately tree to 150 feet and 3 feet diameter, commercially important for timber. Shade tolerant has dense, conical crown with thick, flat dark-green needles and medium-sized cones. Wood is yellow-white. Can live to 500 years.

9. DWARF SIBERIAN (STONE) PINE, "Elfin Cedar," *Pinus pumila*

Common and widespread shrub conifer of northeast Siberia, occurring all across Kamchatka (42 % of the area of forests). Extremely hardy, it grows in dense, impenetrable stands on steep slopes, mountain ridges and old lava flows, from sea level to alpine zone. Tolerant of heavy snows, this fragrant dwarf pine can reach 15 feet in height under favorable conditions. Has curved stems with long needles (in bunches of five) and dense, medium-sized cones containing abundant nuts of great food value to wildlife. Lives to 250 years. (The Russians call this tree, "Kedrach.")

10. ALDER, *Alnus spp.*

Very common small tree/shrub occurring in two main species in Kamchatka. The larger form, *Alnus hirsuta*, is an important small tree along Kamchatka's rivers, reaching 30 feet or more in height and over one foot diameter, occurring in pure stands and mixed with various river willow species. Has gray-brown bark with lobed, oval leaves that turn dark green to black with the first heavy frosts; female catkins are small cones, an inch or less. The shrub alder, *Alnus fruticosa* forms dense pure stands on hillsides, from sea level to alpine zones, along with the Siberian dwarf pine. Up to 15 feet high, it has leaves and catkins like those of the larger form, but bark is gray. Both forms live up to 100 years.

11. WILLOW, *Salix spp.*

One of the most important and widespread group of small trees/shrubs in Kamchatka, occurring in many species along river valleys, forest margins and in alpine and arctic tundra. Tree forms usually to 45 feet, can reach 90 feet in favorable habitats such as along major rivers where it occurs in large, tall dense stands. Bark is green, brown or gray, leaves are long and thin, turning yellow in fall; catkins small to medium-sized. Shrub forms grow prostrate or bush-like to 6 feet tall in marginal zones like snowfields, rocky hillsides, alpine and arctic tundra, etc. Leaves lance-like or small oval; bark gray or reddish-brown. All forms are short-lived, to 60 years or so. (The Russian word for willow is "Iva.")

12. SIBERIAN MOUNTAIN ASH, *Sorbus sambucifolia*

Important small tree of Kamchatka's forests, occurring mostly in southern peninsula. Small to medium-size, to 35 feet in height, with smooth, flaky greenish- gray bark and long, pinnate leaves with serrated edges. Has white flowers that develop into bright orange-red, spherical fruits of great food importance to songbirds. Lives up to 100 years.

13. KAMCHATKA HAWTHORN, *Crataegus chlorosarca*

A fairly common, stout tree like bush to 30 feet in height, rarely more. Found in meadows and birch forests throughout Kamchatka. Has grayish brown trunk and branches with sparse thorns, flaky bark. Leaves are oak-like with sharp pointed lobes; develops clusters of white flowers that become purplish-black spherical fruits of great importance to birds and other animals, including man.

14. BIRD CHERRY, *Padus avium*

An important wild fruit tree growing along rivers of the Central Kamchatka valley. Medium-size, fast-growing, to 35 feet in height, with curved trunk and smooth grayish-brown bark and petiolate leaves. A very strong medicinal, the bird cherry develops beautiful clusters of white blossoms which turn into shiny small black berries of high food value to songbirds. Lives up to 100 years.

GOVERNMENT TOURIST AGENCIES AND OTHER ORGANIZATIONS

The Government of Kamchatsky Krai

1 Lenin Square

Petropavlovsk-Kamchatsky

Russia 683040

7 (4152) 41-24-20

www.kamchatka.gov.ru/

Official Kamchatka government website, with information on Kamchatka's history, natural resources, economy, etc., plus extensive list of visitor services and cultural attractions across Kamchatka (hotels, resorts, restaurants, night clubs, museums, recreation centers etc.)

Institute of Volcanology and Seismology

9 Pip Boulevard

Petropavlovsk, Kamchatsky

Russia 683006

4152 29-77-17

volcan@kscnet.ru

www.kscnet.ru/ivs/eng/index.php

Studying, monitoring and disseminating information on volcanism and related processes in Kamchatka

Kamchatka Search & Rescue

5 Khalaktyrskoye Motorway

Petropavlovsk, Kamchatsky

(415-2) 41-03-95

www.rescue-kamchatka.ru

Emergency response services for all of Kamchatka

Wild Salmon Center

721 NW 9th Avenue, #300

Portland, Oregon 97209

503-222-1804

www.wildsalmoncenter.org

For conservation and sustainable use of wild salmonid ecosystems throughout the Pacific Rim

World Wildlife Fund

27/1 Pobedy Prospect, #109-112
Petropavlovsk, Kamchatsky
Russia 683023
7 (4152) 29-85-35
7 (4152) 29-84-16

Preserving the unique natural ecosystems and habitats of Kamchatka and adjacent seas

Travel and External Affairs Agency of Kamchatka
35 Sovetskaya Street
Petropavlovsk, Kamchatsky
Russia 683000
7(4152) 41-23-55
travel@kamgov.ru
www.visitkamchatka.ru

Promoting Tourism to Kamchatka, with a tourism information portal on the web

Kamchatka Ministry of Fisheries
1 Lenin Square
Petropavlovsk, Kamchatsky
Russia 683040
fish@kamgov.ru
Phone/fax: (4152) 42-10-37; (4152) 42-09-55

For information on Kamchatka's fisheries, including sport fishing licenses and permits

AirRussia.US
InterPacific Aviation and Marketing, Inc.
2211 Elliot Avenue, #200
Seattle, WA 98121
206-443-1614 (U.S. ticket sales)
8-800-100-75-77 (Russia ticket sales)
7-499-749-00-21 (Russia ticket sales)
www.AirRussia.us

Providing Alaska with seasonal international flight service to and from RFE and supporting local and joint venture ecotourism.

Yelizovo International Airport
1 Zvedsnaya Street
Yelizovo
Flight info: 7 (41531) 9-93-42
International Terminal 7 (41531) 9-97-50
www.airport-pkc.ru/

REFERENCES

Pacific Salmon Life Histories, C. Groot/L. Margolis, University of British Columbia Press, Vancouver, 1991

Alaska Fishing: The Ultimate Angler's Guide, 3rd Edition, Rene Limeres & Gunnar Pedersen, Publishers Design Group, Roseville, California 2005

Atlas of Pacific Salmon, Xanthippe Augerot & Dana Nadel Foley, University of California Press/State of the Salmon, Berkeley, 2005

Ribbi Reki Kamchatka, Bugaev, Vronsky, Zavarina et al., KamchatNIRO, Petropavlovsk, Kamchatka, 2007

Systematics and Biology of the East Siberian Charr (Salvelinus leucomaenis), Savvaitova, KA; Kuzishchin, KV; Pichugin, MYu; Gruzdeva, MA; Pavlov, DS, Journal of Ichthyology, Vol. 47, No. 1, 2007.

Charrs, Salmonid Fishes of the Genus Salvelinus, Balon, E.K. (Ed.), W. Junk Publishers, Hague Netherlands, 1980.

Illustrated Keys to the Salmoniform Fishes of Kamchatka, B. H. Leman & E. B. Esin, VNIRO, Moscow, 2008

Raptors of the World, James Ferguson-Lees & David A. Christie, Princeton University Press, Princeton, NJ 2005

Plants of Kamchatka (The Field Atlas), V.V. Yakubov, Moscow 2007

Forest Vegetation of Easternmost Russia, Pavel V. Krestov, from *Forest Vegetation of Northeast Asia*, Kolbek, Srutek & Box, Kluwer Academic Publishers, Dordrecht, Netherlands, 2003

Flora of Alaska and Neighboring Territories, Eric Hulten, Stanford University Press, Stanford California, 1968

Alaskan Wildflowers, Verna Pratt, Alaskakrafts, Inc., Anchorage, Alaska, 2001

Amphibiotic Insects of the Northeast of Asia, I.A. Zasypkina & A.S. Ryabukhin, Pensoft Publishers, Sofia, Bulgaria 2001

Explorations of Kamchatka 1735-1741, Stepan P. Krasheninnikov, Oregon Historical Society, Portland, Oregon 1972

Biological Characteristics of Subspecies of the Arctic Grayling, The Kamchatka Grayling, Thymallus arcticus mertensi, Mikhael Skopets, Journal of Ichthyology, Vol. 30, no. 4, 1990.

Rare, Endemic, and Endangered Freshwater Fishes of Northeast Asia, IA Chereshnev, Journal of Ichthyology, Vol. 32, no. 4, 1992.

A New Form of Pacific Basin Trout of the Genus Salmo from Kamchatka, Saavaitova, K.A., K. V. Kuzishchin, S.V. Maximov and G.G. Novokov, Journal of Ichthyology. Vol. 35, No. 8, 1995

Freshwater Fishes of the USSR and Adjacent Countries, Berg. L.S., Translated from Russian, Israel Program for Scientific Translations. Jerusalem. 1964.

Population Structure of Mikizha (Parasalmo mykiss) from Rivers of Northwestern Kamchatka and North America, K. A. Savvaitova, K. V. Kuzishchin, and D. S. Pavlov, Journal of Ichthyology, Vol. 39, No. 7, 1998

A Review Of Size Trends Among North Pacific Salmon (Oncorhynchus Spp.), Brian S. Bigler, David W. Welch, and John H. Helle, Canada Journal of Fisheries and Aquatic. Science, Vol. 53, No. 2, 1996

Present State of Asian Coho Salmon (Oncorhynchus kisutch) Stocks, V.I. Radchenko, I.I. Glebov, North Pacific Anadromous Fish Commission Bulletin No.2, 2000

ABOUT THE AUTHOR

Rene Limeres was raised on the East Coast but has lived most of his life in Alaska. A longtime wilderness fly fishing guide, photographer and outdoors writer, with hundreds of credits in all major sporting magazines, he also co-authored and published the best-selling, award winning *"Alaska Fishing: The Ultimate Angler's Guide"* in addition to two pocket guides on fishing and wildlife in Alaska and two earlier versions of *Alaska Fishing*. One of a handful of American entrepreneurs to establish successful sport fishing operations in Russia's Far East after the opening of the former Soviet Union in the late 1980's, Rene and his partner, international whitewater rafter Eugene "Goo" Vogt (whose fishing program out of Khabarovsk garnered five IGFA world records, including the largest Siberian taimen ever taken on rod and reel), were among the first American sportfish tour operators allowed to float and fish the rivers of Kamchatka in the early 1990's. He is considered one of the premier authorities on fly fishing Alaska and Russia. For more information on the author and his latest guiding and publishing ventures, visit his website at http://www.ultimaterivers.com.

Other Books by Rene Limeres:

Alaska Fishing (ISBN 0935701516), Foghorn Press, San Francisco, California 1995

Alaska Fishing: The Ultimate Angler's Guide, 3rd Edition (ISBN # 192917011-4; hardback #1929170297), Publishers Design Group, Roseville, California 2005

Alaska Pocket Wildlife Guide (ISBN 13:9781929170333) Publishers Design Group, Roseville, California 2010

Alaska Pocket Fishing Guide (UPC 9079300114) Publishers Design Group, Roseville, California 2007